DECLINING FORTUNES

DECLINING FORTUNES

The Withering of the
American Dream

Katherine S. Newman

BasicBooks
A Division of HarperCollins*Publishers*

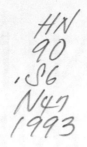

Library of Congress Cataloging-in-Publication Data

Newman, Katherine S., 1953–
    Declining fortunes : the withering of the American dream / Kather-
ine S. Newman
        p.   cm.
    Includes bibliographical references and index.
    ISBN 0–465–01593–X
    1. Social mobility—United States.   2. Middle classes—United
States.   3. United States—Economic conditions—1981–   4. United
States—Social conditions—1980–.   I. Title.
HN90.S6N47 1993
305.5'13—dc20   92-53246
                                              CIP

Designed by Ellen Levine

93 94 95 96 ◆/RRD 9 8 7 6 5 4 3 2 1

For Paul, Steven, and David

Contents

Preface

In the decades that followed the Great Depression, Americans came to assume that prosperity was their birthright: each generation expected to exceed the standard of living their parents had struggled to achieve. The boom years that followed World War II intensified this national belief in upward mobility as the U.S. economy grew at an unprecedented rate and our standard of living became the envy of the world. The two largest living generations of Americans—postwar parents and their baby-boom children—were the prime beneficiaries of this expansion, and the impact of their good fortune went beyond the pocketbook. Both generations were steeped in a culture of optimism that reinforced their confidence in the future.

The economic realities of the 1980s and 1990s have crushed these expectations, leaving behind doubt, fear, and anger. Recessions, widespread bankruptcies, anemic rates of growth, high unemployment, and the relentless pressure of the federal deficit have combined to place the future of the middle class in serious jeopardy. Rarely have Americans been so worried about the future for themselves, their families, and their country. Rarely have they demanded with such force that politicians do something to rescue the nation.

News of economic disaster has dominated the media for the past four years, gathering strength as the election season of 1992 neared. But we lack an understanding of what the megatrends mean in the daily lives of middle-class Americans. Statistics, graphs, and bleak headlines tell us how serious the damage is, but they cannot tell us how the numbers translate into rage, disappointment, and a sense of drift in communities across the land. It is important, indeed critical, that we understand how the problems that beset our economy are shaping the family lives, political attitudes, and personal identities of the people who must contend with them every day.

Declining Fortunes fills this gap by going directly to the source: it is based upon over 150 interviews with ordinary Americans who live in one typical suburban community, a town the likes of which could be found in almost any state in the union. The residents of "Pleasanton" are white-collar professionals and skilled blue-collar craftsmen; they come from a variety of ethnic and religious backgrounds; they are, or were, believers in the promise of America; and they are trying to understand what has gone wrong. I studied this suburb over a two-year period, interviewing school teachers, guidance counselors, and parents and their now-grown children in some sixty families. Having promised to keep their names confidential, I cannot thank them personally for having confided in me. But I can tell their story, a story that is shared by millions of Americans who hoped for better things for their children but now find that promise sorely tested.

It is not a particularly happy tale, for it often involves bitter conflict between generations, antagonism between racial groups, and friction between husbands and wives. The social and economic problems that beset a place like Pleasanton must be explored because they have already set the stage for political confrontation in the 1990s and may well lead to the unraveling of the unspoken social contract that glues America together. The people of Pleasanton are not likely to lose everything they have. But they are not going to get what they believe they deserve either, and the resulting frustrations have colored their most intimate decisions and their most public expressions of discontent.

My own way of exploring the general problem of downward mobility owes a great deal to my training as an anthropologist and my years as a faculty member at Columbia University. Anthropologists strive to understand the worldview of ordinary people as they understand it themselves. While we pay attention to surveys and polls, this is not our medium. Anthropology works through the words of the people under study and tries to represent their perspectives faithfully. My field is also an interpretive art, one that seeks the underlying messages and meanings of culture as much as the surface forms of behavior and custom. Economic disorder is a particularly useful lens through which to examine these often hidden but nonetheless central aspects of middle-class life in the United States, because under stressful conditions, people often lay bare the cultural expectations, collective memories, and internal sources of division that might otherwise be obscured.

Over the years I have worked on this project, many colleagues have listened patiently to me as my ideas took shape. It is always a pleasure to be able to thank them in print, for without such friends the life of a scholar would be a lonely one indeed. Elaine Combs-Schilling, my colleague in the anthropology department at Columbia University, has devoted her life to understanding the Islamic societies of North Africa. But she is also Appalachian, born and bred, a steel magnolia who has been a source of intellectual and personal strength for me during the decade we have been at Columbia together. Herbert Gans, one of the nation's best-known sociologists, has never failed me when I have asked him to read and critique my work. The Wenner-Gren Foundation for Anthropological Research made it possible for me to work closely with a remarkable group of scholars dedicated to broadening the involvement of anthropologists in public policy debates. Michael Blakey, Frank Dubinskas, Shep Forman, Carole MacLennan, Jim Peacock, Carlos Velez-Ibanez, Alvin Wolfe, and I spent many happy moments at the Amerind Foundation in the wilds of the Arizona desert thinking about ways in which anthropologists could increase their contributions to the study of social problems in our own society.

Sheldon Danziger and Mary Corcoran invited me to lecture at the University of Michigan, where I also benefited from the feedback of Greg Duncan and Tim Smeeding. My friends at the University of California, Berkeley—Carol Stack, Arlene and Jerry Skolnick, Phillip Selznick, Doris Fine, Troy Duster, Kristen Luker, Jerry Karabel, Jim Stockinger, Bob Fitzgerald, and Judy Small—have all been stalwart in their support of my preoccupations and stimulating sources of new ideas. The Rampel-Motts welcomed my family to their Berkeley home where I found the peace of mind to finish the book.

My editor at Basic Books, Steven Fraser, is a gift to the world of letters. As his many admirers in the academic world know, he has one of the sharpest minds in the business. He is a fine historian in his own right, a pleasure to work with, and a master of the blue pencil. Hence, to Steve and his family—Jill, Max, and Emma—go my thanks. Kathryn Dudley devoted years of her own time to this project. She was deeply involved in every phase of it, from the interviews to the analysis, right down to the endnotes. Without her, and the last-minute assistance of Katherine Hughes, this book would never have come to pass.

I should also like to thank the faculty and graduate students of the anthropology department at Columbia University for their support and interest in this research. A long and distinguished legacy left by our Columbia ancestors—including Franz Boas, Margaret Mead, Ruth Benedict, Robert Murphy, and countless others—has enriched us all, particularly those of us who have committed our energies to the study of American society.

Declining Fortunes was a labor-intensive enterprise, requiring both human and financial resources. I am particularly grateful to the National Endowment for the Humanities, which, in partnership with the American Association for State and Local History and the New Jersey Historical Society, provided the first grant for my work. This was followed up in a very substantial way by the cultural anthropology section of the National Science Foundation. I realized from the beginning that my research represented a departure from the norm for anthropologists and was therefore doubly appreciative of the generous grant (BNS 89-11266) NSF provided me.

Finally, but most importantly, I must thank the members of my family who, as always, put up with me while I spent countless hours working on this project. Steven Attewell, age nine, is accustomed to my writing habits by now and has started to compete with me for use of my computer. David Attewell, now three years old, twined himself around my ankles as I soldiered on. My husband, Paul Attewell, understood the pull between family and work better than anyone else could because as a professor and a sociologist, he has been in this position at least as often as I have. Without his constant intellectual support—his willingness to debate the issues presented here—none of my work would ever have seen the light of day. For this reason, *Declining Fortunes* is dedicated to the three men in my life who make it all worthwhile.

I edited the final version of this book while sitting in the midst of one of the most beautiful spots in Berkeley, California—the Rose Garden. High atop the Berkeley Hills, the garden treats its visitors to a commanding view of the San Francisco Bay. Ordinarily only the privileged few would have the chance to soak in such a sight, but the Rose Garden is open to all because it was built with public monies during the Great Depression. It is one of the many magnificent monuments created by the unemployed of the nation, courtesy of the WPA. One cannot help but wonder how many other playgrounds and national parks, monuments and roads, and schools and hospitals might be built by the millions of men and women who have been sidelined by the economic downturns of the 1980s and 1990s. There is surely no shortage of work to be done. But investing in the nation's infrastructure and in its people requires the kind of political will that the depression brought forth. In the midst of a far worse crisis than the one we face now, the United States summoned the determination to pull itself out of the abyss. The Jones Beach boardwalk on Long Island, the magnificent train station in Los Angeles, and most of our national park system are living testimony to what can be done, even in a period of declining fortunes.

May 1993
New York City

I

The End of Entitlement

Lauren Caulder was born in the halcyon days of the 1950s, when prosperity was a given and the formula for achieving it was clear. You drove yourself in school, got into a respectable college, picked a practical career, and pushed ahead with your nose to the grindstone. At the end of this long march lay the accoutrements of the good life: homeownership, family, and the security of a middle-class standard of living. Even as the currents of the American cultural revolution of the late 1960s swirled around her, Lauren doggedly followed the prescription for entry into the middle class and landed the kind of job that should have made it all possible, as a midlevel administrator of a federal lending program.

Something went awry in Lauren's life in the 1980s. Just when the fruits of her labor should have begun to pay off, the carrot at the end of the stick began to shrivel. Homeownership, that essential piece of the American dream, became an impossibility. Prices escalated to ridiculous levels and closed Lauren out. Unable to afford her own home, Lauren thought she could at least enjoy the benefits of her hard work through an occasional shopping spree or a winter holiday on a sunny island. Instead she discovered that even without the burden of a mortgage, she was still boxed in by a budget that never seemed to stretch far enough for the odd, spontaneous purchase. These days, every dime in her bankbook is committed: she is reasonably solvent, but there is no room for indulgence. This would not be such a problem if Lauren were just starting out; she could afford to wait her turn. But she is nearly forty years old now. All that lies ahead is endless penny-pinching, without much equity to show for it:

Every time I think I've made a financial breakthrough, something comes along that knocks me right out of the water. You think, okay, finally everything is paid off. Great, now we can start saving for such and such. Car breaks down. No use fixing it anymore. You've got to buy a new one or worse yet pay for a $750 transmission job. There you go. Now you're back in the hole, charged up on your credit card. . . . Something always comes along to wipe out everything that you might think is a winning achievement. You never seem to get over the hump and put it behind you.

Why has Lauren's standard of living fallen so far short of what she thought it would be? Her father, a quiet man of working-class origins and modest means, worked all his life in the advertising industry as a copywriter. Together with his wife, who stayed home to raise the Caulder clan, he was able to buy into a comfortable suburban community and give Lauren and her siblings a solid high school education at the local public school, swimming lessons at "the club," a chance to learn a musical instrument, and occasional travel to interesting vacation spots. Mr. Caulder's life is testimony to the great American dream: his hard work paid off in a better life for himself and his kids. His upward mobility ensured that serious want never intruded into Lauren's childhood.

The Caulder children were raised to respect traditional virtues of family and frugality, but they were also provided the emblems of affluence that were, after all, part of the reason their parents labored so hard. What was an achievement to be proud of for Mr. Caulder's generation became an expectation, a norm, an entitlement in his daughter's generation. If you became a certain kind of person—educated, cultivated, serious, motivated, hardworking—you were entitled to expect the same benefits in your life. Remaining a card-carrying member of the middle class was the most natural state of existence imaginable for baby boomers like Lauren who were raised amid its splendors.

But as Lauren left the 1980s behind—the decade dubbed by the media, the president, and a passel of economists as the longest period of expansion in the economy's postwar history—all she could see was the life-style she had taken for granted receding farther and farther from her grasp. She is better educated than her father; her job pays more than his ever did; she has a professional identity that her mother never even dreamed of—she should be sitting on top of the world. At the very least, Lauren tells herself, she and her husband are entitled to do as well as her parents did on one modest salary. Yet the gap between what should be and what is feels as large as the Grand Canyon:

> I'll never have what my parents had. I can't even dream of that. I'm living a lifestyle that's way lower than it was when I was growing up and it's depressing. You know it's a rude awakening when you're out in the world on your own. . . . I took what was given to me and tried to use it the best way I could. Even if you are a hard worker and you never skipped a beat, you followed all the rules, did everything they told you you were supposed to do, it's still horrendous. *They lied to me*. You don't get where you were supposed to wind up. At the end of the road it isn't there. I worked all those years and then I didn't get to candy land. The prize wasn't there, damn it.

Lauren is a member of the first generation since the Great Depression that can expect to have a *lower* standard of living than its parents. Children of the post–World War II economic boom, they entered adulthood in an era of economic uncertainty, where news of shuttered factories, bankruptcies, junk-bond nightmares, and white-collar unemployment is the stuff of daily headlines. Gone is the notion that each generation improves on the lot of its parents. In its stead comes the dread Lauren feels: she is on a treadmill that will never support a life-style even remotely like the one she knew as a child. Where Lauren's parents could expect to live in a nice house at low cost, have a family when they felt like it, and support their expenses on a single income, Lauren knows that she cannot afford a house, that she and her husband both have to work, and that children are a luxury that will be hard to afford.

Lauren's father, Andrew, a widower for some eight years now, recently sold the house he had owned for thirty years. This lovely New England–style home—too big for a man alone, with its four bedrooms and a large yard—had cost him $15,000 in the late 1950s, nearly twice his yearly income. While that was no small amount of money for Andrew, the 4 percent veteran's mortgage he received as thanks for his military service brought the cost within reach. The Caulder homestead fetched an astounding $400,000 in 1990, a sum so vast it makes Lauren laugh and weep at the same time. There is simply no way she can imagine ever earning enough money to buy her natal home now, or anything even remotely similar.

If Lauren could scale back her expectations, change her ambitions with every fluctuation of the consumer price index, she would have lower blood pressure. Instead, she boils over at being so tightly constrained, so unable to see past this month's paycheck:

> I'm not able to go anywhere. The lack of upward mobility and foreseeing no way out of my current situation is very frustrating. I couldn't take a more expensive apartment, couldn't buy a new car, can't take a vacation I want to take. It's just being frustrated everywhere I turn. Not being able to do the things you want to do with the money you are earning to enjoy your life. Being constantly browbeaten by the economy.

Most perplexing of all from Lauren's perspective is the fact that she always resisted the temptation to deviate and instead stuck to the straight and narrow path that was supposed to ensure that this would not happen. She followed the rules: she didn't party too much or get involved in drugs. She finished a respectable college degree, and she has steadily worked her way up the public-sector hierarchy to a responsible, even important, job. In her youth, the rewards for this good behavior were forthcoming, and she was lulled into the expectation that goodies come to those who work and wait. It seems a cruel hoax:

> I've always killed myself for a reason. I killed myself in school to get the good grades, and that was the reward, thank you very much. I got my A's. All the way along, I was rewarded in just the way I was supposed to be. . . . That was what the book said. And then you get out here to the real world and suddenly the last chapter is a sad joke. You're told you work hard for a living and you can buy a house in [your hometown], or the next town down the line that's a little cheaper. But its not true and it's really very perturbing.

Lauren sees the real world as a rude awakening from a perfect childhood. Her upbringing made her naïve and gullible. Unseen forces have taken advantage of her faith in the work ethic, leaving her feeling duped.

Americans are an optimistic lot. It is part of our cultural heritage, if not our daily experience, to assume that even when times are tough, the situation is bound to improve. Even in the depths of the Great Depression, the government tried to capitalize on the average Joe's belief that prosperity was just around the corner. Unfortunately, the members of Lauren's generation do not see the economy in this light. They are beginning to believe that the slump they have experienced is permanent, something they will have to get used to, even though they find this "fact" difficult to accept. Although they have lost their optimism, they have yet to come to terms with the new reality of downward mobility.

Baby boomers find it hard to accept their lot because more than their own lot is at stake. The fall they have experienced relative to their parents may well have serious consequences for their own children. Wendy Norman, a high school classmate of Lauren's, spends a lot of time thinking about the advantages her parents conferred upon her: comfort and enrichment without extravagance— ballet lessons, the occasional theater trip, and lazy summer days down at the pool. While Wendy was lucky to have all these things, her parents were fortunate too. The economic history of the 1950s made it possible for them to do far more for Wendy than their own parents had been able to do for them in the dreary days of the Great Depression. The Normans took pride and pleasure in being able to provide Wendy with so many advantages. Wendy is fairly certain, however, that she will *not* experience the satisfaction that comes from knowing that she has "done right" by her own kids:

> I guess our grandparents and our parents, what kept them moving and motivated was that they were trying to do for their children. Improve their children's lot. I think they achieved that and for the most part were probably happy in it. That gave them the happiness, the self-fulfillment. I don't think we have that in our generation.

Wendy and her baby-boom counterparts across the nation are worried that those critical advantages, those aspects of personal biography social scientists call "cultural capital," may be lost to their own children in the 1980s and 1990s. Their kids may have to settle for less: for mediocre schools, libraries that are closing down due to lack of revenue, and residence in less affluent communities with fewer amenities.

Today's middle-class parents are only too aware of how disastrous such a scenario could be. Children who do not go to good high schools have a hard time finding their way into competitive colleges. They are disadvantaged in their efforts to get into professional schools or to land high-paying jobs. In short, the connection between cultural advantage and social prestige has never been more definitive, particularly in the eyes of those baby-boom parents who were themselves the beneficiaries of middle-class advantage. Wendy knows all too well that she would be doing even *worse* in the 1990s were it not for the educational credentials her parents bestowed upon her. She is bombarded daily with headlines that proclaim education the key to the nation's prosperity, along with daily public handwringing over the quality of America's schools. The message is abundantly clear: her child's future depends upon the resources she provides. If these are less than what it takes, Wendy's kid will pay the price.

If the baby-boom generation is bewildered and disturbed by this turn of events, their parents—the generation that entered adulthood in the affluent years following World War II—are even more confused. They see themselves as living proof of the vitality of the American dream. Children of the Great Depression who were raised in cramped working-class enclaves of the nation's cities, they came of age in a time of war and emerged into peacetime to the benefits of the GI Bill, the VA mortgage, cheap land, a booming housing market, and a seemingly endless expansion in every conceivable industry.[1] Young men whose fathers crossed the Atlantic in steerage (and were satisfied to land a steady job in a sweatshop), ended up in America's finest universities and fueled an unprecedented expansion of the country's middle class. They became engineers, doctors, lawyers, businessmen—the first professionals in their family lines. Opportunity seemed limitless. As these postwar parents tell the story, those who were willing to work hard could literally make their dreams come true.

John Reinhardt certainly saw the world in these terms. John married Helen, his high school sweetheart, just before shipping out to serve in the European theater in 1945. After John was released from the army four years later, the Reinhardts moved in with his parents to save enough money to find a place of their own. Apartments were scarce in the immediate postwar years, but ironically houses were getting cheaper and more accessible than they had ever been before. The Reinhardts moved to suburban New Jersey and laid down some roots:

> We lived in a small house with two bedrooms and a big yard. It was a corner plot; it was like a quarter of an acre and it was one of those houses that were designed for GIs, right after the war. You could buy it for $11,990—can you imagine that? Ten percent down—all you needed was $1,100! Which I had to borrow from my father!

The Reinhardts had two children in that home. When the third was imminent, they traded up to a four-bedroom colonial in a more affluent community. Moving up was virtually effortless, for it was financed out of the steady accumulation of equity that came to suburban homeowners during the 1950s. By the time Gerry, the Reinhardts' fourth child, came along in 1952, the family was settled, secure, and able to enjoy the spacious country atmosphere of their home. John had always assumed that little Gerry would repeat his own performance and set up a family of his own nearby, but as he sees it now, the mountains Gerry has to climb are far too steep:

> Everything he does now is so much more expensive than what we did at a comparable age. He has to keep up with the times and it isn't easy. . . . We were always raised that your rent shouldn't exceed one week's pay. That's a good rule of thumb. Today the young people can't do that. Today they're spending two weeks pay to keep an apartment! I feel sorry for them. And the young married people today can't go out and buy a house for $11,990 like I did. They have to pay $100,000. Where do they get it from? I'm not talking about people who inherit money or their parents give them money, I'm talking about hard-working kids that have to save. . . . Today a car costs more than what I paid for my house!

John and Gerry, father and son, see themselves as part of a single family unit with a common history. Yet in the space of one generation, so much has changed in the landscape of the U.S. economy that fathers and sons have come to inhabit different Americas. John finds this truth deeply troubling; his effort to understand why his son cannot lay hold to his rightful station as a local homeowner remains unsatisfied. John is not ready to accept the notion that

Gerry's life will never equal his own from a material point of view. He wants to know to whom he can assign the blame for this most un-American reversal of fortune.

Both generations—those who rode the wave of postwar affluence and those who have fallen into the trough of postindustrial decline— pose this question now, largely in the privacy of their homes and in conversation with friends. The declining fortunes of the baby-boom cohort, while the subject of an occasional magazine piece or news- paper article, have yet to become the platform for a social move- ment or the rallying cry of a new-age politician. Indeed, for many Americans the personal strain of coping with disappointed expecta- tions and dashed ambitions is so great that little energy is left for analyzing their own experience as symptomatic of far-reaching, structural disorders in the U.S. economy.

While I will touch on the large forces that have reduced the life chances of the baby-boom generation relative to their postwar par- ents, *Declining Fortunes* is not primarily about trends and numbers or graphs and tables. My purpose here is to explore how transfor- mations in the life chances of these two critically important genera- tions have influenced their lives. Through the words of parents, daughters, and sons who settled in one community in northern New Jersey in the postwar years, I explore how the diminished standard of living of today's boomers shapes the personal and social problems they must live with. From the most personal conflicts in marriage—over children, domestic responsibilities, and obligations to aging relatives—to the relations between neighbors of different nationalities, there is virtually no aspect of daily life that has been left unruffled by the shock of declining fortunes.

And while politicians have yet to capitalize on the inchoate sense of disaster that plagues both the boomers and their parents, I shall argue that these issues will dominate the policy landscape in America as we move into the twenty-first century. For ulti- mately the question of who is entitled to the good life in America and who must pay to help those excluded from the golden circle must be resolved if we are to avoid the unraveling of the social fabric. There is plenty of evidence to show, albeit in isolated ways thus far, that such a process is already under way. If we are to avoid a future characterized by the philosophy of every man for himself, a credo that cannot sustain any society for long, we must look long and hard at the impact of intergenerational downward mobility and ask what it means in cultural as well as practical terms.

The Life and Times of Pleasanton

Lauren Caulder, Wendy Norman, and Gerry Reinhardt all come from one pleasant, but largely unremarkable town in northern New Jersey. Established during the colonial era by French Huguenot renegades, "Pleasanton"[2] was nothing more than a sleepy vacation spot by the nineteenth century, accessible only by rail to New York City dwellers dying for some fresh air and a temporary respite from the congestion of urban living. Farms that are as old as the revolutionary war were still the mainstay of the local economy in those days, and massive old-fashioned country hotels sat at the end of the rail line waiting for the city folk to disgorge from the trains.[3] Little changed in the Pleasanton area until the 1930s, when the Works Progress Administration sponsored the construction of the stately George Washington Bridge, which straddles the Hudson River. This brought the little country enclave into the orbit of the Big Apple in a more substantial way than ever before, and slowly families began to make their way out of the city in search of peace, quiet, and space.

The big boost in the population of Pleasanton came, as it did for thousands of American communities, with the construction of a major state road system[4] and the exponential expansion of the American automobile industry. Cars became an item of mass consumption, the government provided the cash to fuel a national highway system that is the envy of the world, and together these made it possible for families to live far from the city center and commute to work. Although Pleasanton grew fivefold during the 1950s and early 1960s, even by American standards it was never a big community. Some five thousand families lived there, almost entirely in single-family homes sitting atop large lots of land. This was the zenith of its development, and it has remained this size ever since.[5] To this day Pleasanton has no industry and only a few neighborhood stores. It has purposely kept itself a quiet residential community, centered around a small town hall, a beautiful recreation center, a graceful pond, and a few New England–style churches.

When the exodus to Pleasanton began, the newcomers were largely young couples tired of hauling babies up the stairs into small city apartments. With their families expanding by leaps and bounds, these city folk were thirsty for space and freedom from the confines of inquisitive in-laws and neighbors. They were the pioneers, the first to depart the familiar embrace of the extended family, the first to become truly Americanized. The institution of suburbia itself played a critical role in the process of homogenization, for it allowed people accustomed to being grouped into ethnic enclaves like Little Italy or Irishtown to seek out new friends and new identities based more on common interests than on family or national origin.[6] In time, differences made themselves felt, a subject I shall consider in chapter 3, but like the millions of other Americans who happily fled to the suburban ring, the goal was a kind of freedom that was simply not available in the city.

The rising tide of good fortune that swept the country in the 1950s seemed to offer this freedom to almost everyone.[7] Pleasanton's makeup reflected the inclusive, egalitarian distribution of the postwar boom. Elevator operators whose wives worked in the local school cafeteria could afford the smaller houses in town. Skilled blue-collar workers, many of whom went on to establish their own small businesses, lived nearby. Medical residents, who would eventually trade up to the big houses, lived in the same modest part of town. Grander lots went to the businessmen who owned auto parts stores or worked in the many insurance firms that sprang up in the larger New Jersey cities nearby. Older folks, already suburban dwellers in less swank towns, moved into the biggest houses, since they were already able to pull equity value out of earlier, smaller homes. Large Catholic families lived next door to smaller Protestant families. Jews were a decided minority.

Pleasanton was truly a mélange of different classes and occupations, faiths, and nationalities. While neither the very poor nor the rich and famous lived in this bedroom community, almost everyone else seemed to be there. It was the kind of heterogeneous place that many Americans have in mind when they think of the ideal of the melting pot.[8] This is clearly one important reason why boomers who grew up there—including Lauren, Wendy, and Gerry—continue to believe that living in such a community is a reasonable aspiration. If an elevator operator could once manage it, why can they not do it now that they have become teachers, administrators, or business managers?

But Pleasanton no longer looks like the melting-pot paradise of the past. Today's newcomer to this quiet, leafy, gentrified town has a six-figure salary, inherited wealth, or a hefty sum drawn from equity in a previous house. Even in the midst of episodic slumps in the real estate market, there are few homes for sale for less than $250,000.[9] It would be tough for most young couples starting out— like those who came in droves in the 1950s—to find anything in Pleasanton within their reach. First-time buyers must look for less affluent communities now, generally several hours' drive from the big city. Those who can afford Pleasanton are often executives posted to New York subsidiaries of major Asian corporations. These are the families who began to buy into Pleasanton in the 1980s. There is no place left in the community for the baby-boom progeny, although they cling stubbornly to the notion that they belong in Pleasanton or at least somewhere nearby that is just like it.

What Happened to the American Dream?

From the perspective of the boomers and their parents, a series of intertwined forces derailed the "normal" trajectory that is supposed to make it possible for children to surpass their parents. Although Pleasanton residents are not economists and do not lay claim to professional expertise in these matters, they have a fairly good grasp of the immediate culprits that have complicated their lives. Four related phenomena typically crop up when they explain the erosion of their slice of the American dream: escalating housing prices, occupational insecurity, blocked mobility on the job, and the cost-of-living squeeze that has penalized the boomer generation, even when they have more education and better jobs than their parents.

The extraordinary inflation of housing prices comes as no news to postwar parents. By sitting tight and doing almost nothing, they have seen the value of their most important asset rise to levels that are, by their own standards, stratospheric. In the course of the 1980s real estate became a language and a way of life. Dinner-party gossip revolved around how much houses on the block were going for and who was making a killing on what piece of property. It seemed, and still seems to many in Pleasanton, as though there was nothing else to talk about, nothing as captivating as money being made in the form of four-bedroom colonials. The Renfrew family can provide instant quotations on the cost of the homes that run in their comparatively well heeled family. When asked to describe the life-style of their now-grown children, Mr. Renfrew responded with what has become a well-understood shorthand:

> Let's put it this way, our son lives in a million-dollar house, our daughter in Boston an $800,000 house. [Our house] is about a $400,000 house and our daughter [who lives nearby] has about a $500,000 house. So that puts it in perspective.

In public people like the Renfrews would shake their heads in amazement over these numbers. In private they became almost giddy over the sudden wealth acquired by simply staying put.

The odd thing about this sudden wealth was that it made the process of accumulating capital effortless, almost magical. Compared to working for a living, real estate profits were incredibly easy to pile up. Dumb luck—being in the right place at the right time—and some modest resources were all that was needed to get into the game.

Simon Rittenberg was a salesman for nearly forty years for a factory that manufactures security devices for use in businesses and homes. He has the hearty, confident character of the ideal salesman even though he has been retired for some time. Like everyone else who grew up in a little apartment during the depression, his dream had always been to have a house of his own. Simon was always worried about how he would pay it off. It never occurred to him that he could pile up a little fortune just by hanging on to the house. But when he became a widower and the house was just too big for a lone man, he sold out and discovered how much "doing nothing" had done for his bank account:

> I don't think I had the intelligence to know that by moving, coming to [Pleasanton] county, that I would do so well. All I knew was that my father had always rented. He never owned anything. He rented his store, and he rented his apartment. And now I was going to take this big leap into owning a home, which would be mine, my castle. . . . After thirty-five years, my $17,000 became $285,000 when I sold [the house]. So was that brilliance on my part?
>
> Now I'm a big shot: I made some kind of great deal! The economics of it didn't have anything to do with me. It had to do with the world, what happened.

While Simon is happy enough to have this fat bank account, he takes greater pride in the achievements of his work life than in the lucrative side effects of the housing mania of the 1980s. He does not take credit for his good fortune, though he is not unhappy to have it. It has become emblematic of a kind of real estate madness that seems to have descended on the world, or at least his small corner of it.

Were this madness only positive in its impact, Simon would not be troubled long by its benefits. The truth is that his son, Ron, has been driven out by the very same forces that provided him with such fantastic rewards. Ron Rittenberg is nearly forty now and lives in Washington, D.C., where he works for a federal agency that provides information to criminal justice agencies around the country. He has a three-year-old son and a wife who works full-time. They live in suburban Maryland in a community that is nowhere near the level of affluence that Pleasanton represents. Ron just laughs when asked to compare the community he lives in now with the Pleasanton of his youth. The flip side of the father's good fortune is the son's flight to a less expensive community, far away from his kin.

Of course, the escalating cost of housing is not the only divide separating the postwar parents from their baby-boom children. Jobs are harder to find and far more insecure in all respects. Pleasanton's progeny were well-educated by any standard, and they parlayed that advantage into job qualifications that often exceeded anything their parents had had to offer employers in years gone by. The sons of skilled blue-collar workers earned college degrees and became accountants. The daughters of nonworking, high school–educated mothers nearly all went on to higher education, often finding jobs as teachers or managers. Yet even with these credentials, success did not come easily to the boomers. Where their parents found an expanding job market with an inexhaustible thirst for their talents, they have found a crowded, competitive market that often deems them expendable.

Security is not easy to come by these days; it is a concern that looms very large in the lives of those who were raised in the prosperous, stable 1950s and the roaring, expansive 1960s. Contractions, leveraged buyouts, bankruptcies, layoffs, and general despair over the state of American competitiveness—these are the headlines in today's business pages. Nothing in the boomers' upbringing, schooling, or early experience in the labor market prepared them for what we must all confront now: the U.S. economy cannot provide the kind of job opportunities or personal security that the country took for granted only a generation ago.

Martin O'Rourke, now in his early forties, got a firsthand taste of this nasty medicine when he worked for an auto company in the early 1980s. Martin's father was a blue-collar man through and through, but Martin was a talented artist. Ignoring family objections, he decided to become a commercial artist. Ultimately, he started his own small business and continues to make a reasonable living at it today. But his early inclinations were not in an entrepreneurial direction. He thought he would be a company man, until he witnessed what happens to loyal company men:

> The real reason I quit the company was that my office was next door to a man who had worked for the company since 1955. He was the oldest employee in the company, and he was sixty-two years old when I met him. On a Friday afternoon at 4:30 they fired him. He had been a very important man in the company and he lived and breathed his work. He was in charge of all the warehouses across the country—all the parts warehouses. They decided to consolidate the warehouses and figured he would be unnecessary. So they just fired him. I'll never forget that day. He was in his office and he was crying and I asked what happened. I thought maybe his wife died or something horrible happened and he just handed me this piece of paper that said he was no longer needed by the company.
>
> I went home and said to my wife, I've got to leave, quit. I can't go on with this job because I'm just as devoted to my work. I lived and breathed my job too and I was 100 percent a company guy and worked insane hours for them. For what? So I could wind up like him? Be just let off? At age sixty-two, where's this man going to go? And my feeling was that I just had to be in control.

In the 1980s a new habit began to spread through corporate America, a tradition of declining loyalty of firm to worker and a consequent wariness among younger employees of depending upon any job for permanent security.[10] We are used to the fact that our manufacturing industries are on the skids and few of Pleasanton's progeny were headed in that direction. They were, and are now, white-collar material. But this has hardly protected them, their parents, or their friends from the shakeouts and shutdowns that have plagued the service industries. New York City, where many Pleasanton boomers work, has lost over one hundred thousand jobs since 1987, many of them white-collar positions.[11] Martin O'Rourke watched an older, longtime employee get the ax, and it scared him enough to abandon the corporate world altogether. His fear was well justified, since few age groups have been spared the pressure of mounting layoffs and white-collar dislocation. Many a thirty- and forty-year-old has been handed a pink slip in the long aftermath of the 1987 stock market crash.[12]

Among those who *have* managed to escape the abyss of unemployment in the 1980s and the early 1990s, other problems have contributed to an intergenerational decline. Upward mobility within the ranks of American firms is leveling out at an earlier age for baby boomers than was true for their fathers in the expansive postwar period. When business was booming in the United States, management pyramids just kept on growing. Newly minted B.A.'s (courtesy of the GI Bill) flooded into the marketplace and advanced quickly up the ranks. Business growth remained strong as they reached their forties, and this was reflected in continuous career growth. For these postwar men, careers tended to level off in their fifties and to begin the slow descent to retirement as they entered their sixties. While some were caught and crushed by the years of high unemployment in the early 1980s, most managed to escape the crunch of the Reagan recession and are still coasting on reasonable pensions and high home equity.

Sons and daughters who began their careers in the 1970s and 1980s have encountered both tremendous competition for the "good jobs" and flatter job pyramids, which level off at distressingly early ages. Charles Aberstein, whose son Larry graduated from Pleasanton's main high school ten years ago, has noticed how much harder it is to make one's way in the job market now than it was when he started out:

> We're in a different kind of life environment today than we were thirty years ago. There's lots more competition. There's many more college graduates and fewer and fewer positions. Many of the good jobs have been exported to the Pacific. Major industries have fled the U.S. There are that many fewer executive-level positions here and yet many candidates for them. It's a more competi-

tive world than the one that I grew up in. [Larry's] aware of it.
He'll find his way, but it won't be as easy as it was for me.

Charles climbed the job ladder toward a vice presidency in an insurance firm, but he knows that Larry will find the same kind of ascent less assured. Many baby boomers are discovering that the sheer size of their generation ensures that there are too many of them chasing too few options. Moving up from entry-level positions to middle management seemed easy enough; the next step has become increasingly difficult.

Under the best of circumstances only a few of the millions of baby boomers will see advancement into executive ranks. Many will see the zenith of their careers arrive in their forties, leaving twenty or thirty more years of their work lives with unchanged horizons (if they are lucky enough to escape the pressures of downsizing or business collapse). Beyond the boredom that leveling off entails lie important financial consequences: boomers will not see the continued salary increases that might eventually put them on a par with their parents. Leveling off, coupled with increasingly frequent recessions or inflationary pressures, will translate into a long-term erosion of their standard of living, a standard that already falls short of their initial expectations.

The combination of high housing costs, occupational insecurity, and slowing potential for advancement in the workplace has subjected the baby-boom generation to an intense squeeze.[13] Yet the demands upon their resources, far from slowing, have only accelerated. Now in the midst of their childbearing years, they face mounting costs for everything from clothing to child care, from education to transportation. The proportion of their income that must go toward these essentials seems, from their parents' perspective, far more than was required in "the good old days." As one 1950s mother put it, her children are working hard not to get ahead of her but in order to keep from slipping even farther backward:

Our income was so low when we first got married, but we got a brand-new auto for $1,800. Our son David earns $20,000 teaching kids. For him a new car costs $16,000. It's just the proportion! When I went to Radcliffe, it cost $3,200 a year. Maybe my father was only earning $9,000. But for David, Harvard would cost $20,000 year and that's a lot more than one-third of his father's income. . . . Usually there's an improvement in each generation and what they're able to get. But I think with our kids they're going backwards. They have a much more austere kind of life-style.

Disparities between generations along these basic economic lines inevitably leads to strain and a background jealousy. Boomers do not wish their parents ill or feel that their good fortune was undeserved. They just want to know why the run of luck did not hold long enough to include them, why they have to put up with the penny-pinching that Lauren Caulder complains of so bitterly:

> You just sit there and look, and watch how everything that seemed reasonable to wish for has somehow flown—I really think in the last two or three years. Partly because there's so many of us pushing prices up. . . . It's not as if it's a mystery why this should be happening. It's just a shame that you have to wake up and smell the coffee like that.

Lauren believes that an arbitrary force intervened to ruin things for her. She has to pay the penalty for living in an era of economic disarray, for being part of a generation so huge it has overwhelmed every market it touches—from the schools, to the professions, and no doubt some day to the retirement homes. But it is often hard for her to hold on to this structural explanation, this macropicture of demography and economics, interest rates, and international competition. What she *can* see is the discordant biography that puts her own childhood experience of normal middle-class existence out of reach now that she has reached middle age.

Many boomers have had the good fortune to exceed their parents in education and in occupational prestige. Unfortunately, superior credentials no longer seem to "buy" a superior, or even equal, life-style. Mary Flory's experience is a case in point. Her parents are working-class people who were able to settle in Pleasanton when that was still possible for families of modest means. Mary and her husband have moved up in the world; he, in particular, is an educated white-collar man. Nonetheless, they have fallen way behind Mary's parents in terms of the life-style they can afford:

> My father was an elevator operator all his life. My husband is a teacher. I would have thought right away of course we could afford to live in Pleasanton. We have better jobs. But we couldn't.

There is no way we could live there. I really couldn't believe that
I couldn't live in the town that I grew up in. I don't know what it
says.

American culture is based in large part on an underlying social
Darwinism that sees justice in the rule of survival of the fittest. We
believe that those who are well equipped to compete will reap
material rewards and that, conversely, those who cannot "cut the
mustard" will (and should) suffer deprivation. For the past fifty years
or more the dominance of white-collar work in the U.S. prestige
hierarchy has meant that we define the "fittest" as those who are
educated and who can lay claim to a professional identity.[14] According to this view of the natural order, blue-collar employment should
not be rewarded nearly as well as "mental" work. Jobs that require a
strong back are honorable enough, but they do not deserve the kind
of payoff that "thought" jobs do.

In Mary Flory's case, the reverse rule seems to apply. Her respectable but unskilled father could afford to buy into Pleasanton, but her
educated, professional husband is locked out. The upside-down quality
of this arrangement is entirely illegitimate from Mary's point of view,
and there is considerable cultural support for her way of thinking. There
is no justice in the notion that Mr. Flory was in the right place at the
right time, whereas Mary and her husband had the bad taste to be born
at the wrong historical moment. It is an arbitrary feature of postwar history. Yet arbitrariness barely begins to capture Mary's response. She is
angry, frustrated, and above all bewildered by this reversal of what
"ought to be."

Rhonda Carland is younger than Mary, but she too has seen this
peculiar inversion of the rules that link rewards to personal credentials. Rhonda's father is not a blue-collar man. If anything, he is better
educated than Rhonda, for he became a professor at a well-respected
university near Pleasanton. Mr. Carland traded high income for the
flexibility and freedom of the academic life and he is happy enough
with this equation. When Rhonda started college in the 1980s, she
was determined to follow another, more lucrative path. She wanted
something a little less ivory tower, a little more high powered than
what her father had. Law school looked like the way to go. In
absolute terms, there can be little question that this strategy has
paid off: Rhonda now works for one of the good law firms in the
Big Apple; her husband is also a lawyer. Nonetheless, she finds it

hard to see how this has any advantage relative to her professor father:

Both of us together make more money than my father does as the sole supporter of his house. So it seems absurd that we have to worry about how out of control our finances are lately. But the fact is that we can't duplicate his life-style. We get out of bed at 6:30 after sleeping for maybe five hours, go to work and put in thirteen hours to reach the same life-style that my parents had, which I never thought was particularly impressive. It just seems like [my father] had an upper-middle-class, reasonable kind of affluence on his salary alone. He could take a vacation now and then. He didn't own a summer house. He budgeted. That *should* be attainable now for people who work hard, or have an education. But now that doesn't seem as clear. We just aren't getting ahead!

Rhonda struggles with the fact that by all objective standards she is enormously privileged. She has an interesting, well-paying job and a husband with the same professional profile. Yet they cannot seem to support the kind of life-style that her father was able to manage on a far more modest budget. This too represents a reversal of the cultural rules that distribute benefits in life: professors are allowed to be modestly comfortable, but lawyers are supposed to be among the most affluent professionals in America. Not only has Rhonda failed to pull ahead of her father, but she realizes that the day she stops working to have a baby, her family's life-style will plummet. She knows not to expect genuine sympathy for her position, since her economic worries are far less serious than those of many other Americans today—she keeps her dismay private. Nonetheless, the Rhondas of Pleasanton continue to feel that something is amiss.

For most of Pleasanton's boomers, the cost-of-living squeeze is here to stay. They do not see any way out of this mess, and this conclusion in and of itself is a source of depression. Weathering hard times is one thing; accepting that the intergenerational slide is a permanent fact of life is quite another. Nevertheless, as Cathy Larson sees it, there is no reason for the realistic person to see the situation in a rosier light:

This has gone on for so long, I don't know why it should be any different tomorrow. You know, you tell yourself constantly that you can get over the hump. But it's just an ongoing thing. It's a life of credit cards. It's a life of bills. It's a life of living beyond your means.

In Cathy's life, financial limitations create what she calls a "low burning thing," a subtext of constraint, a feeling that she is not free. This, above all, is the meaning of the intergenerational slide: the freedom to consume is cut short, the ability to plan for the long run is limited, and the bitter sense of rules turned inside out makes people feel, to use Cathy's words, like "it was all a big lie."

A Private Morass

Financial pressures facing the baby-boom generation have profoundly affected their private and public lives. From the most intimate decisions about whether or when to have children to the most pragmatic questions of career choices, virtually every serious decision they have to make has been dictated by conflicting desires. On the one hand, the boomers are loath to give up the hallmarks of middle-class life, and they cling tenaciously to the idea that by working harder (more hours, more workers in a household), they can claim their share of the American dream. On the other hand, they face pressures to conform to ideals of family organization and child rearing that were feasible in the 1950s and 1960s but are no longer easily achieved. Despite the revolution of the women's movement, which has brought millions of women (including mothers of young children) into the workplace, the image of the nurturing, omnipresent mother has yet to fade away. Indeed, for the boomers themselves, she is a vivid memory, not just an abstraction. The postwar generation was largely raised by women who either retired from the factories and offices they had worked in during the war or never worked in the paid labor market at all. The domestic front, they were told, was a woman's natural destiny.[15]

While the women's movement did succeed in dismantling the notion that women belong in the kitchen and the kitchen only, it did not succeed in shifting the burden of child rearing to a fifty-fifty proposition. As Arlie Hochschild has pointed out in her remarkable book *The Second Shift,* women are still fighting that battle and mainly losing.[16] American society still looks upon women as the crucible of the moral development of the young and charges them with the responsibility for making sure the kids "turn out right."

Women are told in so many ways that they cannot afford to "mess up." Where social movements encouraged women to broaden their horizons and take up their fair share of the burden of earning a living, personal history and cultural norms tell the same women that they had better be sure they have done a good job raising their children. Can this be done from the vantage point of the workplace? No one is sure it's possible; many are skeptical.

The problem, of course, is that by the early 1980s it was clear that a middle-class life-style mandated a two-income household. How could husbands support their families alone? How could wives live up to their obligations as moral mothers when their incomes were needed to make the mortgage payments? We will see in chapter 4 that this core contradiction has found no easy resolution, for these cultural and political dilemmas, while often treated as moral issues, are fundamentally tied to the declining fortunes of the baby-boom generation.

There are those—even in Pleasanton—who might ask why the postwar parents do not help out. Having benefited so much from the boom years, do they not have the resources to rescue their kids? Even if Pleasanton parents were inclined toward rescue missions, inclined to ignore the cultural prescription that calls for every generation to stand on its own two feet, they lack the wherewithal to prop up their adult children.[17] The generation of the postwar parents had children while comparatively young and hence has many years of retirement left to finance. Baby boomers in their forties often find themselves with parents in their sixties, parents who can expect to live for twenty years or more on the resources they garnered during the boom years. In particular, the equity value of their homes—generally the largest single item of value in their personal portfolios—will serve as the main bank account they will draw upon in their retirement years. Where growing old once meant growing poor, social security, public and private pensions, and home equity now mean that the golden generation that hit the postwar boom will also enjoy the most comfortable retirement ever made available to an American generation. They will, that is, if they can hold on to their resources and fund their sunset years themselves.

Medical care costs have skyrocketed in the last decade, as have the cost of nursing homes. Pleasanton parents are all too aware of the expenses involved in the long haul. Moreover, they have little faith that they will be able to depend on anyone else, whether government or members of their own family, to provide for them as they age. Whatever pressure they may feel to help the younger generation over the hump, especially over the hump of homeownership, collides with the knowledge that they must marshal whatever they have for the long years ahead.

Were the future their only concern, many Pleasanton parents would undoubtedly try to do something for their struggling boomers, but they are already experiencing problems in the present. For the fiscal crisis that has beset many a suburban community has generated demands for property tax revenues that are proving ever more difficult for the postwar generation to meet. In Pleasanton itself, property taxes have increased nearly *sixfold* in the last twenty years. For many old-timers who moved to Pleasanton when it was a modest town (on the strength of modest incomes), taxes have proved to be the last straw.

Kate and Sam Kensington moved to Pleasanton in the 1950s, even though they could barely afford a down payment. Sam owned a local hardware store that was bought out by a chain. He now does construction work in the city, driving a tractor trailer. Kate works for a perfume franchise that has concessions in big department stores, work she has done since her youngest child was ten. Married fresh out of high school, the Kensingtons raised four kids in Pleasanton and lived in one house for almost thirty-eight years. It has not been easy for them financially, but they scraped by and thought things would ease up once the kids were on their own. Tax increases have put an end to the dream of coasting into retirement. When Sam retires, they plan to sell and move South to join their oldest son, who long ago concluded he could not afford to live in Pleasanton either. Their neighbor, Mrs. Floury, found the tax problem an even bigger burden. She was a widow who simply could not meet her legal obligations. Mary Floury speaks with considerable bitterness about the way her mother was pushed out by the tax bite:

> The reason my mother moved to Florida was because the taxes had gone up again in Pleasanton. My father had died. She was still working at the local restaurant. This was in 1977. She was housepoor. She was the only one living in a three-bedroom house, and it was a struggle to keep afloat. She went to Borough Hall and said that she was really having trouble paying her taxes. What should she do? They told her to leave. She was so hurt. She had been liv-

ing there since 1951. They don't have a heart. They just want her money. It really hurt her that they said leave.

Although many of the postwar migrants to Pleasanton have found themselves sitting on residential gold mines, the tax consequences have made it increasingly difficult for them to remain in the community they consider to be their own. Pressures to move out grow as they age and face the prospect of declining income.

A growing uneasiness with the social character of Pleasanton is also responsible for making the old-timers feel that they are no longer entirely welcome. By all accounts, Pleasanton was a very ordinary community in the 1950s and 1960s. It was (and still is) pretty and peaceful, but it was not socially exclusive. Mary Floury's father, the elevator operator, and Rhonda Carland's dad, the chemistry professor, lived together and accepted their differences, since few in the community were "really rich." Pleasanton families thought of themselves as ordinary middle-class people (even though by national standards they were quite well off). People who wanted to "put on airs" did not move to Pleasanton; they settled in other, nearby communities that already had established reputations as havens of the wealthy, replete with country clubs, chauffeurs, and mansions.

Yet as the cost of housing grew, the new families who moved to Pleasanton in the 1980s were far more affluent as a group than many of the old-timers. A social gap has opened up between the skilled blue-collar workers and middle-level management types who founded the postwar community and the very highly paid professionals who are the only people able to buy into this desirable suburb these days. There are no manual workers, jewelry store clerks, or hardware store managers among today's migrants to Pleasanton. Newcomers are partners in big-city law firms, executives in large corporations, and specialist physicians. Their tastes, their desires, and their more privatized life-style have subtly eroded the communal flavor of life in Pleasanton, setting the tone for a more genteel, uppercrust local culture. Long-time residents like the James family do not feel entirely comfortable with this shift. Keith James, who is in his late twenties now, looks back upon the change with the sense that something has been lost:

By the time I graduated from high school in 1980, the town was just barely affordable. But there were still all the same kind of families. I feel now that Pleasanton has totally turned around. It's become basically a very affluent neighborhood, you know, because it's near Manhattan. You see a lot of new . . . groups coming into town. And we're getting a lot of doctors. It's pushing people out. I can remember when someone's parents lived in town, maybe someone's grandparents lived in Pleasanton, and there was some sort of return to the town. But that's totally changing.

It is not unusual to hear those who know they cannot afford to live in the community now argue that it has changed so much they would not really want to locate there anymore. As one of Keith's classmate's put the matter, "I wouldn't really want to live in Pleasanton now. They have a lot of rich people that have moved in that are kind of snobby." As the burden of the high cost of living mounts, the change in the social climate in town leaves old-timers feeling that the community they may need to vacate is no longer quite the same place anyway. It belongs to a different class of richer Americans.

Mindful that their worries may be dismissed as so much bleating by spoiled, demanding, perfectly comfortable baby boomers to whom the nation owes nothing, Pleasanton's boomer progeny are quick to point out that in an absolute sense they have much to be grateful for. Neither the boomers nor their parents confuse their experience with that of the poor or believe that they deserve an outpouring of sympathy to soothe their disappointments. They understand that relative to the "truly disadvantaged,"[18] they lead a charmed life.

Nonetheless, they live with a vague sense of dissatisfaction and an underlying desire to blame someone for their grief. They are especially perplexed by the arbitrary character of the trends that have had such a profound influence over their standard of living. It has escaped no one's attention that two generations living side by side have encountered drastically divergent life chances. As Martin O'Rourke puts it, "Times have changed. I don't expect to walk in my parents' footsteps. I won't have the same opportunities they had."

Americans think of themselves as a resourceful people. If there are obstacles in the way of prosperity, we will clear them away. If the rules of the game have changed, we will learn to play by the new ones. Unfortunately, it would appear that we cannot figure out what today's rules really are. We are drowning in a kind of national confusion, floundering in our attempts to find a way out, all the while wondering why the old formula no longer works.

For millions of families in communities across America, problems like these dominate the conversation within and between generations. They are beginning to surface as matters of policy debate also, though often in the form of single-issue arguments whose common threads are hard to discern. Political questions as seemingly divergent as school bonds, catastrophic health insurance, property taxes, and welfare payments are superficial expressions of a deeper struggle in the United States at the end of the twentieth century. We are facing the critical question of just who deserves a share in the bounty that defines the great American middle class. And when there is not enough to go around, as is clearly the case at this juncture, how will we respond to the demands of those who are deserving but disenfranchised? We must consider how American culture defines the responsibilities of one generation to another, of one ethnic group to another, of one town to another, when scarcity is the rule.

Paul Kennedy has written eloquently in *The Rise and Fall of the Great Powers* of the habit that dominant countries have of over-reaching their capacity to exert military control in the world, straining their fiscal resources and hastening the demise of the empire.[19] In his work we see how difficult it is for nation-states to reconcile themselves to the limitations of their power, how they strain against evidence of fading domination and exacerbate their decline by engaging in military adventures they can ill afford, simply to prove to themselves and the rest of the world that they are still superpowers. Few empires have mastered the fine art of decline; few nations have developed the cultural means of letting themselves down gently when the tide of history turns against them.

This is as true in the mundane domain of domestic well-being as it is in the annals of international relations. From the myth of Horatio Alger to the legacies of real-life robber barons, we have built a national culture around the idea of progress, and its cornerstone is our standard of living. Though the United States has weathered economic catastrophes like the Great Depression, we continue to think of these debacles as aberrations that pass like massive tornadoes. They wreak destruction across the land, but being the pragmatic, can-do people that we are, we pick up the pieces and rebuild our lives in a bigger and better fashion than before. This is the best our culture seems able to offer about the problem of economic decline: that it is a temporary problem, and we will overcome it.

Americans cannot adjust their expectations with every fluctuation of the consumer price index. Instead, they search desperately for some person or political party to rescue the nation from its unhappy pattern of recessions and anemic recoveries. From Jerry Brown on the left to H. Ross Perot in the quirky middle to Pat Buchanan and David Duke on the far right, voters have turned to outsiders and political renegades, hoping they will turn the tide and bring back the prosperity that is central to the self-definition of this society. It is a dangerous time to be an incumbent of any stripe, for the status quo has rarely been so unacceptable.

We are uncomfortable at the thought that the squeeze play tightening around the baby-boom generation is anything more than a momentary glitch. Yet evidence is mounting that this is a long-term phenomenon. Experts in economics can tell us about the large-scale trends that are transforming the United States, endangering the middle class, redistributing wealth away from those in the middle toward the rich, impoverishing those already unfortunate enough to be at the bottom of the pyramid. This big picture is worthy of review and will be presented in laymen's terms in the next chapter.

The larger task of *Declining Fortunes,* however, is to understand what these trends mean in the lives of the two most important generations alive in America today: postwar parents and their boomer progeny. We need to know more about the kind of values that were nurtured in the suburbs when the boomers were growing up, about the ways in which the experience of social change in the 1960s and 1970s reshaped the views of the older boomers, and how the experience of growing up in the shadow of the Reagan White House conditioned the younger boomers to expect more material rewards than they have found. For the baby-boom generation is truly a house divided. The liberal political culture of the older boomers, those who came of age in the 1960s, departs sharply from the more conservative culture of the younger boomers. In a fundamental sense, they are different kinds of Americans.

Never has it been more critical for them to unite as a generational interest group and never has it been less likely that they will do so. Fissioned by their cultural and political history into two antagonistic groups, the boomers greet each other across a chasm of differences in expectations, desires, and values. These divergent generational cultures have thus far prevented the boomers from recognizing their common complaints, their common needs. Hence, where other generations are organized to claim their share of the national pie, the boomers are strangling on their internal differences and fail to articulate their own demands.

Coming to terms with the political, social, and cultural significance of declining fortunes means exploring the meaning of generational identity in modern America, the way that expectations nurtured in different moments of our postwar history are continuing to shape responses to the disappointments accumulating in our lives.

2

Winners and Losers in the Eighties and Nineties

History will not be kind to the America of the 1980s. A decade-long binge of red ink, savings-and-loans scandals galore, the near bankruptcy of the Federal Deposit Insurance Corporation, monumental tax cuts for the rich, and deep consumer debt for the rest all added up to the largest federal deficit in the history of the United States. We have avoided the real fallout of our declining fortunes by passing the political buck back and forth from the Congress to the president and by passing the bill to our grandchildren. The well-worn cliché about "no free lunch" haunts the nation: interest payments on the national debt consume 15 percent of the federal budget, leaving that much less behind to pay for the social services we need, the roads we travel, the financial aid our students require, and the social security our elderly depend upon. The deficit eats into our savings and consumes funds we might otherwise invest in new plants and machinery, a crucial element in any return to economic growth.[1]

Though we may believe that the long-term damage we have sustained is a matter to be rectified in the future, many Americans live with the consequences of economic retrenchment every day. The decade of the 1980s saw steep declines in the purchasing power of the vast majority of Americans and a widening gap between the haves and the have nots. Sympathy for the down and out has declined, as those who are supposed to be enjoying "the greatest economic expansion since World War II" (the standard Republican refrain) discover that they cannot afford health care, child care, mortgage payments, or any of the other needs that constitute the bottom line of a middle-class life. There appears to be no end in sight to the economic downturn of the late 1980s, as the prolonged recession of the 1990s digs deep into the pocketbooks of the American middle class. Anemic upturns in consumer confidence dissipate within days, as one bank or brokerage house after another announces layoffs. The encouraging possibilities of lower interest rates are of little help as long as unemployment remains high and serves to remind the average person of his or her own vulnerability.

This dismal portrait of a stalled, floundering economy may lead readers to imagine that our problems have rightly given *everyone* a bad case of the consumer blues. A closer look tells us that this is not so. Some people—indeed, some generations—made out like bandits in the 1980s and continue to reap the benefits of having been in the right place at the right time, while others are playing a game of catch up and doing poorly at it. I do not speak here of the genuinely rich, who are always better able to withstand the ups and downs of the economy.

I do argue that underneath the national trends lie vast generational differences that began to take form during the long, expansive upswing of America's postwar economy that came to a halt in the mid-1970s, catching the baby boom as a whole unawares and ill prepared to contend with the slide that followed. The result is a striking difference between the economic fates of two generations: the postwar generation, beneficiaries of an expanding private sector and generous government benefits, and the baby-boom generation, heirs to the vagaries of deindustrialization, deregulation, speculative gains in the housing market, and unprecedented competition driven by their own numbers. Their divergent fortunes are abundantly clear if we look underneath the surface of national averages to see how changes in the affordability of homeownership, the increasing inequality in the distribution of income, and changing family structures and career trajectories have caught different Americans at different points in their lives.

Home Sweet Home—For Whom?

Between 1980 and 1989 the United States saw the first downturn in rates of homeownership since the 1930s.[2] After fifty years of sustained increases, we began to see shrinkage in the proportion of people who could lay claim to the most fundamental aspect of the American dream: the family home. Rising real estate prices, more stringent lending standards, and higher interest rates all contributed to falling rate of homeownership in the 1980s. According to the National Housing Task Force, a congressional panel formed in 1987 by Senators Alfonse D'Amato and Alan Cranston, nearly two million *fewer* families own their own homes today than would have if the rates of homeownership common just a decade ago had held throughout the 1980s.[3] Yet even as these numbers went down, some people were doing fairly well in the housing market: Americans over the age of sixty and whites in general increased their share of the homeownership market. For one or two demographic groups to improve their lot while national averages decline can only mean one thing: somebody else has done much worse in the housing sweepstakes. The somebodies were members of the baby-boom generation, who have been locked out of the American dream in increasing numbers.

Table 2.1 shows very clearly that homeownership has become the province of the postwar generation. Older Americans saw their

TABLE 2.1
Homeownership Rates by Age of Household Head

Age	1973	1976	1980	1983	1987	1990
Under 25	23.4	21.0	21.3	19.3	16.1	15.3
25–29	43.6	43.2	43.3	38.2	35.9	35.9
30–34	60.2	62.4	61.1	55.7	53.2	51.5
35–39	68.5	69.0	70.8	65.8	63.8	63.1
40–44	72.9	73.9	74.2	74.2	70.6	70.4
45–54	76.1	77.4	77.7	77.1	75.8	76.1
55–64	75.7	77.2	79.3	80.5	80.8	80.4
65–74	71.3	72.7	75.2	76.9	78.1	78.7
75 and over	67.1	67.2	67.8	71.6	70.7	71.0
Total	64.4	64.8	65.6	64.9	64.0	64.1

SOURCE: Joint Center tabulations of the 1973, 1976, and 1980 American Housing Survey and the 1983, 1987, and 1990 Current Population Survey. From "A Shift in Who Owns Homes," *San Francisco Chronicle*, November 29, 1991, pp. A1, A20. © SAN FRANCISCO CHRONICLE. Reprinted by permission.

rates of homeownership climb dramatically from the mid-1970s to the early 1990s. Particularly advantaged during this period were people in the group aged fifty-five to seventy-five, the very group that benefited in the first place from postwar government policies that provided low-cost mortgages, making it possible for them to get into the housing market early and stay there. As William Apgar, associate director of Harvard University's Joint Center for Housing Studies, put it:

> After World War II, we made homeownership much more avail-able to people at a younger age than before, with the Veterans Administration and Federal Home Authority and other programs. [The postwar generation] was able to start earlier and own their own homes longer, and that's where the equity build-up comes from. Now that process is reversing.[4]

Baby boomers had exactly the opposite experience. In every age group under forty-four, homeownership rates dropped dramatically between 1973 and 1990. Boomers now in their mid-thirties suffered a drop of nearly 10 percent over that period, with younger people sustaining similar declines. Figure 2.1 tells the story in graphic terms: Americans under the age of thirty-five, which includes many

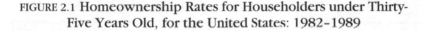

FIGURE 2.1 Homeownership Rates for Householders under Thirty-Five Years Old, for the United States: 1982–1989

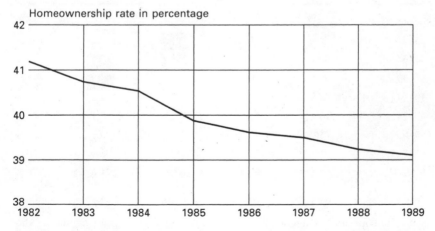

Homeownership rate in percentage

SOURCE: U.S. Department of Commerce, "Homeownership Trends in the 1980s," Series H-121, No. 2, December 1990, fig. 8, p. 11.

of the nation's boomers, found themselves excluded from the home-buying market. The younger members of the baby-boom generation, the men and women who came of age in the Reagan era, were especially disadvantaged: in 1973 over 23 percent of the people in this group owned their own homes; by 1990 that figure had dropped to about 15 percent. Not surprising, these figures were reflected in a substantial jump in the average age of first-time home buyers. In the early 1980s, the median age of the first-time buyer was twenty-seven. By 1991 it had risen to thirty-five—an astonishing jump in less than a decade.[5]

Baby boomers did not meet this downturn on equal footing. Those on the leading edge of this colossal generation, who entered the labor market when the economy was still expanding in the early seventies, were able to jump over the homeownership hurdle before it became prohibitively expensive. The trailing edge of the boomer group, those born after 1955, lost the race almost before it began.[6] As Table 2.2 shows, in 1976, when the older boomers were in their mid- or late twenties, about 43 percent of all Americans

TABLE 2.2
Baby-Boom Divider: Owning a Home

Percentage of People in Each Age Group Who Own a Home

■ Largely people born from 1946 to 1954   □ Largely people born from 1955 to 1964

Age	1973	1976	1980	1983	1987
Under 25	23.4	21.0	21.3	19.3	16.1
25–29	43.6	43.2	43.3	38.2	35.9
30–34	60.2	62.4	61.1	55.7	53.2
35–39	68.5	69.0	70.8	65.8	63.8
40–44	72.9	73.9	74.2	74.2	70.6
45–54	76.1	77.4	77.7	77.1	75.8
55–64	75.7	77.2	79.3	80.5	80.8
65–74	71.3	72.7	75.2	76.9	78.1
75 and over	67.1	67.2	67.8	71.6	70.7
Total	64.4	64.8	65.6	64.9	64.0

SOURCE: Population Reference Bureau, from Census Bureau data. "A Shift in Who Owns Homes," *San Francisco Chronicle,* November 29, 1991, pp. A1, A20. © SAN FRANCISCO CHRONICLE. Reprinted by permission.

aged twenty-five to twenty-nine owned homes. By 1987, when the trailing edge of the boomers had reached the same age, the proportion of those in that age group who owned a home had dropped to about 36 percent. A gap of this size represents more than just a set of abstract numbers: it encapsulates a sharp, painful variation in the ability of Americans to put a roof of their own over their heads simply by virtue of the fact that they were born a mere five years too late. Serendipity is never a satisfying explanation for those on the losing end, and it is small wonder that the younger boomers feel especially cheated.

The age profile of homeowners was not the only demographic variable to shift during the 1970s and 1980s: the kinds of families who could afford homes also changed in striking ways. Married couple families over the age of fifty were able to hold their own; young families were in trouble. Homeownership rates for married couples under the age of twenty-five decreased by about 5 percent. Nontraditional families,[7] a group increasing in size, lost ground as well. Particularly damaging is the trend evident among young families with children. Unless they were over the age of thirty-five and able to get into the market before the rapid price inflation of the 1970s and 1980s, the 1980s saw them increasingly shut out.[8]

Underneath national averages of this kind lie some important regional and racial differences. Not surprisingly, rates of homeownership are higher in areas where house prices are low and sharply lower in regions where the costs are high.[9] The South and the Midwest are favorably blessed in this respect, while the Northeast and the West have suffered. Racial differences became even more extreme than they had been in the past. In 1980 about 44 percent of black households owned their own homes; the comparable figure for white households was nearly 70 percent. The downturn that followed was devastating for black families, particularly for those in the baby-boom generation: those families whose household heads were under thirty-five saw their homeownership rates drop by an astounding 21 percent compared with the black family average of 1980.[10]

To understand better why these differences developed, why Americans otherwise closely positioned in age and background faced wildly different climates for homeownership, we need to look at the question of affordability. Who has the financial wherewithal and who does not? And why did these differences develop in the first place? Using the standard of the median-price house and a conventional, fixed-rate mortgage of thirty years, the Census Bureau discovered that by the late 1980s less than half of all American families could afford to buy the median-price house in the region where they lived.[11] Even more telling perhaps over 90 percent of the nation's renters could *not* afford a moderate house. The people best positioned to move into the market in the late 1980s, the proverbial yuppies—married couples with no children—were better off than anyone else, but they represent the minority. Families with a single wage earner, including those headed by single women, were virtually locked out. And married couples with children, the iconic image of the homeowner in the 1950s, found the going increasingly rough.

Affordability is, of course, largely a function of the income a family has to spend on housing. The higher a family's income, the easier it is to amass the funds for a down payment. Lending officers in local banks also look upon higher-income families with greater favor, granting them mortgages while turning down households living closer to the margins. As the economy cycles through its periods of downturns and upswings, families often find their credit card bills and conventional loans rising, a practice that may place them outside the bounds of an acceptable mortgage risk. When money is tight and interest rates are high, families that carry a high debt burden do not fare well in the mortgage market. By the late 1980s the Census Bureau showed that even current homeowners would not be able to buy median-price houses in their areas, partly because they could not afford the down payment or monthly costs and partly because their debt level had risen too high. Renter families were even more disadvantaged: 80 percent of the nation's renters could not qualify for a mortgage on the average house in their area.[12]

The relationship between house prices and American wages explains a good part of this story. Between 1973 and 1989 the average price paid by first-time home buyers *increased* nearly 19 percent.[13] Meanwhile, the average income of the nation's young renters *decreased* from $27,860 to $26,000.[14] In most regions of the United States median household income dropped during this period, and in all areas of the country house prices rose.[15] To add insult to injury, mortgage rates began to skyrocket in the late 1970s and early 1980s, a trend that would have increased the burden on buyers even if prices had remained flat.

For those fortunate Americans who have the income to sustain the monthly costs of homeownership, amassing the down payment can often prove a barrier nonetheless. To make the transition from renter to first-time buyer, a household must lay its hands on a stock of wealth through saving. But as we know, the savings rates of U.S. families have been declining for some time now. Many families, especially young families, simply lack the margin of affluence to stockpile the cash for a down payment.

Postwar parents often look at this situation through unforgiving eyes. "If Johnny and Susie would just stop spending their money on every new gadget," they complain, "in a few years they would have enough for that cute starter home they want so badly." Indeed, the inability of the baby-boom generation to buy homes is often attributed to their shortsighted patterns of consumption; conversely, their parents' high rates of homeownership is attributed (by the parents themselves, of course) to their frugal habits and assiduous savings.

Are the boomers squandering their money and therefore to blame for destroying their chance to own a piece of the American dream? Economists argue that only part of the acceleration in spending in recent years can be chalked up to the discretionary items typically associated with yuppies: cars, VCRs, and the like. Much of the increase in discretionary spending has been soaked up by medical care and legal/financial services; the increasing cost of these services has outstripped inflation by a substantial margin. Moreover, people tend to use them more as they get older.[16] From this point of view, it would appear that the aging of the boomers will contribute very little to boosting overall savings rates, a key to increasing the rate of homeownership.

The notion that boomers are frittering away their down payments on items they could do without is not wholly without support, however. Data from the 1987 Consumer Expenditures Survey show that the total share of household expenditures given over to the purchase of cars among those aged twenty-five to forty-four increased substantially in the late 1980s. The National Association of Realtors—a group understandably worried about boomers spending their way out of homeownership—has concluded that this enormous generation is indeed discouraged about the difficulty of getting ahead and is spending now rather than saving for the future. The spiraling costs of essential goods and services—health care, for example—has put the price of homeownership out of reach for many. They may indeed be spending what is left over on VCRs, since the kitty will never amount to enough to buy the white picket fence.

Spending the leftovers is not the only impediment to saving. Boomers are also more indebted than previous generations were at the same age, a trend that is also interfering with their ability to save. Student loans left over from their college years and other "nonrecreational" debts are biting into the funds they might otherwise use as a housing nest egg. Prospective first-time buyers surveyed in the mid-1980s showed that more than 20 percent were paying back on loans of this kind. Among these housing hopefuls, average loans were twice the amount carried by homeowners.[17] This level of debt makes it hard for first-time buyers in the twenty-five- to thirty-four-year-old age group to accumulate the kinds of assets that could be liquidated to make a down payment on the average home.

Table 2.3 compares the 1986 financial position of baby-boom households, their postwar parents, and elderly Americans who were born before 1925. The average net worth of these three generations differs rather dramatically, a trend attributed in part to the increasing equity value of their homes, which grows over time, time that the elderly have by definition had longest to accrue. America's seniors are far better off than any other age group in the country, a trend that is accelerating. In 1983 households headed by someone under the age of thirty-five had an average net worth of $45,700. Three years later that figure had slipped to $38,600! At the same time households headed by those sixty-five and older increased their net worth on average from $208,000 to $218,000. All age groups under fifty-five got poorer, while all age groups over fifty-five grew richer.[18]

In 1963, according to a Federal Reserve Bank survey, households headed by those sixty-five and older made up about 20 percent of our population and owned about 26 percent of the country's wealth. By 1986 the size of this elderly population had increased only slightly (to 21 percent), but its share of national wealth had grown to 33 percent. During the same period households headed by the under-thirty-five set—the baby boomers—grew much larger in terms of the proportion of the population they represent but stagnated in terms of their share of the wealth at just 6 percent. To put

TABLE 2.3

Financial Well-being of Three Generations of Americans*

Financial Characteristics	All Households	Baby Boomers	Postwar Generation	Elderly
Liquid assets[†]	$3,000	$2,000	$4,200	$5,601
Net worth (minus home equity)	$42,630 ($14,365)	$20,634 ($9,480)	$70,542 ($22,628)	$59,898 ($16,427)
Income[‡]	$21,137	$22,333	$28,662	$12,115
Number of households in sample	2,338	721	934	683

* Generational membership is based on year of birth of the head of household. Households headed by individuals born between 1946 and 1964 inclusive are referred to as "baby boomers"; those headed by members born between 1925 and 1945 are labeled as "postwar"; those headed by members born before 1925 are labeled as "elderly."
† Liquid assets are defined as stocks and mutual funds, bonds, checking and savings accounts, and money market accounts and CDs.
‡ Income is the average of the median 1983, 1984, and 1985 annual incomes.

SOURCE: Adapted from table 4.6 of National Association of Realtors, *The Housing Ladder: A Steeper Climb for American Households* (Washington, D.C., 1991), p. 81. Data are drawn from the 1983 and 1986 surveys of Consumer Finances, published by the Board of Governors of the Federal Reserve System.

the matter in dollar terms, the average baby-boom household had about $63,000 in net worth to its name, compared with $153,000 for the postwar generation ahead of them.[19] The generational divide is largely a function of the dynamics of the housing market, dynamics that have been particularly unkind to the boomers as a group.

Married boomers in rental households should, in theory, be the prime movers in today's real estate market. Their family needs should propel them to buy houses in unprecedented numbers, for they are perfectly positioned as parents of young children to fill the vacancies left behind by the large number of "empty nesters" among their parents generation looking to sell their homes. But the median liquid assets of baby-boom renters ranged from $500 for married couples with children at home to $2,000 for those without children at home, an insignificant amount when compared with the costs of buying a place of their own in most regions of the United States.[20] Given this, it is hardly surprising that only 9 percent of the nation's renters are able to afford a home, a small number that gets even smaller when we consider the country's most expensive housing markets: only 8 percent of American renters are in the running for homeownership in the Northeast and the West.[21]

The situation is bad enough for renters who are white, the one group of Americans most likely to fare well in the employment market. For minority families and single parents, the news has been worse: 98 percent of black and Hispanic families that rent could not buy a median-price home; 97 percent of single women with children were in the same position. For all families in rental housing, the high cost of rent is itself a barrier to saving the money needed to become a homeowner.

Delayed entry into the ranks of the homeowners imposes a lifelong burden on families headed by members of the boomer generation: the longer it takes to leap the hurdle of homeownership, the shorter a period of time they have to reap important financial benefits of ownership—equity. Few people today earn enough money to amass large amounts of capital out of their regular earnings. We see from Table 2.3 that the net worth of the postwar generation and the elderly drops by more than 75 percent when the accumulation due to home equity is subtracted. Housing is clearly the major mechanism for accumulating wealth in the United States, outside of those few who are lucky enough to inherit.[22] Along with various entitlements provided by the federal government—Medicare and social security—these equity nest eggs are the main reason for the comfortable retirement enjoyed by today's elderly.[23]

While boomers are painfully aware of the economic frustrations they face in the here and now, they have not yet begun to contemplate what this delay in entering the housing market will mean for them as they age. Compared with their parents, they have "missed" an important opportunity to begin the capital accumulation process, a misstep that will dog them for the rest of their lives.[24] They will find it harder to save for their own retirement, since for most Americans increasing home equity is the only way to squirrel away money. When we couple the boomers' declining ability to save and increased indebtedness with the pressure that continues to mount on the federal social security system, pressure that may threaten the system's integrity when the baby-boom generation needs it most, we are looking at a time bomb.[25] Boomers assumed they would live adult lives akin to those their parents had and have been crushed to discover that this is not to be. Their dismay has been compounded by the realization that they may not be able to do as much for their own children as their parents did for them. Multiply this litany of frustrations with the prospect that their retirement will lack many of the creature comforts that the postwar generation now enjoys—condominiums in Florida, travel, and medical care—and we have a recipe for bitterness.

Inaccessibility has not stopped the boomers from *wanting* to follow in their parents' footsteps: along with the chicken in every pot and the car in every garage, boomers still want that white picket fence. Indeed, according to a nationwide poll conducted by the *New York Times* in 1991, 84 percent of Americans still consider home-ownership to be the best long-term investment. This holds true even in regions of the country that have experienced instability and decline in housing prices. While affirming the importance of home-ownership, 80 percent of those surveyed agreed that "younger people today have a harder time buying a home than their parents did, and may never be able to afford the home they need."[26]

Why has homeownership become such a hurdle? Many trends have contributed to this problem, some of which have benefited older Americans at the expense of younger ones. We have seen a rapid growth in the number of high-income households that fueled a strong tradeup: families who were doing well wanted something to show for it, families that were growing in size needed larger homes. These fortunate Americans pushed prices up by increasing the demand for larger homes and for renovations and repairs. This, added to the trend toward strict local zoning that limits house construction and the steep cost of land, makes it even less likely that the nation's renters will make the transition into the landed class.[27]

At the other end of the spectrum, however, slow income growth expanded the number of households unable to afford even minimally adequate housing. In essence, the housing market has bifurcated into haves and have nots, with those at the high end benefiting in terms of equity value and the sheer size/comfort of their homes, and those at the low end sinking even farther below the homeowner threshold. The age distribution of these haves and have nots is hardly random, however. In the twenty years from 1970–90, the median price of a starter home for a typical married couple twenty-five to twenty-nine years old *rose* by 21 percent in constant dollars. The income of John and Jane Doe *declined* by 7 percent during the same period of time. This has left the Does in the unhappy position of having to devote a much larger proportion of their household budget to housing costs: in 1970 the typical family spent 28 percent of its income on housing; in 1990 housing soaked up 44 percent of the household budget.[28] Not only were younger families priced out of the market, but they also have less money to spend on other goods (cars, food, vacations, and so forth). Americans ten or more years older than the Does had the opposite experience: their income stayed even or increased. This group took advantage of their improving finances to increase their share of homeownership and expand their luxury spending.

One might imagine that the recession of the early 1990s would cure some of these affordability problems by cutting housing prices. No such luck. Boomers who have waited with bated breath for those prices to fall have discovered that just when it appeared that a buyer's market was around the corner, their own economic security has been severely shaken by rising unemployment. Even in the New York region, where the crash in home prices has been among the most severe in the nation, the goal of homeownership is more difficult to realize than it was ten years ago.[29]

Bringing Home the Bacon

To understand why some won and some lost in the battle for the American dream over the past two decades, one must look at some fundamental trends that have changed the distribution of income in the United States, the demographics of the work force, and the behavior of households in different generations. The basic message here is clear: on virtually all counts it was better to have reached adulthood by the early 1950s than at almost anytime afterward. During the postwar years jobs were not only increasing in number, but they were also increasing in quality, in prospects for advancement, and in financial reward. As Harrison and Bluestone point out, real weekly wages of the average American worker rose steadily from the 1950s until about 1973.[30] Thereafter, it was all downhill: the average wage has been falling or stagnating ever since those fateful days when the OPEC cartel formed and pushed oil prices into the stratosphere. The United States is still reeling from the resultant economic downturn.

Moreover, as wages began their slow descent, their distribution became increasingly unequal as well. Indeed, we saw a marked increase in the divide between haves and have nots over the course of the 1980s: record numbers of American families were pushed into poverty, while those fortunate few who were already at the top of the income scale added enormous sums to their coffers. The census shows that the top 1 percent of American families reaped the lion's share of whatever economic gains were to be had throughout the 1980s. As the *New York Times* put the matter:

> An outsized 60 percent of the growth in after-tax income of all American families between 1977 and 1989—and an even heftier three-fourths of the gain in average pretax income—went to the wealthiest 660,000 families, each of which had an annual income of at least $310,000 a year for a household of four. . . . The average pretax income of families in the top percent swelled to $560,000 from $315,000, for a 77 percent gain in a dozen years. At the same time, the typical American family—smack in the middle, or at the median, of the income distribution—saw its income edge up only 4 percent, to $36,000 and the bottom 40 percent of families had actual declines in income.[31]

The pattern of concentrated income is paralleled by data that show increasing inequalities in the distribution of wealth. In 1983 the top 1 percent of American households accounted for approximately 31 percent of the private net worth of the country.[32] By the end of the decade, that share had increased to 37 percent or $5.7 trillion. This is an astounding jump in a period of only six years. It left the wealthiest Americans—again, the top 1 percent—owning more than the bottom 90 percent of the nation's households.[33]

What accounts for the surge in the economic strength of the richest Americans? Politicians and economists alike will have a field day attempting to explain the enormous increase in inequality these trends represent in a society that sees itself as open to all comers, a level playing field in which Horatio Alger may triumph at will. Some argue that tax policy was the prime mover in the concentration of wealth: Ronald Reagan's legacy may be defined by the rollback of capital gains taxes and ordinary income tax rates that greatly advantaged those in high income brackets.[34] Others point to the stratospheric increase of executive pay levels: it is no longer unusual to find CEOs earning in excess of $5 million per year, a figure that would have been almost unthinkable as recently as the 1960s.[35] Still other economists point to the steep increase in the value of real estate as the major reason for the upturn in the fortunes of the very rich. Whatever the cause—and no doubt all of these factors played a role—there can be little doubt of the conclusion expressed so clearly by Harvard economic historian Claudia Goldin: "Inequality is at its highest since the great leveling of wages and wealth during the New Deal and World War II."[36]

And what of the people on the other side of the tracks? Earnings in the vast majority of the nation's households have failed to gain ground against inflation since the early 1970s. Annual raises have been overtaken by bigger gains in the consumer price index that have eaten away at purchasing power. According to the Census Bureau, median income in 1990, adjusted for inflation, was $29,943—$1,000 less than it was in 1973. For the 80 percent of the population with annual incomes below $80,000, income has stagnated.[37] Deciding what conclusions to draw from these facts is more a matter of political persuasion than of economic philosophy. Republicans look at the experience of the 1980s and see that the median family income represents a record high for American families, even though it represents barely a 2.4 percent increase over the past ten years. Democrats counter that the only reason that the American middle class has managed not to fall through the floorboards is that a record number of families are bankrolled by two wage earners. Without the massive entry of women into the labor market—a move stimulated both by the feminist movement and by the declining average wages of men and the rising needs of families for more earners—household incomes would look decidedly more anemic.

Frank Levy and Richard Michel, economists well known for their research on long-term trends in income distribution, conclude that most of our economic woes can be explained by the following "central fact": "The years since World War II divide into two major periods: 27 years of rapid real wage growth followed by at least 13 years of real wage stagnation."[38] The 1950s and 1960s were years of high labor productivity and increasing wages. This rosy picture reversed in 1973, when a fourfold increase in the price of oil pushed the United States into recession and inflation; labor productivity began to fall as well. The downfall of the Shah of Iran and the subsequent Iran-Iraq War compounded our domestic economic problems by boosting the price of oil once again.[39] Employers in the United States responded by slamming the brakes on wage increases.

Why is wage stagnation so important? The rising standard of living that followed World War II was built on a foundation of increasing income flowing into American households. Most of the material goods that we think of as constituting a middle-class standard of living came to us because rising wages made them affordable. That gravy train has long since left us standing at the station, and along with it goes any hope that baby boomers can look forward to the same rising trajectory of comfort their parents experienced. As Levy and Michel put the matter:

> Rising real wages were an important part of the assumption that each generation lives better than its parents lived. Consider the example of an 18-year-old man who is getting ready to leave home for college. As he leaves, he looks at his father's salary and what it buys and he keeps the memory as a personal yardstick. In the 1950s and 1960s, the young man would have quickly measured up. By the time he was 30, he would have been earning about 15 percent more, in real terms, than he saw his father earn 12 years earlier. . . . In 1986 (after 13 years of slow wage growth) a young man of 30 earned about *15 percent less* than his father earned 12 years earlier and it is an easy next step to say, as many have, that this is the first generation that will not live as well as their parents.[40]

Wage stagnation hits American families where it really hurts: in the pocketbook; but it also has indirect effects that will impinge upon us in the long run. Policymakers have been complaining for years that Americans do not save enough money, that we are well behind our counterparts in Japan and Germany in the amount we squirrel away. Declining savings rates are a direct reflection of slowed income growth: the only way to maintain a level standard of living in the face of stagnant wages is to use all the available cash to pay for daily expenses.

Wage stagnation is largely responsible for the slow bleed of Americans right out of the middle class. Current estimates suggest that if our present trajectories continue, fewer than half of all Americans will be in the middle class by the year 2000. Throughout the 1980s a larger proportion of middle-income Americans descended into the lower-income category than in previous decades, while a much smaller group of low-income families moved up the ladder.[41] The Panel Study of Income Dynamics (PSID), an annual survey that has tracked the fortunes of five thousand representative American families every year since the mid-1960s, shows the change in the profile of income distribution. The percentage of Americans living in households earning $18,000–$55,000[42] fell from 75 percent in 1978 to 67 percent in 1986.[43] By the end of the 1980s only six out of ten Americans were middle class—*a 20 percent decline in barely a dozen years*.[44]

The squeeze on the middle class creates political agitation for tax cuts: the more Americans need their income to pay for essentials, the less generous they feel toward Uncle Sam. It is no accident that the tax rollback revolutions stretching from California (the infamous Proposition 13) to Massachusetts (the equally infamous Proposition 2-1/2) came about after many years of stagnant wage rates. It is equally unsurprising that these tax revolts were coupled with an unwillingness to see cuts in government entitlements for the middle class. We need those services and subsidies all the more since our income has been flat. Ultimately, these are not merely matters of abstract public policy: they too hit the average family in the pocketbook, for the government must respond to this whipsaw of demands either by cutting services (which families must make up with their own resources) or by borrowing to provide the same services with less tax revenue (driving up the interest rates we pay for mortgage loans, car loans, and the like). Few in this country can escape the personal financial consequences of these alternative actions.

Why did this pattern of stagnation develop and how have families responded to it? Conservatives tend to argue that declining productivity and overpriced labor were responsible for the leveling of income growth in the United States. From this perspective, our competitive position in international trade has declined precipitously because our workers do not work hard enough and because they earn too much money, particularly in comparison with their blue-collar counterparts in Third World countries (or even in Japan) who earn a fraction of American wages for doing the same kind of work (faster and more efficiently).[45] Not only does the conservative posture blame a bloated work force and its unrealistic expectations for its own problems, but it also labels them as the responsible party for the problems the rest of us have experienced as a result of competitive decline. The solution to the problem, by this account, is to force workers to be realistic about the true value of their labor and to insist that they accept a drastic decline in their standard of living, which in turn will lower the cost of American goods and restore our market position. It is all too clear who will bear the cost of this "realism": labor.

Liberal economists, including well-known figures such as Bennett Harrison and Barry Bluestone, see the picture quite differently. Stagnant wages have developed, they argue, because the economy is no longer generating decent jobs. In their recent book, *The Great U-Turn*, Harrison and Bluestone turn a critical eye on the changes in the American job market and conclude that

> the proportion of jobs that are low-paid has been mushrooming since 1979. . . . The nation is producing jobs by the bushel, but corporate restructuring, aided and abetted by permissive government policy, is producing a startling deterioration in the quality of those jobs and consequently in the standard of living of a growing proportion of our citizens.[46]

If the economy continues to produce a large number of "bad" jobs and a small number of "good" jobs, entrants into the labor market will be disadvantaged over time in terms of wages and prospects for mobility.[47] One might respond that only the poorly qualified will suffer this fate and that this pressure will eventually force young people to invest in their own education and training. It is true that the vast majority of poorly paid workers are those whom we expect to be trapped at the bottom of the job market: women, minorities, and high school dropouts. But a growing number of people who never expected to find themselves among America's low-paid workers are landing in that category despite their college training. As of 1986 almost three million people with some college training were among those unfortunate Americans who work year-round at full-time jobs that pay less than $11,000 per year.[48] Harrison and Bluestone warn that it is no fluke:

> The trend in the low-wage population since 1963 suggests that those workers traditionally most favored in the U.S. labor mar-

ket—whites, men, and workers in the high-wage Midwest—are joining the low-wage segment in record numbers.[49]

Things are bad enough for workers who can find year-round full-time employment. For the fifty million Americans who work part-time (or less than the whole year), including the growing army of temporary workers, the income picture is even less encouraging. Nearly 80 percent of these part-time workers earn less than $11,000 per year. Apart from paying poorly, low-wage jobs are notorious for having poor benefits and little job security. For the millions of workers who have been able to do no better than this, life is looking ever more precarious.

By now we are all familiar with the rapid demise of America's heavy-manufacturing sector. The specter of "deindustrialization"[50] has stranded millions of blue-collar workers in states like Michigan, Indiana, Ohio and in the northeastern rust belt cities that were once dependent upon the now-defunct steel and auto industries. The loss of these unionized, high-paying, benefit-rich jobs has permanently changed the face of blue-collar America. Many have given up on reviving this sector and look instead to strong growth in the service industries as the panacea for the nation's economic ills. Indeed, there has been a surge in employment in the service sector.

Some of those jobs are every bit as good as, perhaps even better than, the blue-collar jobs they have replaced. On the whole, however, jobs in the service sector are skewed toward the low wage end of the spectrum. For every doctor in the country there are scores of hospital orderlies; for every stockbroker there is a fleet of clerical workers; and behind every elegant restaurant owner is a passel of poorly paid waiters. Job growth in the United States has been confined largely to these low-end service jobs, which are more likely to be part-time and without benefits than their counterparts in the manual trades used to be. Hence, growth in the service sector does not solve the problems of the American labor force, particularly when the problems include growing income inequality.[51]

But what of those fortunate workers who land managerial jobs in the service sector? Are they not riding high in an expanding part of our high-tech economy? Many an economist and many an ordinary manager would like to believe this is so. Unfortunately the late 1980s have shown us that there is nothing magical about white-collar managers; they too are subject to the winds of recession.

Their educational credentials, years of service, and specialized expertise offer far less protection against hard times than many had thought.[52] In October 1990, *Business Week* ran an article that sent chills down the spines of many a manager: "This Time, the Downturn Is Dressed in Pinstripes," read the headline. The text was little comfort:

> Since August 1989, the number of unemployed workers has jumped by 485,000 and 65% of them are managers, professionals, and the clerical workers who work for them. If the U.S. is in a recession, as many economists believe, it's one that is wearing a white collar.[53]

In 1990 over 170,000 permanent white-collar staff cuts were made across a diverse group of American industries: computer manufacturers dug deep into their managerial ranks to trim costs, defense contractors let go engineers and project managers even though the war in the Persian Gulf was gearing up. Financial services were in a tailspin, with bankers reeling from the impact of mammoth mergers, real estate agents turning in their licenses in record numbers, and insurance companies cutting their managerial staffs back as business fell.[54] *Business Week* complained that the recession of the late 1980s and early 1990s was doing disproportionate damage to their managerial readership, leaving blue-collar workers "escaping practically unscathed." The truth is that blue-collar employees have already been so sharply reduced in number that there is virtually no one left to cut. White-collar managers are now likely to be unemployed longer on average than blue-collar workers.[55] With manufacturing on its knees, the service industries appear to be next: few of these managerial jobs are going to return, even if economic growth picks up.

Having depended upon the service sector to be our engine of growth, we are now learning that when times are bad, it is just as vulnerable to downturns and high unemployment as any smokestack industry ever was.[56] There is no comfort in this egalitarian distribution of pain: every well-paid job lost is another blow to a consumer-led economic recovery. People who are unemployed—coupled with those who are worried about following in their sorry footsteps—are not good candidates for high spending. When they cut back on their purchases, companies respond by laying off more workers. A vortex of unemployment, declining demand, and more unemployment sucks everyone down. When economists wring their hands over "consumer confidence," they need look no farther than the unemployment lines to understand why Americans are tightening their belts and cutting back on their credit card purchases. Widespread fear of unemployment makes even well-paid executives feel the need curtail their spending.

In the New York region, the main market for the citizens of Pleasanton, job losses for the three years ending in 1992 reached record levels. Not since 1939, the year the state began keeping records, have so many jobs disappeared from the scene.[57] In the Big Apple, the fallout from Black Monday, the stock market crash of 1987, has been felt in real estate, the restaurant business, and the thousands of other tertiary service industries geared toward the well-heeled life-style of the denizens of Wall Street. Massachusetts, New Hampshire, and Rhode Island were in worse condition. Even the formerly prosperous sun belt state of California found itself in deep trouble, as unemployment rose to record high levels. Few parts of the country were immune to the impact of prolonged recession.

How has all this affected the divergent pathways of postwar workers and their boomer children? To some extent the two generations have been equally damaged by the trend: wages have fallen across the age groups, leaving everyone behind the curve. But thereafter the similarities end. Boomers entered the labor market just as the long period of postwar expansion was starting. From the mid-1970s onward, newcomers to the labor market faced a less favorable set of opportunities. Wage declines hit them particularly hard and have continued to place serious constraints on their ability to claim their share of the American dream.

The impact of the slowdown first surfaced as a form of credentialism: a high school diploma was no longer enough. College degrees became the sine qua non of white-collar employment, however lowly the job. The gap in earnings between college and high school graduates widened into a chasm, with college-educated men outstripping their less credentialed counterparts by 16 percent. The gap among women widened as well, by 12 percent.[58] Those who failed to learn this lesson fell behind precipitously and have never recovered: the less educated are also less likely to own homes or have savings or retirement benefits. They are essentially locked out of the middle class.[59] Boomers who followed the credentialist impulse, including the vast majority of Pleasanton's high school grads, also found it rough going. College admissions were more competitive, in part because of the sheer size of the generation, and the professions that pay well were similarly oversubscribed. Applications to law school, medical school, and above all business school rocketed throughout the 1970s and 1980s; the salaries of successful professional school graduates followed suit. Those who made it through these ever-tightening entry gates did extremely well. Those who did not, by definition the majority, were confined to less exciting and less lucrative jobs in the white-collar world.

In the past they might have been able to look forward to success in the business world. However, the fits and starts of the American economy put the brakes on upward mobility even for those who were gainfully employed. The growing glut of college graduates cannot be absorbed into a labor market with shrinking professional opportunities. In the 1980s one in five college graduates ended up in jobs that the Bureau of Labor Statistics defines as not requiring a college degree: sales clerks, typists, file clerks, and laborers.[60] Men who expected to move up in their organizations found the escalator slowing down for them at a surprisingly early age. The feverish thinning of managerial ranks of the 1980s left fewer layers of hierarchy and fewer opportunities for promotion. "Lean and mean," the watchword of the business community in these struggling times, could not have come about at a worse time for the baby-boom generation: record numbers of them, including thousands of newly minted business school graduates, came of age just when managerial opportunities were being phased out in droves. Hitting a plateau at forty, when you expected to continue to rise well into your fifties, lets a white-collar man know in a particularly personal way that he should not expect bigger and better things in his business life.

Boomer women newly arrived in the business world were even more likely to see their prospects for advancement damaged. The "glass ceiling" that prevents them from ascending into the executive suite is only partly caused by gender bias: it is exacerbated by the general slowdown, the lean-and-mean philosophy that has translated into reduced middle-management opportunity, and the extreme competition that the bulge of boomers has brought to the labor market. The result is a decline in the standard of living of the baby boomers as well as a crushing blow to their expectations for a career and a life-style that would approximate the dreams their parents inculcated in them in the rosy days after the war.

Divisions within the boomer group are widening as a result of the slowdown in job opportunities. The leading-edge boomers were fortunate relative to their trailing-edge counterparts, for they were able to get into the job market and work their way up for a period of time before the sharp decline in promotion opportunities of the 1980s. A decade later, when the youngest boomers (born in the 1960s) began to seek their own fortunes, entry into the market was far more problematic. Unemployment was at record levels in the early 1980s, as the impact of the 1979–82 recession devastated the younger boomers. There were far fewer jobs, even for the highly qualified, than there had been in the early 1970s when the leading-edge boomers got their toehold in the working world. And, unfortunately for the nation's youngest boomers, the sheer size of the group just ahead of them will foreclose opportunities that might otherwise have been available.

How have boomers responded to the combination of rising costs and declining opportunities? Enter the gods of demography. They tell us that boomers have reacted to reduced opportunities by making fundamental changes in their patterns of marriage, childbearing, and household composition. At the turn of the century the average age of first marriage for men was 26, while women married at 22. The mid-fifties changed all that, bringing the age of marriage down to 22.5 years for men and 20.2 for women.

Fertility rose accordingly, with the average size of the American family climbing to an all-time record of slightly more than three children between 1954 and 1964.[61] As Arlene Skolnick explains in her book *Embattled Paradise: The American Family in an Age of Uncertainty,* the 1950s was an aberrant time on a number of counts, however much it may appear to us now as the benchmark of "Leave It to Beaver" normality.[62] Women married young, had far more babies than their own mothers had had, and stayed home in record numbers to raise them. They could do this because their husbands' wages were rising fast enough to make such domestic bliss possible even for families of modest means.

As the economic slowdown that began in the early 1970s gathered force, and the feminist movement kindled the desire of women to work, the age of marriage began a long climb back up toward levels common at the turn of the century. In 1980 the average age of first marriage was 26 for men and 22 for women, a considerable increase compared to the Ozzie-and-Harriet era. The 1990 census confirms the persistence of this trend: men stand at 26.3 and women at 24.1 for age of first marriage.[63] Fertility rates have declined drastically to slightly fewer than two children per women, cutting the childbearing rate to nearly half what it was when the mothers of today's boomers were having their kids. The sheer number of baby-boom women of childbearing age is high enough to produce a record of number of births in absolute terms, but the trends tell another story—that women are marrying later, having fewer children, and bearing them much later in life than was characteristic in the 1950s. For many women, these adaptations exacted a considerable cost: they had to chose between maintaining a middle-class standard of living and having and raising children at the time and in the manner they wished. Nonetheless, the choice was clear and many opted to keep their family's standard of living high by delaying or limiting their childbearing in favor of working.

It is clear that the wholesale entry of women into the labor market is practically the only thing that kept the average middle-class family afloat. With men's wages stagnating and the cost of living rising, it was women to the rescue. The labor force participation rates of women twenty years of age and older rose from 43 percent in 1970 to 59 percent in 1992.[64] Their earnings, once mere pin money, have become mainstays of the family economy, a fact that still seems to catch American politicians by surprise. Absent this trend, the United States would have faced a future of massive downward mobility. Indeed, for families that did not follow this pattern, the consequences are clear enough: they fall farther and farther behind with every passing year. The price they pay for maintaining an Ozzie-and-Harriet household has been a steady decline in their standard of living.

What of the price paid by dual-career households? As long as children are not part of the picture, households with two wage earners live better than any other kind of American family. They are, in fact, the only ones who can pull ahead of the stagnation that has plagued the rest of the country. However, the "young urban professional" (yuppie) of the 1980s was never more than a short-lived demographic phenomenon. The vast majority of Americans—even the liberal boomers—eventually marry and have children. When they do, they quickly discover that they cannot manage financially without both incomes and cannot easily manage children with two workers slogging it out in the business world. Not only do they have to maintain two incomes, but they also have to work longer hours just to stay even. The Bureau of Labor Statistics found that in 1989 more people than ever before held both a regular job and a part-time job. Moonlighting among women has soared, particularly among single mothers struggling to keep their families afloat. The result should surprise no one: leisure time has shrunk from 26.2 hours per week in 1973 to 16.6 in 1987.[65]

Who is taking care of the kids while their boomer parents are out working? This is one of the great unanswered questions of social policy in the 1990s. As a society we have failed miserably in providing an infrastructure capable of responding to the needs of the millions of boomer households with full-time working parents and kids who need supervision. Conservatives rail against the very idea of professional child care and prefer to provide tax breaks to families with "stay at home" moms. Liberals know that child care matters but seem wary of putting much in the way of national resources behind their convictions. Families are essentially left to fend for themselves, an approach that would astound our European counterparts, who accept day care as a given, in nations as diverse as Italy and Sweden. Americans seem to have no trouble with the notion that providing for the elderly is a social responsibility, paid for through a taxation system that hits today's workers hard in the pocketbook so that yesterday's workers can retire on social security. When it comes to children, however, the view seems to be that these are private problems to be dealt with by every family on its own.

Many of the demographic responses of boomers to wage stagnation are predictable, but there are also some surprising developments that are changing the landscape of the American family. According to the 1990 census, married couples make up a smaller percentage of the nation's households than at any other time in the last two centuries.[66] One might be tempted to attribute this pattern to an increasing rate of divorce, but it turns out that divorce rates have been declining slowly since the 1980s.[67] The more telling explanation for the decline is that young people have been delaying marriage: the proportion of adults between the ages of twenty-five and thirty-four who have formed their own families plummeted from 83 percent to 65 percent between 1960 and 1990, a finding explained by the declining economic opportunities of the baby-boom generation.

Where are all those young people living if they are not marrying? A record number of them are "boomerang" kids who have returned home to live with their parents after completing their education or children who never left in the first place. The number of adult children living with their parents fell steadily in the years after World War II, but started to climb in the mid-1970s and has continued to do so ever since. The Census Bureau reports that by 1990 more than half of all young adults between eighteen and twenty-four years of age were living with their parents, compared with 42 percent in 1960. One in nine adults (a total of five million) between the ages of twenty-five and thirty-four lived in his or her parents' home, an increase of more than 25 percent in the boomerang rate since 1960. These figures may actually be an underestimate since this transient population is difficult to track, but even the numbers we have document a startling reversal in the earlier pattern.

Clearly at work here is the whipsawing impact of rising housing costs and stagnating paychecks. Young people who want to live on their own can expect a considerable drop in their standard of living. Those who stay with Mom and Dad are looking to hold on to the comforts they knew as dependent children, comforts that they cannot easily afford on the strength of their own incomes. Young people face steep increases in the cost of rents, up 28 percent since 1982. If wages had kept up with rents, this would not be a problem, but workers aged twenty-five to thirty-four were earning only 77 percent of the wages earned by people ten years older than themselves, down from 86 percent in 1980. Boomers were clearly at an economic disadvantage and are paying a price for their relative lack of earning power: they are having to compete in the rental market with older generations who entered the market when wages were rising.

One might expect that children from affluent communities like Pleasanton would have more resources at their disposal, resources that could underwrite the task of becoming independent. However, it is precisely among the more affluent of America's families that the drop in standard of living is most acute when the young strike out on their own. Hence, children living in households with annual incomes above $50,000 are more likely to remain at home with their parents than those in households less well heeled.[68]

Gender differences are also evident in the reaction of young people to the soft job market and the soft marriage market: among twenty-five- to thirty-four-year-olds, 32 percent of single men were living with their parents in 1990, while only 20 percent of single women were in the same situation. Given the stronger earning potential of men compared to women, we might expect to see the reverse, yet it is among young men that the most dramatic shifts are apparent. In 1970 less than 10 percent of single *and* married men in the twenty-five to thirty-four age group lived with their parents. By 1990 the figure had grown to 15 percent, a fairly steep increase.[69] The rates for women increased only half as fast.[70] These figures suggest that the slump affecting the baby-boom generation has hit sons harder and has pushed them back into the natal home at a greater pace than it has daughters.

The postwar expansion was enormously kind to the men and women who had the good luck to enter the labor market during those years. With wages rising, housing costs falling, and a generous package of government mortgage and educational benefits at their disposal, it became far more common than ever before for Americans to go to college, marry young, buy homes on the strength of the husband's income alone, have large families tended by mothers who could afford to stay at home, and sit back to watch their equity value grow. These favorable conditions in early adulthood set the stage for equally favorable retirement prospects: the postwar generation is set to reap the advantages of high equity in the form of a relatively comfortable sunset period in their lives.

Their children, the nation's boomers, face virtually the opposite set of conditions: the training and credentials a college degree confers have never been more important in deciding an individual's economic fate, but that education cost them dearly.[71] They were more likely to emerge from their years in college burdened by debt and less likely to find high-paying jobs that would help them relieve it. With opportunities in the job market constricted by serious periodic recessions throughout the 1980s and into the 1990s, boomers have been forced back into Mom and Dad's lap as they seek to protect their standard of living without the resources to do so in independent households. The combined effects of rising rents and stagnating wages have kept them at home long past the age when, at least in generations past, they would have been considered ready for independence.

Staying home longer, and lacking the ability to amass much capital, boomers have developed patterns of family formation that stand in stark contrast to those common only one generation before. They are marrying later, having fewer children, and paying for what they have with the efforts of two wage earners. Despite these adaptations to economic decline, they have not been able to catch up with their parents with respect to the single most important asset: homeownership.

Whatever disappointment and frustration this causes boomers, it may pale in comparison with the impact delayed access to housing equity will have on their retirement prospects. Boomers will lack the wherewithal to pay for the kind of retirement they have come to expect. In short, once the golden years of affluent childhood were over, boomers found themselves at a disadvantage every step of the way. They are not happy campers. And since they constitute such a large chunk of our population, when the boomers have the blues, the country as a whole is headed for a serious crisis of confidence.

3

The Making of the Boomers

The declining fortunes of the baby-boom generation capture our attention precisely because their lives stand in such stark contrast to the experience of their parents, the men and women who graduated from the war, spearheaded the exodus to suburbia, and in many respects organized and defined the middle class we take for granted today. We rarely think of the postwar generation as pioneers; they are not credited with having transformed American culture. The "cult of domesticity" they are identified with—a culture that placed men in the boardroom and women in the kitchen—is considered by many Americans a fossilized form of family life suitable only for the past. Yet consigning postwar suburbanites to the garbage heap of traditionalism blinds us to the cultural revolution they set in motion. These Ozzies and Harriets created a new suburban society. Far from the urban metropolis, the nation came to understand what the spread of affluence beyond inherited wealth could mean, what economic stability could produce, what the American dream had become.

In a very real sense, postwar parents represent one of the few living examples of the Horatio Alger story (on a grand scale) that the United States has ever actually produced. The Great Depression was the crucible of their generational culture, an experience that left a dark and lasting imprint upon their lives and formed the bedrock of the moral code they attempted—often unsuccessfully—to transmit to their baby-boomer children. The extraordinary success of the postwar generation, their flight from the cramped ethnic neighborhoods in the nation's cities to the expansive, Americanized suburbs of the postwar era took place against the vivid, unsettling subtext of the 1930s. Developing back-to-back, the two experiences—disaster followed by triumph—laid the groundwork for the truths these parents passed on to their own children. Hard work leads to success; living close to the margins is a recipe for disaster; caution is better than taking risks. These were the lessons taught to the boomers out in the great beyond of suburban America.

It is possible, the boomers tell us, that the odyssey of the postwar generation may represent the last great experiment in mass upward mobility. For in the lives of postwar parents, all the promise of prosperity materialized, the reward for waiting out hardship. If we are to understand why this historically contingent fact mattered so much in the lives of the baby boomers, why the suburban pioneers were so confident about the value of waiting while their adult children are so skeptical and frightened, we must return to the beginning and ask what kind of society these parents built in the safe enclaves beyond the city gates. What were they running from? What were they looking for? And how did it happen that the lessons the boomers actually learned from their own childhood experiences differed so radically from the ones their parents wanted them to imbibe?

One common understanding of suburbia, bequeathed to us largely by the intellectuals and critics who attacked its very legitimacy as a form of social life, is of deadening conformity enforced by people who were tired of being defined as outsiders to the American mainstream.[1] Herbert Gans effectively demolished this notion in his classic sociological study, *The Levittowners*. He argued that underneath the uniform appearance of neighborhoods of tract houses was a community that allowed for as much individuality as any urban neighborhood ever did. Gans urged his audience to dismiss critics' complaints that suburbs were the spawning ground of one-dimensional people bent on monitoring the condition of each other's front lawns. Instead, he argued, this new American subculture represented a kind of freedom that former city dwellers had never known before—freedom to associate with whomever they pleased, freedom to spread out and relax, freedom from the watchful eye of ever-present, overbearing, patriarchal (and matriarchal) authority that was so much a part of the fabric of life in the urban village.[2] People could remake themselves, and this was to be applauded rather than condemned as antithetical to choice and diversity.

Although nearly half of the population of the United States now lives in suburbs, very little research has been done on the culture of these communities since Gans's seminal work.[3] They have become so much a part of the fabric of the country that we feel we know, without really looking, what people are like out there.[4] In truth, suburban communities are as complex and surely as important as the urban areas that are typically the focus of sociological research. This is particularly true where the problem of downward mobility between generations is concerned. For although there are urban variants of this problem, it is in the suburbs that the disparities between postwar parents and their baby-boom offspring have become most acute.

Understanding the meaning of these divergent fates in the lives of both generations—how they interpret the problem of declining fortunes, diagnose it, politicize it, or steam over it in private—requires a look to the past. We have to consider who came to the suburbs and ask what they were after, for the ambitions they bequeathed to their children reflected their own aspirations and desires. Their image of what decent, hardworking individuals could aspire to in terms of an acceptable but not extravagant standard of living set the stage for the boomers to develop their own expectations. The children's sense of entitlement did not emerge in a vacuum. To understand why boomers feel cheated or burned, we must ask how their parents created a new sense of what was normal, reasonable, and natural for suburban people like themselves to expect.

Most of all, we must explore why it was so important for postwar parents to consolidate their own arrival in the middle class via the ascendance of their own children. It was imperative that the children of the postwar generation follow in their parents' footsteps and demonstrate the permanent arrival of entire lineages of newcomers to the landed middle class. This process derailed in the 1980s and in the early 1990s shows no signs of getting back on track. This very fact has become a familial, social, and political problem that binds the two generations in common disappointment.

To understand what suburban parents of the 1950s and 1960s were looking for in their children's lives, we must begin with the formative events of their own lives, the Great Depression, World War II, and the long upswing that followed. The historical events are, of course, well known. What is less well understood is the retrospective meaning assigned to these watershed moments in our history.

Buddy, Can You Spare a Dime?

I was too poor to have parents! My father started an ad agency in 1929, but he died in 1933. I was four years old. My mother had been an opera singer. The depression was on. After the death of my father we went on welfare, lived in a tenement with only cold water. The only heat came from the kerosene stove in the kitchen. I grew up that way with welfare clothes. They would give us shoes and overalls. Then my mother decided to leave and go someplace and I went to live with relatives in Massachusetts.

Norman Krasdale lives in a spacious split-level that bespeaks relaxed comfort. He likes to chat in the family room, with its cathedral ceiling and its enormous picture windows looking out on a tree-lined backyard. Norman has come a long way from the cold-water flat he shared with his widowed mother in the bleak years of the Great Depression. Yet the impact of that period has remained with Norman, shaping the way he marvels at his own good fortune, reinforcing in him the view that prosperity can be ephemeral.

Norman's experience of deprivation was somewhat unusual in comparison with the experience of his friends and neighbors in Pleasanton. Few of them had plunged so far; most were fortunate enough to ride out the depression without going hungry. Yet they knew what it was to sacrifice one's plans for the future or defer a dream. Families demanded help from their youngsters. Boys went out to work at a younger age than would have otherwise been required and turned over their paychecks to help pay the rent. Girls were less likely to go out to work but were often responsible for a great deal on the home front, particularly if their mothers went out to work.[5] While many of Pleasanton's depression survivors point to these kinds of experiences as proof of their capacity for hard work, their memories are colored with resentment. It was not considered normal, even in their day, for promising young people to have to defer all their own plans for the sake of family survival. It was a necessary sacrifice, perhaps, but not one that anybody welcomed. Whether they begrudged their parents this help or not, they had little real choice in the matter.

Samuel Donnerstein graduated from high school in 1938, at the age of sixteen. He was gifted in science, a genuine wizard with technical engineering problems. Sam was hungry for a college degree. Times were very bad, though, and his family was in real financial trouble. He felt the pressure to leave school and get a job, any job. Sarah, his wife of forty years, was from a more fortunate family, but they have been together so long that their memories have become one. Sarah speaks for Sam about how he subordinated his own plans to the needs of his parents and siblings:

> Sam had no possibility or expectation of anybody paying his college [expenses]. What he needed to do was to bring money home so that they could eat. The reason it took him so long to go to college is because he couldn't afford to take more than one or two courses at a time because of the tuition. His pattern is really the product of the depression years and the difficulty of getting an education. You know, Sam is very modest. He was an unusually brilliant child in terms of his scientific knowledge, but he just had to find a job that would provide food for himself and his family and do his studying on the side.

Sam got a job as an apprentice and enrolled in night school at a junior college. Luckily he was able to parlay this work experience into ever more responsible jobs in a university laboratory and to continue attending school on the sly, his employers fooled into believing he already had a degree. He does not really complain about his adolescence today, but he realizes that he had the potential to do a first-class college degree, potential that was never fully realized.

In retrospect, Sam realizes he was fortunate to get through school at all, even though it took him twice as long as it should have. He knew many who had it worse:

> I had friends who I worked with in high school who were brilliant and some of them said, "I'll steal the money and I'll go to school.". . . Some people would steal for bread . . . they would steal to go to school . . . and they did. One of my closest friends said that he didn't care if his family starved. It didn't matter. His parents had had their life, and "Now it's my turn. I'm going back to work and make the money for school, and I'm not giving it to them."

Sam faced his obligations squarely and supported his mother both before and after he got married. But he could understand his friends' frustration at the thought of compromising their own chances for the sake of their families. People like Russ Santino, who lives just down the road from Sam and Sarah, ended up permanently "derailed" by the economic slump:

> I was never able to go to college. My folks couldn't afford it. I resented that. I picked up a job, was an office boy, and attended school at night. Carrying twelve [high school] credits at night. I worked five days a week. I worked Friday, Saturday nights at my uncle's pizzeria. I was helping my folks. My Dad was ill and I had a younger brother. It was my responsibility and I resented it. I couldn't go out. My friends used to come to the pizza parlor at 1 A.M. and I would still be working. I was a waiter and my uncle didn't pay me anything. I resented that too! I used to work for tips, so if I made $10 for three days that was a lot of money; I was only earning $24 a week. I used to study at work when I could at lunchtime.

Lacking any real opportunity to continue his schooling, Russ worked at odd jobs until the outbreak of the war. When he returned home five years later, he took up the job he has held ever since, selling insurance. It is not an occupation he enjoys, even though it satisfies his financial needs. But he blames the need to work at a job he dislikes on the fact that family obligations (and financial limitations) prevented him from realizing his potential.

From the late 1920s to the early 1940s, millions of Americans saw their hopes dashed, their businesses collapse, their homes and farms foreclosed, and their families pulled apart as young men hit the road in search of work.[6] Official unemployment figures crested to 25 percent, and many others found themselves reduced to a part-time wage. Most of Pleasanton's postwar parents had been children or young adolescents during the depression. Their own parents bore the brunt of the economic slump, for it was they who had to put food on the table and figure out a way to avoid eviction. Nevertheless, their children were hardly immune to the disruption and frustration it visited upon their families. Indeed, adolescents who entered the labor market during the 1930s often found the entire course of their adult career trajectories changed by the unfortunate timing.[7]

Even those who were either too young to understand the severity of the situation or who came from families comfortable enough to be spared the worst were marked by the era. Indeed, the phrase "the depression generation" connotes not only the actual experience of deprivation but also the ethos or culture of hardship that arose in the 1930s. Americans who grew up in those dark times developed a perception of themselves as having been formed in the cradle of desperation, a perception that even the prosperous decades that followed the war never erased. Postwar parents never reconceptualized themselves as the fortunate cohort that rode the wave of growth that catapulted them into the middle class. They continued to speak of themselves as children of the Great Depression.[8] As Sarah Donnerstein put it:

> Our whole attitude about spending money [was affected by the depression]. Our children call it "Daddy's Depression mentality": you can't . . . you just don't go and spend that kind of money for something. You ask, do you need it? Is the value there? I feel guilty if I go out and spend money on something that I really don't need. What do I need another dress for? I have enough. . . . I wasn't brought up with the kind of economic hardship that Sam was, by no means. . . . My father was a lawyer; he was established. I never felt any economic insecurity. Maybe, now that I think back on it, there were probably times when things weren't as easy. But with us, we had the best teachers, the best education, there was no question that I was going to college, my brother was going to college, the money was there. Sam didn't have that kind of thing. And yet because of the times, and listening to the stories, and hearing my father and grandfather talk, I still don't get myself to spend the kind of money freely as my son and daughter-in-law can.

Like millions of her age-mates, Sarah thinks of herself as a survivor who learned the lessons of the depression well and carried them as a private code of behavior into more fortunate times. Sarah is joined in her view by many Pleasanton parents who readily admit that they were too young to appreciate what really happened during the 1930s. Helen Reinhardt's parents struggled to get through the depression, but since she was only a youngster at the time, she never noticed that she was poor:

My parents had a tough time during the depression because my
father lost his job in Bausch and Lomb, they closed up. And then he
went into the WPA and went from being an optical engineer to a
bridge gear engineer, which is a real switch. The depression had a
big impact on my family. Things didn't get better until Roosevelt
came in and the war started. Then my father was real busy. But you
know, people say we were poor then. I never thought of us as poor.
I always thought that we were okay, but when you're ten years old
you don't think in those areas. You know, your life just goes along.
If I had been older I would have thought of that at the time.

Helen knew that her father had suffered through unemployment
and downward mobility, but to a child these were not terribly
meaningful events. Only as she grew older, as her memory of those
years began to crystallize, did the motif of hardship form in her
mind. In a very real sense, the meaning of the depression only
assumed the iconic forms we know today—the face of the migrant
mother—in the process of retrospection.

The depression is not unique in this sense, for the meaning of
any generational experience is largely created in retrospect. Visions
of the past—whether of the 1930s or the 1960s—are constructed col-
lectively as a generation comes to grips with the impact of a shared
historical experience on their lives. Lasting memories were carved
into the souls of depression survivors, memories that were not just
personal or individual, but also collective. For the era of the 1930s
was the kind of cataclysm that unites survivors in a way that tran-
scends differences of class, national origin, or geographical origin.
As the depression passed from view, to be replaced by the war and
the good times that followed, it never faded from the consciousness
of the generation that lived through it. It remained their leitmotif
and continues to be the central, defining experience of their lives.

Most Americans who came through the depression remember
the mass fear it instilled, the deep and pervasive hopelessness of a
nation that felt rudderless until Franklin Roosevelt assumed office
and began, ever so slowly, to catalyze the recovery. But more than
memories emerged from the process of retrospection. Morals, prin-
cipals, maxims—the architecture of dos and don'ts that one derives
from such a critical experience—were also an important outcome of
that collective reflection. Pleasanton's senior generation learned
some lessons from the past, lessons they think of as universal, not
as historically contingent.

For Tammy Dean's parents, the most important "rule" to emerge from the depression was the importance of always keeping one's expectations low. The Deans escaped from the 1930s unscathed, but they saw that those who were foolish enough to consume all their resources left themselves in a vulnerable position. In some respects, they reasoned, those caught short in the prewar years had only themselves to blame, for they had been too quick to spend what they had. Saving, living well *below* your means, doing more with less—these are the Franklinesque maxims that have guided Tammy's parents ever since:

MRS. DEAN: We live a life-style that is not ostentatious. I remember when my husband gave me my diamond ring he said, "Take good care of it cause some day we might have to hock it." But we've never lived beyond our means, and I think for a long time we lived beneath our means. We never lived to the full. My husband's advice to me was, let's live in such a way so that if things get rough we don't have to back up. We can still keep going on the level we're living on.

MR. DEAN: In my lifetime I had seen too many people that lived up to the last buck that they earned and they earned a lot of bucks and all of a sudden they had to retrench and the retrench was so bad they felt as though they were living as paupers when they were probably living as well as people in the lower-middle-income bracket. I saw too many people hurt during the depression.

From the Deans' perspective, the trick is to sustain a life-style that is modest enough to protect your family from the pain of a devastating slide. If you never rise very high, you cannot fall very far.

Many of the parents in the educated, professional families of Pleasanton had survived the depression with their own middle-class status intact. Nonetheless, the aura of calamity had been all around them: they saw friends, neighbors, and even relatives fare poorly. They remember the headlines of banks collapsing and the apocryphal stories of stockbrokers plunging out of windows. They carry this collective memory with them to this day. It is indeed a tribute to the power of the depression to shape the culture of a generation that its lessons have not dimmed in better times.

Baby Boomers and the Great Depression

Boomers are often portrayed as wallowing in affluence, oblivious to the fact that life can take unexpected turns. Yet contrary to what many Pleasanton parents believe, their children are fully conscious of what the 1930s represented in the lives of their elders. Boomers understand how the depression shaped their parents' morality, created powerful and lasting fears over economic security, and generated a kind of penny-pinching attitude. Suburban-born children of affluence rely upon their secondhand understanding of the depression to understand why their parents think the way they do. They know that such a calamity grips its victims and holds them even in the face of years of upward mobility and economic prosperity.

Martin O'Rourke—now nearly forty—has a deceptively Irish name; his family are actually Italians of peasant stock who joined the flood of Mediterranean immigrants at the turn of the century. Growing up in Pleasanton, Martin was well aware of just how far his clan had come since Ellis Island. He also knows that the legacy of the depression has followed the O'Rourkes in an unbroken chain of memory:

> My family came out of a lot of poverty and were eager to escape it. . . . We always had to do something for tomorrow. There had to be food put away in the basement. That had a lot to do with [my parents] being depression babies and the fact that their parents were discriminated against as Italians. My [mother's parents] worked in sweatshops. My grandfather to the day he died never .earned more than $14 a week. My grandmother worked in knitting mills while she had five children. They spoke Italian at home, and my mother didn't learn English until she went to school even though she was born in the U.S., which was a stigma for her. She felt inferior and she talked about this at length.
>
> My father quit school when he was in eighth grade and supported his mother and his two sisters when he was twelve years old. My [paternal] grandfather died when [my father] was four and [he] basically raised his sisters. He got a man's job when he was twelve and took care of the three of them.

Martin's parents were saved by the outbreak of World War II. His father joined the Marines at seventeen and learned a trade as a plumber's assistant. With the end of the war, construction boomed and a skilled plumber could cash in on the bonanza. The O'Rourkes were lifted out of two generations of hardscrabble struggling by the postwar boom, but they never forgot the bad times.

Although Martin is now a commercial artist with his own firm and therefore decidedly middle class himself, he thinks of himself as a "blue-collar son," the last in a long line of simple, hardworking people. He has never shaken loose from his origins or rethought his own identity according to his present-day circumstances. He is therefore an extraordinarily fortunate blue-collar son who happened to make good. Because of this cultural continuity, he appreciates even more the importance of the depression era in generating a family identity.

Some of Martin's other equally middle class, equally professional high school friends did not approach the matter in the same way. Oran MacDowell fully understands what the depression did to his parents, but he defines his own life as a break from (rather than a continuation of) their lives.[9] Hence, he refuses to adjust his plans to meet their conservative standards:

> Till this day we hear it, "Don't change jobs! The depression is coming!" [The thirties] left a terrible impression on my parents. It's a way of thinking. We can change gears faster than our parents. They were locked into a mind-set where we're not. We look at something and evaluate it. [We think about] whether we like it or we don't. We make a decision about it.

Oran understands that he has been blessed by freedom from serious economic worry. His parents' cautious attitude wells up out of their own very different life experience. But from Oran's perspective, the conservatism that is the legacy of the depression, while understandable enough, is not the best way to approach the world. It impinges on one's freedom to choose; it reduces the individual's latitude to the safest, most secure course of action, rather than allowing a person to take the path that leads to the greatest benefit.

Martin and Oran have both appropriated the experience of the depression, once removed, but to different ends. For Martin, the depression explains how he came to have a pragmatic, frugal attitude about his own life and the sense of continuity that links him to his parents. For Oran, the depression explains why his expectations are so different from those of his parents. They labored under extraordinary burdens; his life has been the more normative one. The appropriateness of his expectations is confirmed by the very extraordinary nature of their past.

Interpretations vary as well about another important attitude linked to the depression (one that is also a more general aspect of American culture): self-reliance. Ironically, the 1930s and the early 1940s represent a period in which nuclear families were forced to rely upon their relatives to an extent that has few contemporary parallels.[10] Those who had jobs ended up supporting parents, siblings, aunts, and uncles. It was not unusual to find a single wage earner bringing in a paycheck that had to support multiple families, often living under the same roof. As George Milano put it:

> My father worked and slaved for sixteen hours a day as a chef. I remember him walking through snowstorms to get to work. My father worked like a dog all his life. Good provider. Made good money, even during the depression when people were out of work. He was a chef and people always found money to eat. He was supporting three families in the house where we lived!

Ironically, this elaborate support structure—necessitated by the absence of government programs[11]—became the gospel of self-reliance in Pleasanton. Parents boast that they are self-made, that they knew early on that they would not be able to rely upon their own parents for support once they became adults. They contrast their attitude with the cosseted dependence of their boomer children, forgetting that they are themselves products of an intergenerational support structure that brought their own families through the depression. Boomers, say parents like Paula Stein, fail the test of self-reliance. They can afford to be "laid back" because they believe their parents will always be there to back them up, to make up the difference between what they do for themselves and what they really want:

> In our day there was a need to strive. Now there isn't. If [kids] need or want anything, there's a backup for them. Whatever we wanted to do, we assumed we'd have to do it on our own. We couldn't fall back on our parents. Our son knows that his choices at present don't have to be based on economics. If he were broke, he wouldn't like it, but it wouldn't be a disaster. He would have a place to live [with us], and clothes.

This view is widely held among the parents of children in their late twenties who have in fact "boomeranged" back to the homestead in record numbers. Not since the war—which led to severe housing shortages that forced families to double up—has the United States seen such large numbers of adult children returning to their parents' homes.[12] Even though many postwar parents concede that their children face a tough road, they also perceive their children as tied to the family home in an unhealthy fashion, as the following dialogue between Mary and Francis Riley suggests:

MARY: Prices are out of hand. Our son [Jim] is one of the few in his age bracket who has a house. They don't have the starting salaries equivalent to buying a home that we may have had then.
    Proportionally they're way out of whack. Sure I think it's a tougher time today. It's hard to get that dream house of one's own. Seems like it's way out of reach.
FRANCIS: It's tougher, but it's also more convenient. . . . The minute it gets tough on [kids in Jim's generation], they come back home.
MARY: That's different from our day. Once you left home, you never went back. You didn't leave home until you got married. There was a lot of pride. You might have been broke, but you didn't want to say that you didn't make it. But these kids know that they can always come home.

Francis and Mary *want* their children to see the family as a haven from the storm, as the one place where they will always be welcome. But they also want to see evidence of tough, no-nonsense independence and gumption that will never admit to need. These maxims of independence are not particularly accurate as descriptions of what the depression was like, even for the parents of Pleasanton. Nonetheless, they are the moral lessons the postwar generation carried out of their childhood.

Ethnicity, Class, and Suburban "Sorting"

For most Americans, the hardship of the depression became a thing of the past with the onset of the war. Employment levels rose as factories geared up to produce armaments, clothing, and everything else needed to supply the armed forces. Women went to work in large numbers, bringing home salaries to add to their husband's army pay. Dole lines began to shrink.[13]

Though we like to remember the war era as one of unfettered unity and universal struggle against fascism, there are other legacies that are less attractive but no less true. Discrimination, racism, religious bigotry—these too are part of the legacy of the war years. Japanese Americans were among the first to discover that the melting-pot effect did not hold for them. German Americans also felt the sting of rejection, even those whose families had been in the United States for decades. Leftists, socialists, and anyone else who did not wholeheartedly and vocally support the war effort were suspected of being fifth columnists and subjected to political persecution that would later explode into the McCarthy red scare.

Many Pleasanton parents, themselves only one generation removed from the shtetls of Eastern Europe or the rural poverty of the southern Mediterranean, remember with some bitterness that the collective sacrifices of the war failed to make everyone equally American. The Silverstein family encountered a hefty dose of American racism in the most civilized places, after the war. Their reminiscences about the 1940s offer the reminders of the extent to which prejudice was an accepted part of American culture. The war that was fought to liberate the world from the Nazis failed to eradicate the prejudice directed at Jews in the United States. All kinds of barriers prevented them from moving freely throughout the job market:

MR. SILVERSTEIN: I got out of City College in the middle of the war, class of 1942. I had become a Naval Commissioner. The Navy took college graduates like me and sent them to school. I was sent to be a bank officer because I was a commerce major. But the only place a Jew could get a job was as a statistician in a government office.

MRS. SILVERSTEIN: There was a long history of discrimination. No Jewish people. At AT&T, the banks. You simply knew that those fields were closed to you. When I went to the University of Michigan, the application always indicated what your religious persuasion was, what the maiden name of your mother was. They didn't have dormitory housing. They had rooming houses. They were asterisked "Jewish Rooming Houses." And that's where you lived. Every fraternity or sorority was all Jewish or all non-Jewish in the 1940s. They had quotas for Jews everywhere.

Those lucky enough to go to college often encountered unofficial segregation or elected to stick with their own kind by participating in social clubs for ethnic groups. This was how they found their future spouses. The flip side of ethnic division, then, was a kind of special bonding among the members of each group, a bonding that often cemented marriages that have lasted for the succeeding fifty years. This had its pluses and its minuses. Many a bride and groom owe their union to the closed networks of ethnic communities. Pleasanton's senior generation often met in Catskill camps or clubs that catered to Armenians or Jews or courtesy of meddling relatives eager to fix up their bright-eyed girl with some promising boy of the appropriate background.

Yet once those connections were made, it was not uncommon for the World War II generation to seek to escape the ethnic claustrophobia. Indeed, part of the reason they settled in Pleasanton was their desire to be liberated from the intrusions of ethnicity and religious identity. The war drove home the importance of identifying as Americans, rather than as Italians, Irish, or Jews. This was part of the ideological appeal of military service and an equally important aspect of war-inspired patriotism. For the war was a national struggle and a national victory, not a partisan effort of one ethnic group or another.

In pursuit of that elusive melting pot, the postwar generation sought out the suburbs as places where the distinctions of the past might at least soften. The ethnically uncharted territory of the new suburbs at least offered the potential of making good the promise of an American identity. Unlike the familiar divided landscape of the inner city or suburbs settled in earlier decades along religious or racial lines these suburbs seemed ripe for a nondenominational form of settlement.[14] The Silversteins had considered moving to an older, familiar suburb where they had relatives but finally decided to strike out in a new direction:

MR. SILVERSTEIN: It was a greater decision to cross [the Hudson River] than it was for my grandfather to come from Poland.
MRS. SILVERSTEIN: It was years before I would agree.
MR. SILVERSTEIN: The areas we originally considered were on the south shore of Long Island or maybe the north shore. All our friends and family were there and still are there. My mother, father, brother. But we found that the environment on Long Island was very ethnic and they tended to be ghettoized. All the Jews live in this community. All the Anglo-Saxons here. All Catholics there.

The Silversteins owe their marriage to a form of ethnic solidarity that they no longer found so attractive when it came time to settle down and create their own family life.

Indeed, one of the most striking characteristics of Pleasanton in the postwar period was its heterogeneity. The Silversteins called it a little "League of Nations," since people from every conceivable white ethnic group settled there and made no effort to separate themselves from others. The families of Pleasanton did not even notice the absence of African Americans in their midst. Not that blacks were targets of active discrimination—they did not have to be openly turned away. Real estate agents simply steered them away from the town, hence the issue "never came up."[15] Housing segregation was a custom, a practice that did not require hardened attitudes or overt racism. Pleasanton's profile did not truly reflect the population of the United States as a whole—merely those parts of it that were dubbed "meltable": young white families looking to shed ethnicity as a primary marker of social identity.

Pleasanton was truly a hodgepodge of economic status groups, and the social organization of the community worked to bring them together. Volunteer fire departments linked the men; PTA brought the women together. Little League threw all the kids into a common frenzy of team spirit. The ideology of upward mobility, for many the main motivation for coming to Pleasanton in the first place, transcended many class differences and bound families together in the pursuit of the good life. "We came," it was often said, "to make a better life for our kids"—to find open space, clean air, freedom from the worries of urban decay and crime. Overtly at least, they set aside differences that might have mattered a great deal elsewhere to give birth to this new kind of community, structured less by ethnicity and class than by common orientation and interests.

Yet a subtext lurks beneath the "motherhood and apple pie" version of the Pleasanton experience. Ethnic division persisted, less onerous, surely, than its older urban form, but it was present nonetheless. Scratch the surface and the anthropologist finds accounts of young boys who organized themselves into (fairly benign) Italian and Irish gangs who challenged each other to games or mild fights in the woods.

Mrs. Sullivan, a dark-eyed mother in her early fifties, grew up in the Bronx, a working-class girl who lived in the shadow of the church. Her childhood revolved around the stoop culture of the neighborhood. Summer's heat would bring families out to the street late into the evening, fire hydrants shooting water, kids running in and out in search of relief from the blast furnace of August nights. Many of her neighbors were cousins, aunts and uncles, or friends of

the family close enough to be considered kin. This cast of characters moved around into each other's apartments with fluidity born
of total acceptance. Kathleen Sullivan came to know her Irishness
through this urban medium. What it meant to her was a kind of intimacy that was hard to duplicate in the suburbs:

> When we lived in the city, we didn't have a car. Nobody did. You
> passed around everything. I had two or three cribs and two or
> three high chairs. I always did because I was always loaning my
> things out. Nobody had anything. You operated on a shoestring
> and so did everybody else. You operated on hope and a little bit
> of prayer, a lot of prayer, actually.
>
> I won't say you were in each other's pocket, because there
> was a privacy. Your private affairs were not—there was a level you
> didn't discuss. But you discussed your children, you talked about
> what was going down, what was the food bill, and who had bet-
> ter deals. Your children played together, you'd sit and gab.

When Kathleen moved to Pleasanton with her husband and the first
three of her six children, the adjustment was difficult. In many
respects, she still has not acclimated to this new, somewhat alien
form of living. The Sullivans like the space, but Kathleen misses the
front stoop. For many years after she moved out of the city, Kathleen would gather her babies on her lap and ride the bus back to
the Bronx to spend daytime hours with friends and relatives from
the neighborhood. She never did learn to drive; that is, she never
became a genuine suburban matron.

The Sullivans found it hard to blend into the new scenery because
as Irish Catholics, they never quite fit in. No one in Pleasanton openly
expressed anti-Catholic sentiments. Ethnic/religious epithets—Papist,
dago, and the like—were not heard in Pleasanton's polite society. But
the traditional penchant of Catholics for large families set them aside
from the smaller, seemingly more orderly Protestant families and
from the intellectually oriented Jews of Pleasanton. To an extent,
these were stereotypes. But they are categories that mean something
to Kathleen, because they define exactly what she was. Her family
was big and sprawling, devoted to the church and the parochial elementary schools. In the familiar embrace of other Irish Catholics in
Pleasanton, these distinctions were almost invisible. But in more
public suburban settings, where all sorts of people rubbed shoulders, the differences were pronounced and Kathleen could sense
the disapproval:

Coming from one culture to another, I was the outsider. Our neighbors had two or three children. I had one of the biggest families around. I was told, Why don't you ever control yourself? I had people up here that really were very uptight that I was going to have another child! I felt like saying to them, "You don't have to pay for it."

They'd hold their breath when I'd walk into the A & P (the only store around). I would go in there shopping with my four children, because I wasn't going to leave them home. You'd have to check heads—if one of them drifted off on you, oh! People would watch how they behaved; I could feel them watching us.

One time, a policeman brought a little boy and dropped him off on my front lawn, a little redhead. And I said, "He's not mine." The man was embarrassed, because he thought the child was mine (since I had so many). He was just being nice, I suppose. But other times people had not been so nice, simply because they thought I had too many children.

So, you didn't bother with a lot of people, you picked your friends, and you kinda blocked out the people who were not so nice.

Family size was not the only feature of the Sullivans' life that set them apart. The fact that Catholic fathers born and raised in the urban working class were themselves less affluent than their Protestant neighbors meant that the life-style of the Catholic minority was recognizable, distinct, and not always approved by the abstract "mainstream" of Pleasanton. Mrs. Sullivan knew it. She felt it in the way people looked at her.

How did the postwar generation respond to the subtler forms of hierarchy that emerged in this new suburban society? For Mrs. Sullivan and many of the other Catholic working-class families, the answer was to opt out of the competition. It was important to her to instill a desire for upward mobility in her children: she wanted them to do better in life than her blue-collar husband had done. She knew they would need white-collar credentials. Education in itself was not particularly important, but it was critical that the kids (especially the boys) did well enough in school to get into a local college. Kathleen had to find a way to inspire a respect for credentials but at the same time prevent her children from walking into a competitive milieu in which they could not compete and for which she had little tolerance. She did not want her six kids to weigh in against the likes of the more intellectual, cultured, refined children in the Pleasanton school system. If anything, she felt a certain resentment or disdain for these pretentious kids and their ambitious parents. "Over in the city," she would say with exasperation, "children were just children. Up here, there's a lot of climbing":

> These upwardly mobile people who came [to Pleasanton]! They were always striving; they wanted their children to be the best. They were always pushing their children and I didn't. Maybe I should have, but I didn't. I found this very stressful. People drew back from me because I didn't participate.
>
> I grew up where children were just children. They just grew. They weren't pressured. You did your thing and you did your best. If it wasn't the best, well, that's alright too. But in this town, that was not acceptable.

Kathleen had to navigate her way around this culture of competition and it was not an easy matter. Her husband, Dave, was busy working two jobs. He was not around to help her manage the status system of Pleasanton, so she had to do it herself:

> It was just me [the kids] had to figure all this out. Maybe they needed two people to kind of fend it off . . . buffer them along. But they had what they had. We did our best.

The main arena of competition was the school system, the institutional custodian of the culture of upward mobility. Kathleen, like many of the other Catholic parents, was suspicious of the teachers and the principal in the local high school. They would have been more comfortable with the parochial school, but after eighth grade it became too expensive, what with so many children to educate. Out of necessity, then, the Sullivans turned to the public high school, but they never ceded their moral authority and did not push their children to make school the most important thing in their lives.

Many Pleasanton parents of working-class origins[16] held the same view and conveyed it to their kids. Pleasanton's children did not entirely heed the message. Some, like Martin O'Rourke, went ahead and got their art degrees, having decided to go their own way against the advice of parents who counseled a safer career course. Nonetheless, Martin intuited the dangers of straying too far from the blue-collar life-style of his childhood, of being too much a middle-class type of risk taker. In the end he retreated from the kind of fine art he really loved, and took the middle road of becoming a commercial artist. Throughout his childhood in Pleasanton, Martin felt pulled between two poles: his parents and extended family on the one side, and his more middle-class, Ivy League–bound friends like John Ellwood. He felt as though two people inhabited his mind: one wanted to be just like John and go on to a top college; the other wanted to be safe and secure and not allow his ambitions to run amok. He knew it, and his close friend John sensed it as well.

John and Marty shared many interests in high school. Both were interested in writing, both were talented artists. These common loves drew them together into a tight friendship, a bond that became all the more important because they were surrounded by jocks and hippies, groups neither of them fit into. In all these respects, John and Marty were the same kind of kid. But when the sorting process began in earnest, when it was time to chart the way out of Pleasanton, the differences of class background began to emerge. As John explains, when high school was over, he went one way and Marty went another:

When we applied to college, Marty's aspirations, partly because of his class background, were very low. The only place he applied to was the State University in Binghamton. He really didn't apply anywhere. I don't fully understand why. It was hard for me to evaluate the intelligence of a guy like Marty. I was certainly more educated, just from my family background. I had absorbed fairly high literary standards. So whereas Marty was writing very funny stories inspired by John Lennon's short stories, I would throw in a healthy dose of Dylan Thomas and *Finnegans Wake*. My language was very elaborate, much more than his. I also suspected that his stories were really better than mine. I was too pretentious. He was very plain. But he didn't have the class equipment to succeed, to excel academically. He went to Binghamton, I went to Columbia. We continued to be friends, but there were big differences between us.

Had he had the support I had, he might have also ended up living in downtown New York with artists in a loft, but he didn't. He married a girl who went to high school with us and moved to a small town in upstate New York where her cousins lived. He just didn't have the class background to lift himself out of that life-style, and neither did his wife. He couldn't bring himself to be as irresponsible as I was, to take the risk.

Martin himself was hardly unaware of these class differences. He knew well the ways in which his parents departed from what he felt to be the "white-collar norm" of Pleasanton. When he visited John's house and talked with John's parents, he could see right away that his own family was a cut below:

> Most of my friends [in Pleasanton] had families or fathers that were professional people, stockbrokers, lawyers, engineers, doctors. I lived on a kind of hillbilly road; we were all in the dirt. And that's the way I perceived it. In reality, my father's income was probably greater than or matched a lot of the professional people's at the time. I mean there were years when my father was making probably $60,000, which back in the 1950s was a tremendous amount of money. And then there were years when he lost the amount he made.
>
> But all along I thought of myself as a blue-collar kid. Even though we had a nice house. I come from a huge [extended] family and because my parents were doing well financially and we had the biggest house, we were the ones who had the big family parties. So within my family group, we were doing better than almost anyone.
>
> But when I saw my friends' homes and heard how well educated their parents were, how worldly and well traveled they were, I could see that my parents weren't like that. My parents know New Jersey and they basically stay here. They never went to Europe. They traveled and saw the U.S., but they spent their vacations with the family, that type of thing.
>
> My father was a very, very intelligent man and yet very ignorant of a lot. Ignorant in that he didn't have the opportunity in his life to really explore his thoughts. So, I just saw myself as being from different kind of background than a lot of the kids I knew from Pleasanton.

In some respects, everyone in Pleasanton was middle class. Extremes of real wealth and profound poverty were nowhere to be found. In between, however, were many fine gradations of social status. The well-to-do did not speak openly of themselves as privileged, but in this community that placed a premium on public expressions of egalitarianism—"we all belong"—differences between families nevertheless placed some people in a central, approved social position and marginalized others. June Oldman, mother of three children who grew up in Pleasanton in the early 1960s, recalls how moving in to the community put her family on the low end of the life-style scale:

> For living in Pleasanton, we were economically disadvantaged. Because we had the kids so soon, my husband's salary wasn't as much as people who were older and more established in their careers. We couldn't afford to take them on long ski trips in far-away places. We were a Sears Roebuck family living in a Bloomingdale's community.

There was "nothing wrong" with being at the low end of the economic scale in Pleasanton; adult friendships did not form or break exclusively along economic lines. Even so, however, the whole question of hierarchy in this new subculture was vivid enough as Pleasanton families did a mental calculus to rank themselves and their friends along the socioeconomic continuum. People did not kill themselves to "keep up with the Joneses," but they had some explaining to do behind closed doors—to themselves and their kids—about why these differences existed.

The Fieland family has been in Pleasanton for twenty-five years, a move they were able to make on the strength of George Fieland's job as a machinist in one of the large aerospace companies nearby. Julie Fieland stayed at home to raise her three children but had worked before they were born and again after they started school at various sales jobs in local department stores. Neither parent went to college; it was straight from high school into the work world. The Fielands are hardworking people who figure they got where they are by dint of their own sweat. They made it clear to their children that they would have to do the same if they expected to have a comfortable life.

The message was clear enough to the Fieland kids, who could see with their own eyes that other people in Pleasanton had it better than they did. They were clearly marked as children of the blue-collar class, and although they had many friends who came from more affluent (and well educated) homes, this only served to reinforce the idea of difference, the idea of privilege. On more than one occasion George and Julie had to set their children straight on the subject of what they could expect in the way of toys or vacations, particularly since they had friends who were getting a lot more:

JULIE: There are lots of differences between the types of people who live here. Blue-collar and professional families, they all sent their children to public school. Some of the kids had a lot of money and we didn't. We were comfortable, but they had a lot of money and [our son] Bob would naturally be friends in school with them. One particular family had a gorgeous house and live-in help and tennis courts.

GEORGE: Bob would ask us why couldn't he have whatever it was that Michael [his friend] had and we sat down and explained to him that we don't have the kind of money that Michael's parents have and we just can't afford it. What we can afford we can have and he accepted it. You know, "This is all we can afford and this is all you're getting."

Just as John Ellwood and Martin O'Rourke went their separate ways after high school, so too did Bob Fieland end up sticking with Pleasanton friends who were more like him in background than the wealthy few he played with as a child. As Bob's mother, Julie, put it:

He could always go to Michael's and play big shot over there. He made these friends. But I noticed that when he got in college . . . his friends seemed to be those who were more [like us]. Some did go to college, but one had a landscaping business, or an uphol-stery business. Some joined their father's trades.

The sorting process that stratifies American society was thus murky in Bob Fieland's life, but it was not absent. He saw the Pleasanton kids who had everything, and he knew that he was not one of them. Shared experiences in public settings like school threw people of different means together and for a time obscured the differences between them. But Bob's parents made sure he understood their position in the overall social hierarchy, even though they permitted him to mix with people of higher class standing.

It is probably no accident that the 1950s and 1960s saw the birth of a new genre of popular songs within the larger domain of boy-meets-girl-and-falls-in-love music. Ballads began to play with the idea of class by lamenting the divisions that kept working-class boys from loving middle-class girls and vice versa. The theme of being "from the wrong side of the tracks" was in competition with the bad-boy songs about "the leader of the pack" and other deviant characters whose sex appeal lay largely in the forbidden quality of working-class culture.[17] James Dean's *Rebel without a Cause* brought to the silver screen the same preoccupation with the underside of the working class. During the decades in which the United States saw and celebrated upward mobility on a grand scale, divisions that separate American society along class lines were reproduced in popular culture.[18]

In real life, however, the language of class was rarely invoked in places like Pleasanton. In retrospect John Ellwood can pinpoint the differences that sent him and Martin O'Rourke in distinctly different directions. In their youth, however, what John and Martin actually encountered was sorting by clique. The intellectuals in the high school went one way, the jocks another. Cool kids who were experimenting with drugs, fashion, and attitude separated off from the not-so-cool who preoccupied themselves with the glee club, the debating society, or the literary magazine. Leather-jacket groups shunned the construction-boots and flannel-shirt set. The two groups self-segregated, but even so tension between them boiled over routinely. One of Martin's friends got stuck in the middle:

> Peter was the first kid in the class to have a beard and the abuse that this poor man took. . . . He took so much. He used to get pounced on by the jocks for not conforming. For being a hippie. Peter, all the time I knew him, I don't think he ever did any drugs. He never did anything other than get into rock-and-roll music. He let his hair grow long and grew a beard and he was accused of everything in the book. It did help that he was a brilliant honors student.

Judy Resnick, a woman in the class of 1970 who was part of the same social set as Martin and John, remembers these divisions keenly:

> In my junior and senior years, the honors classes were making experimental films and were exposed to . . . all these foreign films and all these new ideas. We were definitely a crowd. We hung together as hippies, the ones with the angst and the intellectual, political inclinations. We developed our own political newspaper. We would go over to the city, to Columbia, where the sit-ins were going on.

Judy was happy in her own clique and did not mix with the more traditional football crowd. The two groups turned a cold shoulder to one another. At stake in the division of high school society into cliques was something more than style or attitude. Cliques were another means of expressing class divisions in a society that explicitly rejects the language of class. Blue-collar kids were more likely to be on the athletic teams than in the debating society; college-bound children of the middle class were attracted to the school newspaper and showed their disdain for the jocks. Social cliques were, and no doubt remain, the first experience most American children have with the ranking, stacking process that in adult life is based on income and occupation.

Everyone in Pleasanton realized that over the long run some people were going to succeed and others were going to fall by the wayside.[19] No one seriously expected to be poor, but this did not stop Pleasanton's postwar parents from worrying about their kids' future. Those families that eschewed the competition for "most likely to succeed" and counseled their children to forget about the latest fashions and the fancy proms also knew that their own mobility did not in any way guarantee their children's success. The boomers would have to make it on their own, and their parents, particularly their mothers, were responsible for seeing to it that their progeny became the kind of people who wanted prosperity and position.

The Cult of Domesticity[20]

There are few periods that can rival the 1950s and 1960s for the public attention focused on bringing up the kids.[21] The target of all this concern was, of course, Mother. Father, it was (correctly) presumed, was out earning a living, but most women had exchanged the overalls they wore to the factory for the apron and its strings. Raising children became their moral mission, their job. With the landmark publication of Simone de Beauvoir's *Second Sex* and Betty Friedan's *Feminine Mystique,* questions would be raised about the wisdom of this single-minded devotion to home and hearth, but these texts were still some years off.[22] In fact, even when the feminist revolution gained popular support, it remained for Pleasanton adults more of a curiosity or a threat than a movement of personal significance. For better or worse, these mothers and fathers wanted exactly what TV portraits of domestic bliss held up to them as a mirror of their lives. The women wanted to settle down and have kids;

they expected to be sheltered from the demands of the public world of business; and the men intended to throw themselves into their work and be content with part-time fatherhood.

Edith Denman, now nearly sixty, has been a kindergarten teacher in a nearby, slightly less affluent community for the past fifteen years. She loves her job and always considered herself a born teacher, but she came to this work only after her youngest child turned ten. Even then, she worked part-time so she could still be available for her kids. Her husband, Bob, has always been very busy with his construction business. When Edith was growing up, she knew she wanted to teach and did well enough in school to go to college. Even so, however, her overriding ambition had been to get married and have a family, and her desire for a college degree was subordinated to that end:

> My most important goal in my teens was to get good enough marks so I could go to college . . . and getting a date for Saturday night. [My goals were] the same thing in college. I knew I wanted to be married. I was glad I was at a co-ed college. I don't think I would have chosen to go to an all-girls school because I wanted to be married. I never even thought of the [ambitions] people think of now—that you could live the rest of your life and do your thing. What I am doing is what I had always expected—to get married, have children.

Edith's desire to settle into a "Leave It to Beaver" life-style was shared by virtually every other woman in Pleasanton. Françoise Gilbert, who came to the United States from France in the wake of the Liberation, raised five children there and considered them to be her full-time occupation:

> I didn't have a career I can talk of . . . but motherhood was my career, and very totally so. I enjoyed motherhood tremendously. It was a lot of work, but I found tremendous satisfaction in raising my children. I had five; I would have been very happy if I had had five more. It has been the most important thing in my life.

For women of the postwar world everything was oriented around the home. Within this domain Mother was the most important figure: she set the tone of family life, made most of the important decisions about the children's daily activities, and very clearly conveyed the goals the children ought to strive for. Ambition might have been a male preserve, but it was the mother who made ambition "real" in the daily lives of her children. It was she who supervised the homework, organized the Cub Scout pack, met with the teachers for conferences, participated in the PTA, and urged the kids into (or withdrew them from) the local competition in every domain from sports to school.

Mothers also set the moral tone of life in Pleasanton. Their intense commitment to a mother-centered family structure conveyed implicitly their belief in the value of intense female involvement in and devotion to a child's development. Since they were themselves largely removed from the competitive environment of the "outside world," their own sense of achievement was filtered through their children.[23] Every blue ribbon won on the track team, every A paper in history, every painting hung in the high school hallway was a triumph for both mother and child. The task of reproducing a middle-class standard of living was but one more competitive challenge, the key to which was sustaining a constant sense of the importance of becoming (or staying) middle class. It was Pleasanton's mothers who bore the primary responsibility for making their children into achievers. To this day, these postwar mothers see themselves reflected in the successes and disappointments of their adult children.

Of course, fathers were also preoccupied with their children's standing in the socioeconomic hierarchy; but while their wives were busy raising the next generation, they were out of town—in the boardroom, on the assembly line, working the customers, commuting across the bridge. And what a demanding life it was. Pleasanton men were usually away from home from seven in the morning until seven at night. The work world demanded their all, and they in turn invested their own sense of self, their identities as men, in their occupational lives.

Financial security was no small part of what Pleasanton fathers were after. Memories of the depression were still fresh; they knew how quickly comfort and stability could disappear. Hence, these postwar men picked practical occupations, where the payoff was clear and quickly forthcoming. They knew that it was their job, and theirs alone, to provide for the family's financial needs. This was serious business; no one could afford to be carefree or self-indulgent. These fathers simply transferred the no-nonsense attitude they had learned during the war years to the task at hand: securing a foothold in the new middle class for themselves, their dependent wives, and their kids.

Responsibilities like these weighed heavily on men like Ed Winnow. He was not a city boy like so many of his neighbors in Pleasanton. He had grown up in a suburb of Boston and had been able to attend a small college nearby, where he managed in two years what would normally have taken four years to finish. It was wartime and young men had to push through "cram degrees" in order to finish college and enlist in the armed forces. Ed was a talented artist, a natural scribbler, who had always found great pleasure in drawing. His great ambition as a college student was to be a political cartoonist for a national newspaper. When the war was over, and he found himself a married man with little children on the way, these desires took a back seat to necessity:

> When I arrived in New York and enrolled in art school after the war, I had to deviate from my plan [to become a cartoonist]. At that time the Pratt Institute was rated as the top commercial school in the country. Coming out of the army like so many veterans of the day, those who went to art school knew that they had to learn a craft. When they came out of school they were on their own. Daddy wasn't paying the bills any more. It was the golden days of Pratt. The competition was keen; the men were older in school [since they were veterans]. They were not just high school kids going to art school because they didn't want to go to college. There was a definite intent among the student body. The competition rubbed off on us all.

Ed felt the urgency of getting on a career track, a feeling intensified by the high levels of unemployment that followed demobilization and the flood of young servicemen returning to the labor market. The advantage would fall to those competitive young men who were prepared to set aside unrealistic personal desires for pragmatic, hardheaded ways. The specter of the depression was in the background:

> I remember all the songs of the day, "When My Ship Comes In" or "Buddy, Can You Spare a Dime?" and all that kind of stuff. I never realized as a kid the depth to which the depression touched me. I realized it later, that it touched me very deeply, made me very

concerned about economics. I didn't become a greedy person, looking to go to Wall Street to discover how many deals I could turn. But it made me a competitive person. In the art field you tear your guts out. You pour everything into your work. The competition in New York keeps you keen.

Ed's fears, coupled with the more buoyant optimism and can-do spirit of the wartime era, fueled his personal desire to conquer the world of advertising. This was a far cry from fine art, or even from the political cartooning he had once hoped to do, but commercial art at least allowed him to use his genuine talent in a businesslike, real-world way. This kind of compromise was not greeted with despair or resignation; it was a natural outgrowth of the times and of a culture that inculcated the sense that men's destinies were bound up in the competition of the marketplace.

Indeed, Ed's attitude toward work in general was serious, pragmatic, and only partially directed at personal satisfaction. He wanted to work at a job he could be proud of, a job that demanded something of his mind. Like most men of his generation, Ed wanted his life to be a cut above his father's, and for him this meant a professional identity. For others, the same desire for upward mobility meant acquiring a skilled blue-collar job, a trade more elevated in prestige and monetary reward than the routinized factory jobs characteristic of the immigrant working class from which they came. But the most important, overriding concern for men of this generation was to pay the bills. To this end everything else—all forms of personal satisfaction—had to be subordinated.[24] Hence, many took jobs in insurance or sales that were acceptable, but not exciting, respectable but not nourishing for the soul. The meaning of work was first and foremost instrumental. If in the bargain one experienced intellectual challenge or professional achievement, so much the better, but for men like Ed, no sane person would forsake security or stability in order to prove some obscure point about self-worth. They had to keep their eyes firmly fixed on the bottom line.

This attitude was a central feature of male culture in Pleasanton. Working-class women who shouldered part of the financial burden seldom thought of their jobs as meat-and-potatoes; their money went for the luxuries, the extras that the men's wages could not provide. For middle-class women, working in the paid labor market was an anathema. In the 1950s and 1960s it was out of the question, even if there were financial need. When Ed was pushed out of the advertising firm he worked for and was "as broke as the Ten Commandments," it was *his* obligation to find a new job and put the bread on the table. His wife, Yvonne, spent all her time getting the kids to school, to ballet lessons, and to art classes. Yvonne had worked before her children were born, but they came in rapid succession, and she retired from the labor market to become a full-time mother, a domestic organizer, and community participant.

> I was just like my mother, just a homemaker. Having the husband as a breadwinner, taking care of the children, seeing them through thick and thin—that was what I wanted and that was what I had.

Yvonne was scared when Ed lost his job. She had just given birth to their fourth child and had not planned to go back to work; her job was in the home. Fortunately, for the Winnows, Ed eventually landed a position in a major advertising agency, where he has remained for the last twenty-five years. He never felt completely secure again and took to free-lancing to augment his salary. The Winnows still live in their secluded, rambling house on two acres in a wooded area of Pleasanton and look forward to the day their grandchildren will play in the backyard.

The ability to structure family life as the Winnows did—with a full-time working father and a stay-at-home mother—was made possible by two important structural facts: the low cost of housing in the golden years between 1950 and 1965, even in a community as nice as Pleasanton, and the active intervention of the federal government, whose largesse made it possible for young veterans like Ed to move up into the professions.

Listening to young people speak of stratospheric real estate costs in Pleasanton today, it is hard to believe that it was once so easy. Even the senior generation in the community marvels at how affordable the town was after the war. Housing shortages that had forced many a married veteran to move in with his parents (or hers) gave way to a building boom that was nothing short of a frenzy. Farmland became subdivisions overnight, as the unprecedented demand for new houses fueled the suburban expansion.[25]

Pleasanton was not a tract development in the sense of cookie-cutter houses or "little boxes made of ticky-tacky" as the satirical song of the 1970s put it.[26] In fact, many of its 1950s residents came to Pleasanton after a brief stop in one of the Levittowns elsewhere on the East Coast. From the beginning, Pleasanton was more genteel.

Even so, the acquisition of gentility (at least in retrospect) seems to have been a relatively simple matter. Amy James, who grew up in a suburb of Chicago, moved to Pleasanton in 1965. Having been divorced earlier and recently remarried, she was on the lookout for a country atmosphere in which to raise her two sons. As soon as she laid eyes on the home she has now lived in for more than twenty years, she knew she had found it:

> Our house sits up a little higher from the street and it looks like a postcard kind of house. It's a four-bedroom, center-hall colonial. It has two and a half baths, and it had four generous bedrooms. Since we had two children, my husband could have an office in the fourth bedroom. The backyard is huge: we own almost half an acre, both sides of the brook.
>
> The brook is full of fish. In the years I've been here I've recorded forty-three species of birds, and about eight different kinds of wild mammals live back there, including a deer once and a while. . . . The land on either side can't be developed. So, I looked at that brook and I thought, what a wonderful thing for boys to have their own body of water, that's safe and not that deep. A place deep enough to float a rubber raft, but not deep enough to drown, and a place to run your dog and have cats who can hunt stuff like chipmunks.
>
> It just seemed to me to be a wonderful house. Of course, when you come from a little tiny Cape Cod that doesn't have a closet to its name. I went into the closet in the master bedroom and thought, you could make a nursery out of this! It just looked like a sea of rooms. When I saw this house I just saw infinite possibilities. I saw [my son, Keith] descending the staircase to go to the prom! My child was only six years old, but I already saw him coming down in his tuxedo to the prom and having his father take a picture. And I thought, oh boy, I wish I could afford this place.

For Arthur and Amy, "affording this place" turned out not to be a serious problem. Mortgage rates were about 6 percent, the monthly payments were a bit steep but not out of the question. Besides, Arthur's business was doing well, and he could see that the financial burden of the house would lessen over time. They could swing it.

Hal Krauss, a commissioned salesman for a nearby bottled-water company, moved into town at about the same time. He also realized that he would have to budget to afford his house, but in looking back on that decision, he realizes that the move he made in 1964 is likely to set him up for life:

> The best buy I ever made in my life is this home. I put a thousand dollars down and bought this home for $29,000. I got a thirty-year mortgage at 5.25 percent. 5.25 percent!! Can you believe that? Guess what it's worth today. I'll sign it over to you right now for $430,000, but I wouldn't sell it for less. One- or two-bedroom apartments [down by the river] sell for $275,000 to $300,000, and here you have so much more!

The families that had migrated to Pleasanton ten years earlier found prices that were even more attractive. In the mid-1950s, the average house could be had for what now seems like a song. Incomes were, of course, much lower as well. Simon Rittenberg, who settled in the town in 1951, recalls with a hearty laugh how nervous he was about signing his life away for his first new home:

> We started to look in [Pleasanton County], but I wasn't making much money at the time and the prices seemed out of reach for us. We took one more shot with a local realtor who said, "Do you want to live in [Pleasanton]?" I said, where is Pleasanton? He told me to just stay on Old Farm Road and when you see a little trailer, ask for Mr. Riley, who is selling lots. We jumped into the car and found the guy who told us his homes started at $15,900 and if we were interested, he would work things out for us.
>
> A GI mortgage in those days was 4 percent. We had $1,000 left in the bank, after having come out of the service again, and we picked out a home. He had three models and we picked out one, and gave him our last $1,000, frightened to death. But it was probably the best move we ever made. You know, the payments were $100 a month for the mortgage, insurance, everything! Can you believe that?

Pleasanton fathers like Hal and Simon sometimes had to swallow hard before committing the family fortune to a home. Over time, however, as their incomes rose and their mortgage payments remained fixed, housing consumed a smaller and smaller proportion of the family budget, and with inflation their equity skyrocketed. They will both be able to retire comfortably on the proceeds from their houses.

It is tempting to look at such good fortune as one of those flukes of U.S. economic history that bless individuals who just happen to be in the right place at the right time. But the good fortune was also the result of a federal policy. As we saw in chapter 2, government investment during the postwar period in the form of low-interest mortgages made homeownership a reality for millions of young married couples who would otherwise have found this an impossible dream. The WPA projects of the late depression built countless bridges and highways, bringing outlying farmland into the urban orbit and making it possible for workers to commute into the city center.[27] State and local governments weighed in with funds for sewers, schools, and police and fire departments.

It is not part of the cultural legacy of the postwar period to think of these benefits as a form of social engineering, but that is exactly what they were. Federal involvement in the creation of the mass middle class of the 1950s and 1960s was every bit as much an intrusion into the "natural" dynamics of the market as any poverty initiatives taken since that time have been. Curiously, however, current public debate over the appropriate role of government overlooks just how important these Keynesian policies were in shaping the distribution of resources in the United States. To the extent that we remember the policy decisions of this era at all, we are apt to consider the GI Bill and the Federal Home Loan program as thanks extended to our fighting men home from the war. Just rewards, richly deserved—that is how we understand these benefits nowadays.

Yet in their own time, what they really represented was an effort to stimulate the housing industry and enlarge the middle class well beyond its prewar boundaries. Indeed, it could easily be argued that no generation was as profoundly blessed by national investment in their well-being as that one. It was as though the country had decided that they deserved to be lifted out of their depression origins and plopped down in the middle of Oz, where the yellow brick road led to a white picket fence, a manicured front lawn, and a two-car garage. It is little wonder that so many members of this cohort remember the war (and its aftermath) as the best thing that ever happened to them.

On both frontiers—public investment and the roaring engine of the private economy—the postwar generation was positioned to make a dramatic break with the material circumstances of its adolescence. Yet when the members of that generation reminisce about who they are, about what their experience represents in the national panorama, this exciting, optimistic sense of upward movement is not what they recall. Nor does their sheer good fortune figure importantly in what they conveyed to their children about their formative experiences. Most especially the hand of government—the country's national investment in this new middle class—is subtracted from the moral tales they tell about how they became the prosperous citizens they are. When postwar parents taught their own children the lessons they would need in life, it was a different story.

The Prism of Meritocracy

American culture is allergic to the idea that impersonal forces control individual destiny. Rather, we prefer to think of our lives as products of our own efforts. Through hard work, innate ability, and competition, the good prosper and the weak drop by the wayside. Accordingly, the end results in people's lives—their occupations, material possessions, and the recognition accorded by friends and associates—are proof of the underlying stuff of which they are made. When these domains of our lives do not pass muster, the tendency is to assume that this fate is deserved: the unemployed are dead wood. Our failing industries are inefficient, hulking dinosaurs that deserve to be tossed on to the international garbage dump.[28]

Of course, when the fairy tale comes true, the flip side of meritocratic individualism emerges with full force. Those who prosper—the morally superior—deserve every bit of their material comfort. They are made of the right stuff, took the proper decisions, and were sufficiently visionary to meet their goals. Crucial to our understanding of merit is that we must work hard to apply our talents, hard enough to overcome obstacles that might stop a lesser person. It is not enough to be blessed with talent if we do not struggle to use it to advantage. Indeed, we are more admiring of the Horatio Alger character for his fusion of brains and industry than we are of the genius who can solve brain-bending equations. We may marvel at the latter, but it is the former who is enshrined as a mythic hero.

When men and women of the postwar generation explain how

they got from inner-city "little Italys" to suburban Pleasanton, how they moved from the hard years of the depression into the golden light of prosperity, they rarely invoke the Federal Home Loan program or the GI Bill. These items come up as conversational footnotes to a bigger story of depression deprivation, wartime sacrifice, and struggling married couples who never went out to dinner or bought new cars. In collective generational memory, prosperity was earned through the exercise of old-fashioned virtues of deferred gratification. That they pulled it off, they say, is testimony to their gutsy generation: you didn't survive if you didn't have what it takes to begin with.

There is, of course, considerable truth to this view. No one would quibble with the view that the depression caused real hardship. Nor would anyone argue with the notion that the war tested the mettle of the men who went into battle and the women who went into the factories (or stayed home and worried about their menfolk).[29] But absent the economic upswing of the postwar years, these virtuous qualities would not have been enough to boost a whole generation so dramatically. Moreover, without the massive transfer of wealth provided by the GI Bill and the mortgage programs, the whole suburban exodus would have slowed to a trickle.

Postwar suburbia was both a place and a state of mind. As a place, communities like Pleasanton offered space and light, freedom from claustrophobic ethnic enclaves. It was a supremely gendered place, where women organized family life and men were mostly absent. This is not to say that men were unimportant; their status as primary breadwinners ensured their authority.

As a state of mind, suburbia was a riddle—a riddle with consequences for the baby boomers. Becoming a homeowner and joining a community of the similarly landed was supposed to confer some degree of egalitarian camaraderie. People in Pleasanton thought of themselves as a breed apart from the renters in the city. They had ventured out and put down roots, and this gave them a kind of common currency despite their diverse origins. Yet this superficial egalitarianism was undercut by the subtle experience of class and hierarchy, experienced through children's cross-class friendship networks. Hence, it was a schizophrenic existence that espoused one way of thinking as it practiced another. Parents had to explain these hard facts to their children: "We are not as rich as the Joneses; you'll have to be satisfied with what you get." Children in turn had to reflect upon the meaning of class as they moved toward adulthood and formed their own career trajectories and personal identities. Martin O'Rourke had to come to grips with the differences between himself and his friend John Ellwood and figure out how those differences were going to matter over the long run.

Raising a family in a middle-class suburb like Pleasanton appeared to be an easy matter. With men's wages rising steadily and the equity in their homes secure (and growing steadily also), the material facts of life seemed entirely under control. The security of these years of economic expansion allowed a generation with a depression mentality to heave a sigh of relief. Yet it was supposed to be just the beginning. Young marrieds who came to the suburbs in the 1950s and 1960s—often as the first homeowners in their families— had to do more than simply achieve a middle-class life for themselves. They were the shock troops, the frontline warriors in their extended family's quest for upward mobility. It remained for them to secure this claim to membership in the middle class. This could only be done through their children. Only when the long-term identity of the whole family was settled could they sit back and relax.

How does one go about ensuring that the next generation will follow in these footsteps? Pleasanton's postwar parents were sure of the answer to this question. You teach your children the right lessons, school them in the morality of your own generation, and if you do a proper job, they will come out with the drive and motivation to re-create the appropriate identity. These teachings are crucial. Pleasanton parents—like middle-class people everywhere—had few resources to *ensure* their children's succession. They could not hand over their J.D. degrees, their M.B.A.'s, their positions as managers in auto plants. The blue-collar workers among them might have been able to boost their children to their unions, but they wanted something more for their kids. They wanted them to leap the great white-collar divide, to achieve the same standard of living but more respectably. But unlike the truly wealthy, who are able to stake their children to an affluent life and also tack on a profession, the middle class can do very little for its children other than to try and ensure that they have the cultural capital and the motivation to achieve for themselves.

The problem is, of course, that child rearing is not an exact science. It is never possible to guarantee that all children will value those things that their parents hold dear. Parents can invest all the energy they can muster to shape their children in their own image, but then let nature and the economy take over. The process of grooming the next generation is thus fraught with uncertainty, laced with worries that kids will depart from the straight and nar-row path toward a good college or a favorable marriage and never recover. To the extent that the outcome—the persona of a child—is a referendum on a parent's efforts, indeed a parent's very identity, the task of re-creating the middle class is a total preoccupation.

Pleasanton's postwar parents took the matter very seriously. They staked much of their own sense of success on the lives of their children. No amount of personal achievement could make up for disappointments in the lives of their progeny. Only when their kids moved up to take their places in the right part of the class spectrum could they relax and say, "This was a job well done." Only this could confirm the essential correctness of their own remarkable ascent up the social hierarchy, from urban, working-class ethnic enclaves to the suburban American middle class.

Things did not go according to plan. Boomers are in trouble. They may never repeat the success of their parents' generation. Many are discovering what it means to go backward. This tangled reality has become a problem that everyone—boomer and postwar parent alike—must explain.

4

The Problem of the Moral Mother

MRS. AMES: I don't have any [career] aspirations for my daughter. I'd like to see Karen marry a great guy and have some great children that could sit on my lap. No other things going.

MR. AMES: If she makes $100,000 next year, it couldn't matter less for me. I'm pleased, but that's not the goal.

MRS. AMES: I share his opinion. I think now that she's too career-oriented. It dominates her thinking as far as family and marriage is concerned. She's not interested in it right now. I'd like her to marry somebody strong, bright, and have a family.

Karen Ames was born in 1962, the third child in the family and the only daughter. A dedicated student, an enthusiastic performer in high school plays, Karen was, on all counts, a model member of the Pleasanton High School class of 1980. Mindful of the tensions that developed in the family when her older brothers caught a whiff of Woodstock, Karen stuck to the straight and narrow path more characteristic of the Reagan generation. Indeed, she thinks of herself as a probusiness conservative: her primary ambition (at the moment) is to be the best sales manager her company has ever had, to break every record that has ever been set, and to make her mark in the business world before she turns thirty. She has fixed her sights on these goals and refuses, for the moment, to be deterred by her mother's insistent complaints that she ought to settle down with Mr. Right and be a good wife and mother.

Instead, Karen looks to her father as a role model and business adviser. And for all his protestations that he "couldn't care less" whether she breaks the $100,000 mark in sales, John Ames is secretly amazed and proud of his daughter's success. Karen's job has brought the two of them closer together than they have ever been before. Yet on occasion, John's reflex ideals of femininity are jarred by his powerhouse daughter. He is more familiar with the version of womanhood his wife adheres to: the organizer of the home front, who leaves the real world, the real decisions, the real power to her husband. Hence, as much as he enjoys trading war stories with Karen, when called upon to comment on his daughter's future, he feels compelled to say that making a lot of money is not "the whole point."

Margaret, Karen's mother, finds her daughter's goals intensely confusing. She cannot figure out why a girl like Karen—attractive, talented, always popular with the boys—has turned out to be so different, so distant from herself. Margaret is convinced that in the final analysis, nothing is more important in a woman's life than finding a good husband, settling down to raise a contented family, and taking satisfaction in doing good works in the local community. This is what women should want, and it is an enduring puzzle for Margaret that Karen has apparently shelved (if not rejected) these aspirations.

As for the object of all this controversy, Karen herself is something of a split personality. She thoroughly enjoys the cutthroat competition of her job. She likes nothing more than to grab an account out from under her competition, watch those monthly totals climb higher than anyone else's in her sales region, and reap the admiration of everyone around her. As far as her career is concerned, the sky is the limit. Yet when Karen thinks about her personal life and projects herself into the future, she thinks about how nice it would be someday to marry her long-standing boyfriend and settle down to have a family.

What kind of mother does Karen plan to be? The only image of motherhood with which she is familiar is her mother: the mother who was always there when Karen got home from school, who had the time to bake chocolate-chip cookies, sew Halloween costumes, and soothe a little girl's hurt feelings on the days when her best friend decided someone else was a more exciting playmate. This is the kind of mother Karen knows—wouldn't her own children deserve just as much from her? In mind, if not in deed, Karen is not as far away from her mother as Margaret believes.

If Karen Ames could reconcile these two selves by dealing with them in sequence—business ambition first, followed by domestic bliss—she could resolve the conflicts. She could fulfill the goals she set for herself in the heyday of the Reagan years and move on to the seemingly timeless reality of a prefeminist motherhood. Had the financial realities of the 1990s worked out differently, doing things in sequence might have solved Karen's problems (and given her mother some reason for hope). But the clash of Karen Ames's selves is destined to endure because there is simply no way that she and her boyfriend could re-create the domestic organization of their youth, where stay-at-home moms looked after the kids and worldly, distant fathers handled life beyond the picket fence. As long as it remains important to Karen to have a standard of living that can approximate her childhood in Pleasanton, she will have to work and continue to break those sales barriers. How she will manage to do that and still "do right" by her own (future) children is a mystery Karen has yet to solve.

Were this conundrum simply a matter of logistics and finances, the problems would be hard enough for the boomer generation to manage. But like virtually all such difficulties, the organizational problems of family and work life are shot through with moral dilemmas. What should a young woman want out of life? How should the responsibilities of mothering be organized? What claims can a family reasonably make on a father's attention? Just how far should the demands of the workplace intrude into the private realm of parent and child? The solutions to these social dilemmas are circumscribed by the pressures the work world imposes upon those who bring home the bacon. Rare are the individuals who can carve out their own hours, decide which demands to take seriously, and retain the right to say no to the boss when duty calls on the home front. Most people are not that free.

At some level, Karen's parents realize that she cannot ignore these constraints, but they often suspend this knowledge when they evaluate the way Karen has structured her life. They focus instead on the moral acceptability of her life-style. She could manage her life differently if she really wanted to, the Ameses assert, if only she were the kind of woman they want her to be. The fact that she has chosen a different path, one about which they are ambivalent, is evidence of a moral problem.

A war of words and emotions is raging behind the scenes in Pleasanton, as postwar parents challenge the legitimacy of their children's family lives. This is not the public, explosive generation gap of the days of flower power and radical politics. It is a quieter kind of friction.[1] These two generations, born of dramatically different moments in American economic history, are competing camps with opposing views of how private life should be organized, how gender should be defined, how a moral family life should be lived. Though the two generations come to this conflict with vastly different economic profiles, the mundane facts of income trajectories and housing costs are rarely invoked. Postwar parents have delivered a trenchant critique of not only their children's material expectations but also of their character and their values. "Our children would have perfect family lives," they complain, "if only they didn't want too much too soon." They anguish over the thought that their children are "sacrificing" those values and practices they consider essential (like full-time motherhood), all because they insist on a standard of living that is beyond the means of a one-income family.

Postwar parents are not the only ones to voice this critique. Baby-boom mothers who have decided to leave the labor market in favor of full-time child raising are often equally critical of their neighbors who are working mothers. They too will argue that dual-career families are not just trying to survive; they are trying to live a high life, an affluent life, and as a result are failing to meet their responsibilities to their children. Pam Tomasi, herself once a dedicated career woman, now looks out her kitchen window to the houses in her neighborhood in suburban Dallas and frowns at the sparkling new cars parked next door, the swimming pools in the backyard. Pam believes her family has sacrificed a claim on those kinds of luxuries but has gained a spiritual renewal in the bargain—all because she quit her high-powered job to be with her kids. In Pam's opinion, her working-mother neighbors have chosen the wrong path. They have given up on what is most important—the family—in favor of what is least important—the BMW.

I see families where they put their emphasis on materialism. Things. You wouldn't imagine. These homes have bathrooms that are larger than the kitchen my mother had. Garden tubs, huge windows, tennis courts, swimming pools. Let's face it. There's part of me that would like luxury like that. But the people are choosing that. That's their focus. They have to drive a certain type of car, wear certain types of clothes, their kids have to be enrolled in preschool, after school, so that they can work to afford all that. Things are not all right here. We have one of the highest teen suicide rates.

I have a little girl, seven years old, in my Holy Communion class. She came in late one night and said, "I'm sorry I'm late. I had a tennis match, a play rehearsal," and then she had to stop, throw down some food, and change her clothes and come to Communion class. I thought, God bless her. She's just a baby. I don't know, I just couldn't do that.

I don't see the need to be in such a hurry and make so much money. We don't have a whole lot of money compared to what we had when we were both working full-time. But I have less stress and more joy and I wouldn't trade that for all the money in the world. I can do right by my kids.

Pam sees eye-to-eye with many of her mother's friends, women of the Eisenhower generation. They do not accept the notion that women work because their families need the money, nor do they believe women should work because they enjoy being part of the world outside the home. If they lowered their material expectations, they would not "need" the money, they would not "need" to postpone starting their families. In postmodern jargon, need is a social construct not a biological given. You can change what you need reconsidering what is really important. If a woman convinces herself that she does not have to have a big house before she starts a family, she will find that she can go right ahead. Everything does not have to be in place; the really important things will come in good time.

To listen to Pam, one would think that all this anxiety is unnecessary, that it could be waved away if people dropped their expectations for the high life. Many Pleasanton boomers reject this portrait of their aspirations. As Carl Anderson explains, great wealth is not his objective. He just wants to build a firm foundation before he starts a family:

I want to be able to afford to give a good education to my children. I don't want to spoil them, so I don't need to wait until I'm a millionaire to have kids. But at the same time, I want to reach a certain level of security, where I can feel as though we can afford to have these kids. I need to feel that I know what I'm doing, that I can make our lives work. I don't want to be in the position I'm in now where things are very tight and I have to really worry about what our future is. I want to feel secure and that will allow me to say, Yes, let's have children.

The Moral Mother

If the leitmotif of American culture is upward mobility, the star in its enduring drama is Mom. Even during America's prosperous postwar years, opportunities had to be earned. The culture of meritocracy that flourished in those years dictated that those who prospered clearly deserved their good fortune: they had the right kind of character, intelligence, and perseverance. Where did these qualities come from? Mommy. She laid the character foundation upon which achievement in school, on the job, and in the private life of the family were to be built.[2]

The mother of the 1950s was the first figure of moral authority and the keeper of emotional stability. Suburban mothers were home to soothe hurt feelings, comfort the child who had a hard day at school, and provide an undivided audience for every achievement. Women who were cloistered inside the home with little in the way of adult company (other than other mothers) often looked to their children as confidants and close friends. In Pleasanton, as in many an American suburb, this mother-child connection was reinforced by the physical privacy of the home and the lack of any transportation infrastructure that could provide children with autonomous mobility. The icon of the suburbs was the Ford station wagon, equipped to handle six screaming children and one harried mother, moving between Boy Scouts, ballet school, the swimming pool, and Little League. Pleasanton's postwar mothers sigh at the memory of their days as ferry captains in the endless round of after-school activities. In the end, mothers had little time or space to themselves.

Arlie Hochschild has written of the tendency of elderly women to "live through" their children, to surrender their claims to autonomous achievement by investing their own identities in the worldly accomplishments of their adult children.[3] Shades of this "altruistic surrender" were already apparent in the lives of Pleasanton's postwar mothers long before they became senior citizens. They adopted as nearly their own their husband's achievements in the world of business and their children's milestones in school, camp, and church. Having few outlets for independent achievement, save the pride they took in the immaculate condition of their homes, these women looked upon their children as clay they could mold.

The rewards for a successful mother lay in the hurdles their kids jumped. Success in school or in the Cub Scouts was taken as a sign of a good future. Childhood was a proving ground for later challenges in adulthood, and mothers were the inspired coaches. While Pleasanton's veteran full-time mothers have their qualms about the paths their children have taken in their adult lives, they are absolutely certain that the positive achievements of those children reflect the virtues of the mothering they provided. Boomer "children" of Pleasanton recognize the truth of their mothers' convictions. Convinced as they are for the most part that mother did know best, they also believe in that tried-and-true model of mothering, even if circumstances prevent them from realizing it in their own lives.

Three pressures combine to make today's mothers feel that they too ought to uphold the natural law that invests mothers with primary responsibility for their children's success. The first is very personal and close at hand: their own mothers offer persistent advice to this effect, backed up by their own personal experience. The second derives from the boomers' experiences with competition generated over a lifetime as members of the largest generation in American history. The third source of stress is a troublesome background noise: the declining position of the United States in the international economy. Our competitive weakness has made visible inroads into our standard of living and has made Pleasanton's middle class realize that when the going gets tough, only the very best will avoid the landslide. Each of these trends bolsters the critical significance of "quality" child rearing as the first bulwark against competition, even as economic conditions undermine the possibility of doing the job the old-fashioned way.

Who Is a Moral Mother?

When I was a kid, I had this image—I could picture myself in a house as a mother. So I never thought about the [pros and cons] of getting married or having children in any conscious way. I think that was an assumption. I thought I would be like my mom. In terms of career, what I was best at and what I enjoyed most (being a teacher), I eliminated because I was very timid and shy. It was scary to think of controlling a class. So I eliminated teaching on two grounds—fear of being the one in charge and teaching people who didn't want to learn. And now I'm a teacher! I've come full circle. But I had to become a confident person before I could become a teacher. . . . The idea of doing anything professionally scared me, and yet when I started working and having more responsibilities in the work force, I do very well. In the end, I wanted to be independent and to be a mother. And I did it.

Robin Model is a thoughtful person who often ponders the contradictory images of a woman's role as it developed during the 1970s and 1980s. She sees within herself two very different people: the woman her mother was, a happy mother who was sheltered from and afraid of the professional world, and her opposite, an authoritative, self-possessed teacher, able to perform as well as any man might. There are days when Robin would like to follow in her own mother's footsteps and retire to the domestic cocoon; there are days when she wakes up thinking it might be better for her three sons if she did just that. Yet Robin soldiers on in what has become the great middle-class experiment of the late twentieth century, the working mother.[4]

The balancing act is not simple. The complex infrastructure Robin relies upon to care for her children occasionally breaks down: the baby-sitter calls in sick, her youngest gets an ear infection and cannot go to preschool, a meeting is scheduled for five o'clock, when she is supposed to take over at home. Yet on the whole, Robin has managed the artful dance fairly well. The hard part has to do less with logistics and more with a nagging sense of being stretched too thin: Robin spends all day teaching other people's kids, and often wonders whether she is sufficiently devoted to the nurturance of her own. She knows she is better off as an *individual* for having a rewarding career. But on the days when she is too busy or too tired to do the myriad things for her sons that her mother always did for her, Robin has to fight off the thought that she has privileged herself over them.

This dilemma is precisely what convinced Robin's classmate from Pleasanton High School, Pam Tomasi, to pull out of the labor market and devote herself to full-time mothering. The decision was not an easy one, but neither was it a simple matter to ignore the guilt piling up inside:

I had this definite goal. I knew where I wanted to go. I was very career-oriented and very successful. I seemed to thrive on that success and I was comfortable with it. All I wanted was to do a good job for my employer . . . but where does that leave my family? It was a real struggle. When I was pregnant with my son, I started looking backwards and remembering my wonderful childhood in Pleasanton. I thought, My kids are not going to get that if I'm out there in the hectic career world. I treasure what I had so much. I loved my freedom growing up in Pleasanton and I didn't want my kids going into day care. I can't do that. I just *cannot* do that. When it really came down to the finances of it, we could have afforded day care. That was no problem, but emotionally it was impossible.

Mary Floury, Robin's classmate from Pleasanton High School, also became a teacher. But once her children came along, Mary decided to stop working. Indeed, although the youngest is now nearly eleven, Mary still believes that a good mother, a moral mother, must devote herself totally to the task of caretaking: there is no room for a professional career:

If I had gone back to work, we could have had a house in Pleasanton. But I would have had to work. I just couldn't have done that emotionally, I couldn't have had it on my conscience that I couldn't stay home. My Mom didn't work until I was ten. I remember when I was the age my son is now, I was taken care of. I couldn't go off to work and leave my kids, especially if they got sick or something.

As Mary sees it, one must make a commitment to one domain or the other. She chose to put her kids' needs above her own.

The women's movement, though publicly committed to the idea of choice, has made it clear in so many ways that the only acceptable choice was to pursue a career.[5] Children were fine as long as they took a back seat to the primary goal of developing a professional identity; any woman who let the family define her priorities was a dinosaur. Mary realizes that career women look down upon her and she resents it:

These [feminists] drive me crazy. They think I just sit and eat bonbons all day. I'm very busy because I'm active in my children's school. I'm my daughter's class mother. I volunteer a lot in their school. When I'm home, I'm here by myself most of the time. I'm just busy keeping the house going, cleaning, taking care of my kids and husband. I'm always here when everyone gets home. Makes you think of "Leave It to Beaver"—the fifties sitcoms. I'm June Cleaver.

If Robin Model suffers from America's suspicion of working women, Mary and Pam suffer from a devaluation of motherhood.[6] For as much as some place high value on the ever-present nurturing woman, others believe that full-time motherhood represents a failure of nerve and a deficiency of intellect.

Conflicting social prescriptions for women's lives in the late twentieth century and the uneasy resolution of these conflicts even among those who appear at peace with their choices show us how deeply intertwined the lives of women are with the fate of their children. Robin loves her job, but her sense of herself as a mother is all too easily undermined when she feels forced to choose her job over her son with a runny nose. She knows that women like Mary Floury feel morally superior to her in the domain of mothering, particularly on those days when she has to ask one of them to watch over her kids because she has a meeting she must attend.

It is not that Pam hated her work or thought her professional future was somehow lacking in promise.[7] Her work was as fulfilling as Robin's. But she is convinced that her purpose in life is to take care of her husband and children. It is hard work, requiring energy, planning, and a commitment to excellence.[8] Nonetheless, Pam realizes that women like Robin, or the even more high powered lawyers and doctors who do still live in Pleasanton, view her "lack of ambition," her willingness to settle for such narrow horizons, as indicative of a serious character flaw.

Susan Faludi, author of the much discussed book *Backlash: The Undeclared War against Women,* argues that there has been a concerted effort to push women back, to eradicate the gains of recent decades, and re-create a subservient, complacent American woman. Faludi argues that advocates like Betty Friedan and Sylvia Hewlett have betrayed women by manufacturing disagreement and skepticism about the feminist agenda and by pointing to the concerns of ordinary women—whom, Faludi suggests, Friedan has never met. Were Faludi to talk with the boomer women who grew up in the unremarkable suburb of Pleasanton, however, she would see how close Friedan has come to the mark. These women believe that the right to work is fundamental; they would be the last to approve of gender discrimination in the labor market. But they worry—a lot—about the consequences for their children of their absence from the home.

Debates over women's roles have divided the boomer generation from within as women square off over the moral correctness of their choices. These same arguments have also driven a wedge *between* generations of women.[9] Young mothers, older mothers, and especially would-be mothers are subjected to subtle "persuasion" from the older generation on the subject of how grandchildren should be raised; and these sage elders are rarely divided in their opinions. It is a rare 1950s mother who does not believe that the best, if not the only, person to raise a child is its own mother—there simply is no substitute. The leading alternatives, for example, day care, are excoriated, even among those who have never entered the door of a child-care center.

Julia Milano, a fifty-five-year-old woman who raised four children in Pleasanton, is a person of strong character. Now divorced from her husband of nearly thirty years, she has a shy smile, a firm handshake, and the stoic strength of a woman who has been through a lot—two of her children died young. She lives alone now, surviving on the income from a part-time job she took up long after her children were grown. When they were little, she often had no choice but to work in the family landscaping business to help make ends meet, patching together a rudimentary child-care system from among her own female relatives. Never in a million years did she consider the option of day care, nor would she be comfortable about the idea of day care if her own son and daughter-in-law wanted to use it:

> Nowadays even with the woman working it's not easy [to manage house payments]. And then if they want a family, the child care. We just outright reject day care. To think of putting [my grandson] Michael in a day-care center where he's going to pick up all these sicknesses!

Her aversion to day care has many sources. It is too institutional, insufficiently individualized to foster proper intellectual and emotional growth. Its collective character flies in the face of the individualistic culture of the suburban middle class. With three or four children to each adult, day care can never substitute for the one-on-one relationship of parent to child. The vehemence with which postwar parents reject child care is reminiscent of the horror with which Americans reacted to stories of Soviet children being raised on collective farms and the visceral discomfort they felt about stories of Israeli kibbutzim. Diluting the intensely intimate bond of parental love with the affection or instruction of professional instructors is something that comes hard to Americans, particularly those who are devout individualists. These Americans understand childhood, and the moral training that is integral to it, as a training period for adult success, where everything rides on the capacity of the individual to surpass the competition. Collectivist institutions have no place in such a scheme, hence day care is understood as a solution suitable only for the unfortunate: poor, single mothers who cannot afford to give their children the attention they need.

Julia Milano's neighbors in Pleasanton rarely had to work after giving birth; their families were better off, more middle class. They took opting out of the work world for granted, as the right, the only thing to do. They know that matters are not so simple for their boomer children. In fact, they define financial success in the 1990s by the following test: can the family afford to let the wife stay home. David Ehrlich's mother, a full-time teacher now that her kids are grown, put the matter this way:

> I hope that David will be able to advance enough in his job that he can have a family and that his wife would be able to stay home. I don't know how close he is to reaching that goal. Housing is so expensive that it creates the need for the two-income family. This makes it difficult with the children. I see the product of that [difficulty]. Children are coming along who have not been raised by a family, but by a baby-sitter or some kind of day care. Now, naturally you think that what you did was the right way. So since I was able to stay home and we could have the house on one income, it seems right to me to be there when kids are little. I see kids [in the school where I teach] wandering the street after school because the parents don't get home. So I had the best of all worlds. David seldom knew I was out of the house. I don't know how they are going to manage it; I do worry about it.

Yvonne Winnow, whose daughter Joanne is now an accomplished artist and college art teacher, worries about the same thing.

She realizes that Joanne and her husband, a musician, need both incomes to afford the rent for their small Manhattan apartment, but she believes that Joanne's children really need a mother's care, and not just in infancy:

> I hate to see that so many children are being brought up by strangers in a day-care center or nursery, even if it's the best one. As soon as your baby's born, you put him on a list for private school and day care—it's absurd. They say the first five years are the most important. That's true, but that's not all. I was fortunate that I was always able to be here when they came from school. I think teenagers need you more than a child coming home in elementary school. If they come home with a problem and you're not there, they might not tell you. I always had children come home for lunch.

The Moral Referendum

Why do postwar mothers have such an investment in the child-rearing practices of their boomer children? Why are they willing to drive their daughters to distraction by impugning their integrity as mothers, by hinting (or proclaiming) that the only moral mother is one who is fully and selflessly devoted to her child? To understand why motherhood has become a generational battleground, we must consider how the feminist movement of the 1970s and 1980s affected postwar mothers, for the older generation's interference in the mothering practices of its daughters is a direct response to the (often unvoiced) frustration they experienced at the hand of a harshly critical women's movement.[10]

The cult of domesticity that gripped the nation in the aftermath of World War II became the normative definition of parental roles; it is a model that still holds sway today.[11] But as the feminist movement gathered force in the 1960s and 1970s, new definitions of women's lives began to give this June Cleaver image stiff competition. The powerful feminist challenge to domesticity reached well beyond women who came of age in the 1970s and 1980s. It cast a glance backward at the lives of middle-class, postwar mothers and implicitly (sometimes explicitly) questioned their "blind" rush into domesticity. Books like de Beauvoir's *Second Sex* or Friedan's *Feminine Mystique* were followed by feminist novels such as *The*

Women's Room. As an ensemble, this cultural criticism painted a picture of stay-at-home motherhood as a refuge of near madness, a form of gender incarceration. It described the domestic life as so bereft of any intellectual or personal reward that women were slowly crushed under its weight, while men hoarded the only glory available, out in the hurly-burly world of business, letters, or politics.

The critique of domesticity buffeted women around, particularly those members of the postwar generation who started having babies in the late fifties and early sixties. Norms of female behavior were so contradictory and confusing that many women did not know which way to turn. Schooled in the stay-at-home philosophy, they were then hit with a blistering condemnation of traditionalism. Doris Reiney had her first child in 1961 and found herself on the receiving end of divorce when her son was just a baby. She was forced into the job market and had no choice but to move back into her parents' home with her young son because she did not earn enough to support them on her own. Several years later Doris remarried and was able to resume what she thought of as a more normal state of existence as a "plain mother." In many respects, her life is testimony to the truths of feminism: she was disadvantaged by her gender in the labor market, pressured by the disapproval of her parents, and wholly without the kind of infrastructural support she needed (for example, child care). She should have been ripe for conversion to a movement that spoke directly to these forms of gender oppression. Yet as was true of many of Doris's postwar contemporaries, rather than liberating her, feminism only confused her and left her feeling that she was hopelessly behind the curve of social change.

> There was a point where everyone was going off to work and asking me, "How can you stand it, aren't you bored? How do you manage [staying home all day]?" And I'm thinking, "Geez, don't put me down, folks. Now that the choice is available to you, this is my choice!"
>
> But you know I was always on the edge of things. I always seemed to be a day late and a dollar short. When I had a fabulous body, people were wearing bathing suits with shorts; when the body fell apart, everybody was wearing string bikinis. And that's the way I felt about the women's movement. When I desperately needed day care, when I desperately needed an equal wage, it was the dark ages. And then I when I finally found someone who

was supporting me, it was out of style—you were supposed to get out there and fulfill yourself!

Doris was outraged by the shifting models of womanhood. Feminism left her bewildered and victimized because she could never quite get it right.

My mother's generation really had the security of being supported. They knew that that was their husband's obligation and that they were supposed to be taken care of. They accepted a lot of crap in exchange for it, but the deal was there. My generation came along and everybody said that the wedding ring was the end of the rainbow, that if you behaved yourself, learned to play a good game of bridge, and stayed attractive, if you did that . . . a man would take care of you forever.

And then partway through the game, they changed the rules and men were running off with their secretaries because they wanted to be fulfilled. You were old hat and old-fashioned. So your husband left you for some lady at the office who was doing really important stuff rather than staying home, raising children, and becoming old hat. My generation is full of displaced homemakers. People who played by the rules and got screwed. So I think my mother at least had society on her side. Every time I turned around, it was a new set of rules.

Suburban mothers like Doris rejected the feminist creed: women's "libbers" were laughed at as bra burners, man-haters, or sexually dysfunctional. They were ridiculed, hounded, and denounced in the press, on the steps of city hall, and in the living rooms of many middle-class homes. Yet the trenchant critique advanced by the feminist movement stuck. It questioned the inevitability of the traditional division of labor and the power of men to define women's choices. Above all, the feminist movement forced women to see their lives in terms of choices for which they had to take responsibility rather than in terms of a narrow set of decisions whose outcome was predetermined: full-time motherhood.

Feminism put Pleasanton's postwar mothers on the defensive, casting a shadow over the dignity of traditionalists who were thoroughly bonded to the home and to the calling that was child rearing. Forced on the defensive, these same mothers now look upon the choices their daughters are making as implicit judgments of their own self-worth. Even though most postwar mothers believed there were no other options, they feel they have to explain to themselves, if not to others, why they "chose" the cloistered life of the model mother and dependent wife. Pleasanton's women squirmed under the spotlight of feminism and found themselves having to justify a lifetime: they were hardly in a position to turn the clock back and redo their lives.

What they could do was continue the argument, seeking to vindicate their own choices by challenging the practices of their daughters. The choices their daughters are making about how to manage motherhood are understood as implicit judgments of their own self-worth, their traditions, their sacred sense of marital sexuality, and their values. Women like Kathleen Sullivan lashed out:

> Women's lib is eroding this country! I listened to my daughter say things that make me furious! The erosion of the family, the erosion of religion in the family. We have kids that drift without purpose, direction, no morals. We are losing things. I have always been my own boss, but the women's lib that they're pushing now has no moral background, no moral code that will keep women from going to sleep with every Tom, Dick, and Harry. I'm seeing it in friends I know, and it makes me sick. They are going to pay for it. Somewhere along the line, their lives will be destroyed. Men will take advantage of them and leave them high and dry. Women are entitled to better than that, but they aren't holding out for it. They are throwing it away with a mess of crap from women's lib. It takes away your privileges and rights and gives you nothing.[12]

Daughters who want or need to work, who must therefore rely upon institutional supports for the care of their children, are subjected to withering criticism from their own mothers. "You cannot be a good mother," they are told, "if you are not there for your children, my grandchildren." Kathleen continues:

> You see children having problems because they do not have the security of the shell around them. They cannot go home and really be home. Children need this stability. It is one of the obligations that comes with having a family. This generation doesn't feel they have to do this. That's women's lib again!

These notions of motherhood often ring true to boomer women who were raised by ever-present nurturing mothers. Hence, they cannot help but respond to this pressure. But the source of the pressure itself is both a heartfelt conviction that mothering can only be done successfully one way and a defensive pride intent on proving that the methods of the past are beyond reproach.

The feminist critique of domesticity became part of the generational culture of boomer women. Daughters who came of age in the late 1960s and early 1970s in particular put their mother's lives under a microscope and did not always like what they saw. As much as they see the value of this model of mothering for the sake of kids, many are leery of its implications for mothers. As one young women put the matter:

> My mother was an extremely depressed person. She was very reclusive. Had no friends. Never went out. Her kids were the extent of her life. Originally I was doing just the same things she did, but I've come to know that there are other aspects [of life]. I felt she was so isolated and unhappy. I felt there had to be some other way.

Of course, not all postwar mothers were depressed and unhappy. There was enough frustration in their lives, enough isolation from the adult world, though, for their daughters to see that what was good for the goslings was not necessarily the best way of life for the goose. Some boomer women conclude that this is a sacrifice a moral mother must make. Others, however, have come to believe that they cannot be good mothers if they are unhappy women and that however strained the choice, they must make it.

No matter which way they go, boomer mothers are torn between opposing visions of child rearing and are easily held hostage to the powerful emotions that lie behind them. Their own mothers—always an important source of advice on the subject of child rearing—have an intensely personal stake in the choices their daughters make. But a daughter who fails to follow in her mother's footsteps does so at considerable risk to their relationship. Such choices by working mothers are interpreted not as responses to economic necessity, or even as evidence for the positive changes brought about by the searching force of the feminist movement, but as a criticism of their own mothers and of the sacrifices they made for their children.

Much has been made of the conflict between traditionalists and feminists over the appropriate way for women to structure their lives. Kristin Luker's well-known work *Abortion and the Politics of Motherhood* argues that the clash between "right to lifers" and "pro-choice" advocates is best understood as a class conflict that largely pits working-class and uneducated women against their more middle-class, educated sisters.[13] The controversy is not only about abortion, but is also more generally about attitudes toward domestic life and the world of work. Luker argues that the abortion controversy, and by extension the image of mothering that each side invokes, is at the core a form of class conflict expressed through the vehicle of women's identity.

Class is clearly a critical factor in the debate over women's identity, but it is not the only one. Generation is at least as powerful a source of conflict over the nature of modern mothering. In the world of the postwar woman, mothering can be done properly only if it is a single-minded pursuit. In the world of the contemporary woman, the lure of the workplace and the demand that she make something more of herself than "merely a mother" is ignored at the risk of becoming socially marginal. Many boomer women aspire to the traditionalist image of motherhood, partly out of conviction and partly because of pressures from their own mothers. Like Mary Floury, they define themselves as having sacrificed an acceptable social identity for the sake of their children. They understand that they have become socially marginal—a cost their own mothers did not have to pay for doing the same thing. Others take the worldly path and suffer the kind of doubts that Robin Model feels, that she may have put her own interests above those of her children, a suspicion that Robin's mother articulates sotto voce. But whatever the choice, it has been made in dialogue—or, indeed, sometimes in the aftermath of a screaming match—between mother and daughter, a dialogue designed to confuse the daughter and reinforce the validity of the mother's own identity.

Kate Lombardi, a heavyset woman in her early sixties, has lived in Pleasanton since 1954. Her three children are all married and have children of their own. Like many of their baby-boom friends from the Pleasanton days, they are finding it hard to manage. Kate is sympathetic to their needs, having brought up her sons and daughter on her husband's blue-collar income years ago. She understands that is nearly impossible to manage today without two incomes. Yet

in the same breath, Kate is quick to blame the two-income household for much that is morally problematic in our society—especially
for children who go astray. She believes that children are more troubled than they were in years gone by, that this sad turn of events
has come about because working parents—especially mothers—are
not there to guide their young ones through the labyrinth of adolescence:

> My son, his wife works, and they have to have a baby-sitter. You
> miss your children growing. You miss . . . I mean, they grew up
> so fast, and I was with them all the time! What is it if you're not
> with them all the time? It's important to stay home with children
> when they're growing up. A lot of these parents today . . . they
> work and they go out a lot, and the kids are home alone, and to
> ease their conscience, the parents give them too much money.
> [Kids] don't know what to do with it. They make friends, and
> their parents don't know who their friends are, but just to
> appease their own mind, they say, "Oh yes, you can have a
> party." No, I never did that. I was there, I was always aware. I was
> there if they needed me. And that's the way it always was.

Kate understands the pressure of necessity; as a depression child
herself, she knows that sacrifices must be made when there is no
real choice. Her mother went out to work when her father lost his
job; her older sisters had to pitch in just to put bread on the table.
Many dreams were deferred and everyone's sense of "what is best"
had to bend in the face of survival needs. But the 1980s and 1990s
bear no resemblance to the depression years. Affluence spreads as
far as the eye can see as far as Kate is concerned. Sure, things are
tough for young people, but not all that tough.

Kate shares with many of her Pleasanton neighbors the suspicion
that self-indulgence fuels this epidemic of dual-career families. Her
children are in hot pursuit of a more comfortable existence than
Kate thinks they need. They could do with less—and spend more
time with their children. Materialism, not survival, is generating a
demand for income that can only be satisfied by having both parents work. They want to go out to eat, they want to take fancy vacations, they want a big house—all things that Kate claims she had to
wait many years to acquire. Are these luxuries worth more than the
value of raising a child properly? she wants to know. If her daughter
reversed the equation, lowered her expectations, and learned to be

patient, she could work less, spend more time with her children, and ensure (as well as anyone can) the quality of their upbringing.

The problem is cast in moral terms, as a matter of choice, and the choices are taken as symptomatic of a debilitating virus that has settled into the souls of the overly ambitious baby-boom generation. These young people are prisoners of inflated expectations, and this (more than economic necessity) is driving them to abandon the only tried-and-true division of labor between fathers and mothers. If mothers are not there to make sure kids do what they are supposed to do and develop the proper values, then no one should be surprised if the nation's children turn out to be troubled.[14]

Boomers like Karen Ames are divided over whether one can ensure the moral development of children without undivided maternal attention. What they do know is that in an effort to satisfy all the demands placed upon them, to love and care for their children, while working hard to provide a comfortable standard of living, they too pay a price. Collapsing at the end of the day, they wonder what of themselves will be left over when they finish responding to all these demands. As boomer men readily admit, the pressure is toughest on women, who are expected to do everything. Paul Cornell (Pleasanton High class of 1970) thinks that the goal of balancing home and work is still as far off as it ever was. He finds the notion that these competing claims can be successfully negotiated ludicrous, another form of the big lie the boomer generation has been feeding itself:

Our generation has been fooled by temptation, by the carrots held out there. The carrot is that you can have it all. This is hardest on women, I think. They are told, "You can have a family, a good job, a summer house, a nice car, and be happy and fulfilled." No you can't. You're either going to have a nervous breakdown or turn to something like alcohol. Otherwise you'll never have time to do anything with all that wonderful money you've earned. It's like a treadmill. Once you get on you can't get off. I think people are getting desperate and it's hardest on the women. They are finding that there is more room for them in the market, but that it's not a substitute for what they were expected to do before. It's an addition. Now they're professionals, mothers, wives, this and that. That produces guilt, stress, and anxiety. Surefire way to end up in a mental hospital.

The Culture of Competition

Baby Boom, a popular movie of the 1980s, took aim at the patently neurotic tendencies of the Wall Street crowd. Diane Keaton played a single advertising executive suddenly burdened with a baby girl to whom she becomes mindlessly devoted. In one memorable scene Keaton sits with her charge in a Manhattan sandbox, surrounded by "real" mothers immersed in earnest discussion of the competition to get into the exclusive nursery schools. Caught completely off guard, Keaton suddenly realizes what a neophyte she is and promptly enrolls her daughter in an art appreciation course for eighteen-month-olds. The audience howls with laughter at the spectacle of the yuppie mother coaching her prelingual child on flashcards of Michelangelo and Rembrandt. They cheer as Keaton finally chucks the whole business and moves to Vermont, where nature takes over, childhood is restored, and love reigns.

Hollywood has its finger on the boomers' pulse. The film touches a raw nerve in a generation that believes children cannot afford to make many mistakes en route to Harvard or even to more modest end points. And while they might brush aside the importance of getting into an exclusive nursery school, elementary school is another matter altogether. From there on out, the world is one big arena of competition where only the well-equipped, superior few can expect to win the right prizes.

Boomers know this scenario all too well. The sheer size of their own generation plunged the boomers into a lifelong competition that began when they were children, crowding into elementary schools that had to go onto double sessions just to accommodate their numbers.[15] It continued as they made their way toward the prestige universities, which accepted only the crème de la crème while the rest had to settle for less. When they reached the labor market, particularly the professional domain, the intensity of the competition translated into disappointment as avenues to the good life were closed off to many, while the few at the top of the heap gained access to lifelong privileges. Applications for law school, medical school, and business school skyrocketed, and well-qualified boomers who might easily have been accepted under other demographic conditions were turned away in droves. These well-paying service professions did not expand fast enough to make upward mobility a reality for everyone in the boomer cohort. Those who were the best qualified did well, leaving the rest to scramble.

Every corner of American life felt the pressure of this great demographic bulge and will continue to do so for the next forty years, as the boomer generation makes its way through the labor market and into retirement. This experience of being part of such an enormous generation has had a deeper impact than simply the practical one of institutional overcrowding: it has seeped into the social identity and psychological makeup of a generation. More than those before or after them, boomers are aware of how fast they must run to keep up with the Joneses, of how dangerous it can be to deviate from the straight and narrow path, of the frustrating reality that there is simply not enough of what everyone wants to go around.

The culture of competition that surrounds today's baby-boom parents is the almost unconscious bedrock of their own child-rearing strategies. Having been schooled in demographically induced scarcity, it has become part of their generational culture to look upon all endeavors as arenas of competition. Under these circumstances, they must make sure that their own children are equipped to face the same kind of pressures. This translates into worrying about everything from whether their kids learn to walk and talk "on time" to whether or not they are accepted into the right college. Laura Nimura is one of the few boomers who has been able to raise her own children in Pleasanton, having married the son of a wealthy immigrant newcomer. By the standards of her generation, she is free of financial worries; she has not worked since she became a mother. Nevertheless, Laura worries about whether her own children will be able to follow in her footsteps:

> Most of the families in this neighborhood, the mothers don't work. They shoulder the most important thing: raising the kids. Even though we all live in this nice upper-middle-class neighborhood, they still worry about the money and college. Because everything is so expensive and a lot of people have smart kids and they want them to go to Princeton, Harvard, or Yale. They know that might be out of their realm of possibility, but they still want it for their kids.

Hollywood has decided to attribute these competitive fixations to a yuppie culture in which these goods have become status items. Such a superficial view obscures the serious nature of boomer psychology, however: these parents worry about their children falling behind. Having been through the mill, they know that besting the competition is the only way to prevent a personal slide.

As much as baby-boom men and women have devoted themselves to shaping their own careers, these concerns pale by comparison with their anxiety about the way this competition will affect their children. The first few times their children fail to leap a necessary hurdle, they panic, not because they are so concerned about trivial aspects of social status. Rather, it unnerves them because they fear that one failure may jeopardize the future.

Joyce Nelson, a fortyish mother raised in Pleasanton, knows how absurd these anxieties can become. "I realized just how out of hand my concerns about my son's future have gotten when we went to his school open house last year":

> The teacher was talking about the poetry projects the [eight-year-olds] were working on. My eyes wandered to the back of the classroom where some poetry had been tacked to the walls. I started reading these incredibly lyrical lines and thought to myself, "My kid could never write poetry like that!" I was getting depressed thinking that the other children were way ahead of my son. But I didn't have my glasses on, so I couldn't read the names of the authors at the bottom of the verses. When break time came, I wandered up to the poetry section and saw the names: Langston Hughes, Shel Silverstein. God did I feel stupid! I laughed my head off afterwards, but it made me realize just how ridiculous my sense of competition had become on my son's behalf.

Boomers redouble their efforts to ensure that their kids will have the best education they can provide, because they, especially, understand how important credentials are. John Ellwood, father of a six-year-old daughter, was surprised at the depth of his own reaction when Adrienne did not get accepted to the private school he had hoped to send her to in Brooklyn. It led him to think about the differences between his parents' experiences and his own where ambition and fulfillment were concerned, and the way the differences informed his own concerns over Adrienne:

> My parents, having grown up during the depression, were very aware of the possibility that people could fall. They were very concerned about money, material comfort, getting that big house in the suburbs, because they saw so many people fail, lose every-

thing in life. We grew up taking that suburban comfort for granted. As children we didn't experience material want. But when Adrienne applied to schools, it was the first time in my life that I saw this flat-out rejection. I was totally unprepared for it. I've had to face competition in my life; I've had [my work] rejected, but I didn't realize how stiff the competition was, what a desperate thing it was going to be for my daughter. In a way, the dog-eat-dog world has made me think, look it's a hard, hard world. I don't want to take a chance that Adrienne might not have what it takes to be happy. . . . You just have to try to get the best that you can for your child.

The Personal Experience of International Decline

Not long ago, *Good Housekeeping* magazine launched a campaign to attract new advertisers. The magazine has been a national institution for decades, offering advice to women about everything from teething, to cooking, sibling rivalry, and birth control. It has a conservative reputation and has long appealed to the kinds of women that flocked to Pleasanton in the 1950s. With the increase in working mothers, *Good Housekeeping* has had to scramble to prove its relevance. A full-page ad in the *Wall Street Journal* in 1990 was supposed to do the trick. An elegantly coiffed Japanese (-American?) mother stands proudly behind her well-dressed young son—perhaps eight or nine years old—who holds a violin to his chest. The copy below the picture notes that *Good Housekeeping* appeals to the "new traditionalist" who is returning to the old way—the best way—of raising her kids.

The picture speaks a thousand words: the enlightened traditionalist is Japanese. The reward for her attention to home and hearth is a son who plays the violin—a young man clearly destined for success. *Good Housekeeping* is playing upon people's anxiety about the declining position of the United States in the international economy. "Real American women" who want to see to it that these foreign invaders do not preempt their own children's prospects will work hard to adopt the traditionalist model, the model that seems to work so well for the Japanese who are famous for their women's dedication to children's development. The magazine is thus hoping to dramatize its own commitment to traditionalism and the rising appeal of full-time motherhood among boomer readers.[16]

Since the mid-1970s the United States has been plagued by economic retrenchment. Companies long considered the bedrock of

our industrial identity collapse without warning, enormous financial institutions—such as Manufacturers Hanover and Chemical Bank
—merge and dump thousands of people onto a hostile job market.[17]
We read about these economic woes daily in the pages of the business section of the newspapers and have become almost inured to
the pain large-scale forces have inflicted on ordinary people trying
to make a living.

In a climate of decline, when no one seems to be at the helm, the
feelings of competition and scarcity that boomers have known all
their lives are heightened. Who will come out a winner in a country
losing its preeminent position in the world economy? How can we
ensure that our children retain their hold on a middle-class life
when the nation has lost control over its industrial destiny? No one,
least of all the economists in whom we vest our faith, seems to have
any answers. All the baby boomers know is that their decisions
about bringing up little Johnny will affect his life chances forever.

Already schooled in the arts of competition, boomers realize that
the key to winning, or simply surviving gracefully, lies in credentials. Our postindustrial economy favors the highly skilled more
than ever before.[18] Children who fall by the wayside will not have a
second chance; they will pay for their mistakes for the rest of their
lives. They read about Japanese dominance of the international
economy, about the declining American standard of living. As Asian
families move into their hometown, they cannot help but notice
that the honor rolls are filling up with foreign names. The indica-
tions are clear: the best places will be reserved for someone other
than their homegrown children unless they see to it that their kids
can cut it in the competition.

In previous periods of history, people could depend upon the
motivation that sheer hardship creates. No one needed to tell the
children of the Great Depression that struggling for a good job is
worth the effort. Thankfully, few Pleasanton boomers have experienced deprivation of this magnitude and they have been careful not
to bring their own children into lives torn by economic devastation.
Kids born to middle-class parents in the 1990s are not going hungry; they have not witnessed catastrophic unemployment. Their
parents have to school them in the competitive ethic without the
pressure of bleak times to fuel their desires.

These private worries are the personal, familial side of America's
declining standard of living. When we put the headlines down, we
can feel disaster creeping up on those we care about. The best we

can do to protect them is to see to it that they are trained to compete for pieces of a shrinking pie. And then it remains the mother who bears responsibility for doing this. It is to her that the world turns to assign blame or credit for the child of success or the child of failure.

If the boomers and their postwar parents had simply squared off with their different visions of the decent life, we could chalk it up to the friction that inevitably accompanies social change. But the matter is more complex, for boomer children do not depart so radically from their parents' own morality, the feminist movement notwithstanding. They too believe, albeit with varying degrees of confidence, that women should marry, have children, and accept primary responsibility for turning their kids into respectable, competent adults.[19] It is this persistent image of traditionalism that forces the baby-boom generation to stand by and wince as their parents shoot their barbs. Their memories of family life are very much in keeping with "Leave It to Beaver," and their admiration of that traditionalism is very real. Few know any other model of family life.

There have been times in America's past where experimentation, the restless quest for a better life, was esteemed. This is *not* one of those times. Conservatism has had a resurgence, and not just in political life. The more the United States flounders in the international marketplace, the more we search for cultural rafts to save us from drowning and protect us from the winds of change that threaten to blow our prosperity, our security, our very identity as a dominant nation out to sea. Under these less than optimal circumstances, who would want to take chances with a child's upbringing? No one really knows whether our modern life-style, with its dependence upon bureaucratic structures like day care or fast-food restaurants, will turn out to have been good ideas long overdue or disasters in the making. It would seem safer by far to rely upon the tried-and-true models of parenting: the stay-at-home mother and the working father. This model clashes, of course, with the demand for a high standard of living, which is manifestly impossible to achieve in many parts of the United States without two salaries.

Adaptations and Their Drawbacks

For many boomers, the solution to these competing demands has been to try to have it all—only later. They have given their attention to their careers and put off feathering the domestic nest, hoping that they can establish themselves financially before indulging in the private pleasures of family life. Boomers who waited to have children have discovered an unintended and unwelcome consequence of their more advanced age: infertility. The relentless biological clock ticks on, leaving boomer couples at the mercy of experimental, high-technology fertility treatments that are as draining as they are expensive. Even those who managed to have their first child without incident often find themselves caught in this medical maelstrom when the second child stubbornly refuses to arrive. Having come from relatively large (baby-boom) families themselves, the idea of being childless or spawning an "only child" are foreign and unwelcome notions.

If they could chalk these problems up to Mother Nature, they might more easily cope; but like so many other (biological or economic) problems, culture intervenes and gives a moral cast to the problem. A misplaced investment in the world of work often gets the blame for the personal pain of infertility. This is especially true for women who have already had one child; they knew they could have had more, if only they hadn't waited so long. Childless boomers can at least blame faulty biology pure and simple. Nevertheless, they all realize that people, mainly family, talk behind their backs about the workaholic mothers and fathers who refuse to slow down long enough to make room for "what really matters." Between their own self-doubt and the skepticism or outright disapproval of others, the problem of infertility becomes a canvas painted in shades of moral approbrium.

If holding back on starting a family was acceptable for the older boomers, the opposite seems to be the case for their younger brothers and sisters. The more traditional Reagan generation, about whom we will hear more in chapter 7, was less interested in these "parenting experiments" than its older siblings. Boomers born in the 1960s are anxious to return to the model their own parents exemplify: having children in their twenties. This, however, has not proved to be easy, for they are too committed to maintaining a comfortable life-style. The two halves of this equation remain irreconcilable nonetheless: unless one partner in such a young marriage has managed to achieve truly spectacular success in the job market, it is nearly impossible to maintain a middle-class standard of living on a single income.[20]

Younger boomers chafe at being pushed by economic forces to do what many of their older siblings did voluntarily: hold off on having kids. A delicate calculus pits the personal satisfaction of having a family against the desire to sustain a standard of living that, for them, is equally essential to responsible parenting. They consider it an affront to have such intimate decisions forced into the realm of cold, rational, economic thinking. For like most people, these young couples believe that having children is an expression of marital commitment, the most personal of decisions. It is outrageous, they say, that we are "forced" to decide when we can "afford" to have children, to have to put pregnancy on a par with buying a new car. For earlier generations, starting a family seems to have been such a simple matter, or so we are told.[21] The question should not be, Can we afford to have a child?; it should be, Are we ready for this new life? The fact is that young boomer families have to make a trade-off: starting a family virtually ensures a sharp drop in their economic well-being.

Frustration is building among Pleasanton's young people, for they had been raised to expect open vistas, choices, possibilities in life. The very generational proximity of their parents renders this change a hard one to assimilate. Women like Jane Fraser want to know why having a family was such a simple matter for the last generation and so difficult for hers.

I worry a lot about whether I could afford to stay home when I have children. My parents just did it automatically. It seems like my mom, all her friends just stayed home and had families. To me that seems like such a healthier way to do things. She got that time with the kids. When Dad comes home, she can make time for him. There's not this competition. Why can't I have that? What went wrong with my generation?

Karen Rosen, Jane's high school friend from Pleasanton, is a successful corporate attorney. She is earning more money than her father ever did. Karen's mother did not work when she was little and although she is not yet ready to have children she thinks about the contrast between the freedom her mother had to raise her kids herself and the pressure she would face if she tried to follow in her mom's footsteps. She would like to believe that the feminist movement got it right in advocating freedom of choice for women. Unfortunately, is it is economically impossible to exercise the domestic

choice, even for a short time, and in this respect she feels she too
was "sold a bill of goods."

> I can't stay home and live like my mother did. And that's just
> ridiculous because my parents weren't all that well off. They
> were just OK, nothing special. It was very simple then. Even
> though I am doing very well professionally now, I couldn't do
> those simple things. Isn't that ironic? The deal was going to be
> that you didn't *have* to stay home. Now it's like you can't stay
> home if you wanted to. It's depressing. God, if we work so hard
> to get where we've got, there should be a better reward for it.
> And instead we're running in place almost. If my husband was the
> only one working we could not just go and buy my parents'
> house and live that way. And that seems crazy—why did I work
> this hard, study in school, get this job, and do all of this only to
> come out with less freedom than they had?

Karen does not blame her parents; indeed, she is grateful to them
for their support over the years. In truth, she does not know
whom to blame. But the fact that her parents are but one generation removed underscores for Karen the arbitrary character of history, the sense that it does not always move in the direction of
progress. It can advantage one group and then disadvantage the
next.

These constraints can place unhealthy pressures on a marriage.
Typically, women are anxious to have children before their husbands think they are economically ready. Disagreement over an
issue so central is rarely trivial and can undermine the psychological equilibrium of all concerned. George Bank talks uneasily about
how he and his wife are dealing with the issue:

> We have no children now. We have a doggie. That's our baby.
> We have a golden retriever; that's our little girl for now. Are we
> thinking about having children? Well, we are really getting down
> to it now, aren't we! You should talk to my wife! [Pause] Well, I
> would say that children are in the future. Right now I'd say it's
> probably mostly an economic problem. A very expensive propo-
> sition, that is. We are classically in the crunch of the whole thing
> of not maintaining our parents' standard of living. We do own a
> house—or I should say, we're renting it from the mortgage com-
> pany. . . . I feel very fortunate to have it, even though it's just a
> small starter home. But kids—right now, basically, we need both

salaries to support ourselves, and we don't have an extravagant style of living.

These matters are exacerbated when George's parents drop their heavy-handed comments about grandchildren they are waiting to spoil. With feet tapping on the floor, the Banks (senior), who had their children young and on a single salary, make it clear that they are waiting—not too patiently—for grandchildren to appear on the scene.

Many younger boomers raise their children themselves. Like their parents, they are skeptical about the quality of day care, certain that no baby-sitter can do as good a job as they can, and determined not to let the demands of earning a living rob them of the simple pleasure of rocking a small baby out of the sleepy doldrums rather than the rushing to catch the 6:30 commuter train. As Jane Fraser put it:

> I want to be home with my children (when I have them). I don't want to miss that. I know that I will not put my child in care and go to a job. That's why I feel that I have to wait until we're set up. If there is such a thing, to be set up. So that I can do it the way my mom did. I really feel like it had a positive effect on me. I can't see missing all those things when they're that young.

Yet no easy solution presents itself. Hence, Pleasanton's boomers stew in frustration and hope that somehow just waiting long enough will ease the crush.

Far, Far from Home

For some waiting in or around Pleasanton is simply out of the question. If they are ever to own a home, that prerequisite of a stable family life, they will have to move to lower-income communities. Indeed, many of Pleasanton's boomers have left New Jersey and settled near lower-cost cities like Atlanta, Houston, Nashville, Albuquerque, or Phoenix. As a solution to the housing crunch, this strategy has many appeals. Even if one drives but a two-hour radius south or west of Pleasanton, farther from the high-priced orbit of New York City, many a lovely house becomes affordable, even for those boomers who are not stockbrokers or lawyers. Smaller towns, off the beaten path, offer older, larger homes that need some elbow grease and tender loving care to become the kind of rambling family home that boomers remember so fondly from their early days in Pleasanton. One need only look at the statistics on increasing commute time to see that many young Americans are prepared to take to the road in exchange for affordable housing. For many, however, this still entails a two-income family, for even the longer commute does not allow them the luxury of a stay-at-home mommy. But for others, this is exactly what has been "bought" by the long commutes into the metropolis.

For the long-suffering driver, however, the nonmonetary costs of such a move are high, measured in grueling hours fighting the traffic, reckless drivers, aggressive truckers, rain, and snow. It hardly helps family relations, for the commuter must devote to the road time that he (and it is usually a he) would rather spend with the kids. When two parents hit the road, the strain is even greater. Who will pick up Johnny from preschool when he suddenly gets sick? How long will the baby-sitter's patience last when Mommy is caught in traffic for the third time this week? Is it only a matter of time before some equally exhausted driver makes a mistake that totals the family car and puts a loved one at risk?

As more and more people adopt the long-distance commute, the problem reappears like one of Medusa's heads: the more refugees from high-priced suburbs like Pleasanton flee to outlying areas, the higher the prices go in those remote outposts. Distant communities that used to be havens of working-class families find themselves in the thrall of this gentrification, which is pricing out both the old-timers and the latecomers. As in all things, those who got in early were safe and those who waited were sunk. Younger boomers often find that they are on the losing end of this proposition and that even the strategy of moving far from work still costs more than they can afford.

Living far from Pleasanton, the place many still regard as "home," brings other complications as well. Communities that have lower housing costs often lack the amenities that make a well-heeled community like Pleasanton so desirable: parks, pools, and the like. They are also more likely to be mixed-income towns where racial or class tension is in the air. Whatever the current economic status of Pleasanton's boomers, there is no escaping the fact that they were raised in a lily-white town, where the schools were good, and the diction, worldview, and style of the middle to upper middle class became part and parcel of their own personalities. People raised in Pleasanton stick out when they "integrate" these modest communities and often find they have little in common with their older, less educated neighbors. Housing, it seems, is only a part of what they were after: a community of like-minded souls is no less important, and it may be a long time in coming.

The gap that separates boomers from their new neighbors can be wider in the low-income areas of the nation's big cities where some former Pleasanton boomers rent in order to escape the long commutes. Andrew Lerner is an intense young man with thick, wavy blond hair and stylish glasses (without frames). He is working hard to make a career switch from the volatile world of advertising to the more stable and satisfying field of business journalism. Andrew hopes to marry his girlfriend and start a family soon. For the time being, however, he has settled into an affordable postage-stamp apartment in New York City. Andrew has "solved" the housing problem by moving into the heart of the beast, to a marginal neighborhood where the down-and-out rub shoulders with the young and upwardly mobile. He finds the contrast between himself and his neighbors troubling:

> Economic reality in New York is very hard. [My girlfriend and I] are very limited here in New York. It bothers me to have to live with people who are depressed and downtrodden, sick, the homeless.

Andrew's "solution" to the cost-of-living crunch has a price—the alienation he feels as he looks around his neighborhood and registers how many people are in trouble, how divided the society he lives in has become, and how impotent he is to address any of these troubling issues. The homogeneous character of Pleasanton hardly prepared Andrew for this. But his resources restrict him to living in parts of the city where the clash between the haves and have-nots is vividly displayed and this troubles him mightily. It surely will not do when it comes time to have children—from Andrew's perspective the city is simply too far gone.

For the competitively inclined boomers, the chief stumbling block in modest communities, whether urban or rural, is the poor quality of the local schools. Katherine MacDowell is a teacher herself, and she knows full well that towns with cheap houses are towns that have not invested much in the public schools. The Mac-Dowells are not about to settle for a substandard education, particularly not in this era of credentialism. If she has to, Katherine will take her (as yet unborn) children to the school where she works, but few parents have that option. Hard choices loom: you can buy a house but not a good school in one and the same place.

Some of the costs associated with moving away from the old homestead are tangible matters of real estate and community quality. Others are more subtle, more intimate, and take longer to manifest themselves. Erosion of the ties that bind the generations together is one of these. Families accustomed to getting together often may find that the only times they see each other now are holidays, weddings, or graduations. With grown children moving to less expensive areas of the United States—chiefly the Southeast and the Midwest—Pleasanton parents find that they hardly know the grandchildren they so longed for. It saddens them to realize that they can do little to reverse the tide. Grandmothers especially have a hard time coping with the loss, for many of them built their own lives around the needs of children. After years of the empty nest, they had looked forward to re-creating something of that maternal experience with their grandchildren. Retired grandfathers, who may have had little time for their own kids, look forward to making up for it with their grandchildren, only to discover that they are too far away to sustain relationships of this kind. They realize that moving away, whether in pursuit of affordable housing or in response to job demands (or both), is often necessary for their children. But they know, as their children know, that something special has been lost in the bargain.

Susan Combs moved to Atlanta in her mid-thirties, lured by opportunities for her and her husband and by decent housing that cost half as much as the most run-down shack in Pleasanton. They have a pleasant life-style in the cosmopolitan South and for the most part do not regret the move. Yet there is no getting around the fact that Atlanta is not Pleasanton. The things that are missing in her life can only develop over long periods of time:

> The family is important. Stability, friends. You know, when I go home to Pleasanton, I'll go over to my friend's house and we'll just sit for hours talking. I feel like I haven't really left. When you move away you meet new people, but they don't know my back-

ground, they haven't lived through the things I've lived through. You don't have those ties. There's an emptiness of that sort. Thank heaven for my kids and my husband. But you lose something. You need those roots and you don't have them. I don't miss Pleasanton as far as trying to afford living there. But I miss the people. We knew each other, we knew our respective families—their parents and brothers and sisters. In Atlanta, I meet people whose parents are far away, brothers and sisters don't live here, and you only come to know them because your kids play together. These friendships feel very temporary. Your long-term friends and family, they are the ones who really matter—and they're in Pleasanton.

Mary Floury grew up in a big family, the fifth of six children born to working-class parents who both worked "all the hours God made" to keep a roof over their heads in Pleasanton. The Flourys were never well-off. Mary's father was an elevator operator, and her mother worked in a school cafeteria to supplement her husband's wages. But Mary holds dear the memories of growing up amidst her rambunctious siblings. These ties matter a great deal to her. She believes that family, extended family in particular, should be at the core of any child's sense of identity. But when Mary grew up to become a teacher and married a teacher as well, she discovered that if she was going to provide her own children with a house, she was going to have to uproot them:

> It's sad. I don't understand why the house that my parents bought for hardly anything could sell twenty-six years later for a fortune. It's crazy. We had to move up here. The prices were so high in Pleasanton County, we just couldn't stay there. All of our family is in Pleasanton County, but we're up here. We couldn't afford to live in the county that we were brought up in—either of us. Families are being separated. You have to go where you can afford to live or both work.

Mary's husband, the sole provider in the family, does not earn enough money as a teacher to allow the family to remain in Pleasanton. That would require Mary to return to work, something she refuses to do, for it would make her job as a mother impossible. So, pushed by the unseen hand of the economy, the Flourys made their choice. But Mary mourns the loss to herself and her children of the intimate, daily contact with her parents, her siblings, and her many aunts and uncles in the old neighborhoods.

Living far from Pleasanton also makes it impossible to be part of a family support structure. Parents who would be only to happy to step in and help with baby-sitting are too far away to depend upon. When a crisis strikes, there is often no one nearby. The Colombardi family has been lucky in this regard. Marie and Joe Colombardi moved to Pleasanton forty years ago and raised four children, most of whom rent houses in nearby towns. They were among the solid working-class families of Pleasanton. Joe had a construction job, and Marie worked part-time in a local restaurant to make ends meet. Joe's career has had its ups and downs. In recent years he has been laid off and forced to take custodial jobs at night to bring in some money. But Joe does not mind because his "real job" now is to look after his grandchildren during the day. Marie allows that he loves giving his kids a hand with the little ones:

> Our oldest grandchild is three and a half. Her mother had to go back to work, so Joe practically raised her. Now, since our second grandchild was born—a boy this time—Joe has had both of them. Our daughter has a baby too and she's home right now, but when she needs to go out she brings the little one over.

Joe's involvement as a grandfather goes well beyond what has ever been typical in Pleasanton, but as children move to distant cities and suburbs, even the more normative participation of grandmothers has become increasingly rare.

If distance prevents parents from helping out with their grandchildren, it also has implications for the assistance their own children will be able to provide in their twilight years. Moving to a less expensive part of the country in pursuit of the good life for one's immediate family does not erase the obligations adult children have to their elderly parents over the long term. As Pam Tomasi is beginning to realize, the day of reckoning will arrive, and for women, to whom these obligations tend to fall, anticipatory guilt is part and parcel of the experience of geographical separation.

> I don't think that I would want to be farmed out to a nursing home and give up my belongings and my family and all that I had held dear because I was considered a nuisance. My mother and my in-laws are still in good health, and my husband and I are just

beginning to talk about how we will help them. We agree that it wouldn't be right to tell them, "Go buy a condo in Florida and if that doesn't work we'll put you in a nursing home in New Jersey. We'll write and call every once in awhile." What's the point of that? I just hope that there will be some middle ground, but it won't be easy since we're all the way down here in Dallas and they're in Pleasanton.

Most postwar parents have hit retirement age by now. If the fates are good to them, they will have another decade of good health in which to enjoy themselves. Moreover, because the boom years permitted them to accumulate considerable savings, they are better set for a long retirement than virtually any generation of Americans that came before them. Yet even they will have to face dependency some day. As their daughters scatter to the four winds in search of an affordable life-style for their own families, the capacity to care for elderly parents has diminished. Pleasanton's boomer daughters are concerned about what will happen when their parents need them, when the need to reciprocate for their parents' many years of loving care becomes an issue. Distance will make it hard.

A mobile society like the United States is advantageous in many respects, but it also makes it harder for people to meet their obligations. Certainly, many families elect to distance themselves from each other, but just as many experience the separation, as yet another example of the way economic pressure has made it impossible to live a moral life. Pleasanton's retired parents may realize that financial need and better opportunities drove their children away—but they do not necessarily embrace these priorities. George and Amy Ortner have watched their children leave the area in search of better opportunities and in some respects they approve, but they realize now that this has made it impossible for them to spend time with their grandchildren. They wonder about the wisdom of this trade-off:

AMY: The house my son has in Madison, Wisconsin, is probably a nicer house than our home in Pleasanton. It's much larger. But they've had to go a long way from home to have that housing. While we think that it's wonderful for them to have it, we find it painful for them to be so far away and for our grandchildren to be that far away.

We would like to have a close relationship with them, but a twenty-hour drive is not my idea of fun.

GEORGE: It's an emotional burden.

What is more important, a job or an elderly mother's happiness? A nice house or a frail father's well-being? Enough money for vacations or the smile on a baby's face when she recognizes her grandmother? Yet again the baby-boom generation seems to come up wanting.

Pleasanton's boomers are in a quandary. If they delay having children in order to squirrel away money, they feel frustrated, unable to follow their emotions, unable to cement the bonds of husband and wife. If they have children "on time," they often find they cannot provide what they consider an adequate standard of living. Those who work double-time to shore up their standard of living sacrifice precious time with the kids. This leaves boomers open to the unsettling thought that they are neglecting their duties as parents and are too dependent on institutional solutions that may prove to be wanting. If they move to lower-income areas to relieve these pressures, they may lose a sense of rootedness as ties to the rest of the family weaken. There seems to be no good solution to the conundrums that face this generation, no plateau where they can feel content and finally relax. Instead, persistent frustration dogs them. It has all turned out to be much harder than they ever expected.

5

The Spoiled Generation

Regardless of what politicians may have to say about the future of the American economy, the public has long since concluded that all is not well. The slippage we have seen in virtually every corner of U.S. industry, the evaporation of the lead we thought we could claim in our "savior" industries (computers, high technology, communications), and the wave upon wave of downsizing, takeovers, and bankruptcies have permanently shaken our sense of security and our self-identity as a preeminent power. These facts are the daily diet of academicians, policymakers, and frustrated politicians who have to find ways to stretch Band-Aids over our malfunctioning public sector; they are all over the front pages of our newspapers.

But economic decline also has a personal and moral face—the face of ordinary people whose private aspirations for themselves and their children have been crushed by the weight of macrolevel forces. Declining fortunes must be given a cultural texture that turns impersonal trends into people-sized moral problems, problems we might be able to do something about. That we are not successful in reversing the tides of the economy is beside the point. We must find ways to make ourselves feel like meaningful actors on this stage, ways we can influence the course of our lives or the trajectories of our children. The role of a puppet on someone else's string is not a happy one. Our very desire to be active agents in our fortunes and take some control of our lives leads us to see moral purpose and moral flaws in the ups and downs of the market and the dynamics of our own careers.

Had this decline come about gently and gradually, it might have provoked less angst. Instead, side by side sit two generations whose experience of social mobility has been so dramatically different that one cannot help but ask why one group was so favored and the other left out in the cold. The baby-boom generation does not resent its parents per se for coasting into the propertied middle class; it was after all the prime beneficiary of this good fortune. They just want to know why the gravy train gave out before it got to their doorstep and who is responsible for the unfairness they have been subjected to.

Oran MacDowell and his wife, Katherine, are in their late twenties. Oran grew up in Pleasanton during the 1960s. His father was an insurance salesman for a good, solid company. Oran's life was nothing fancy, and he never developed yuppie aspirations. In fact, he thinks that the yuppies are a disgusting lot who have given his generation a bad name. But what really bothers Oran and Katherine is the fact that whereas just a few years ago his parents could lay claim to their modest share of the American dream without sweating too hard, for them no amount of sweat is going to make a difference. The life-style they took for granted in their youth is completely out of reach:

ORAN: We are always trying to save to get a house. We're working on it slowly.

KATHERINE: That's our goal. But it's not as easy as it was for our parents. It's just the two of us. Oran's parents were able to raise him and have his mother not work. They could save enough for a house. Now it's the two of us working and we can't save anything. It's *very* frustrating!

ORAN: The area [around Pleasanton] is skyrocketing. When my parents moved in in 1978, they bought the house for $35,000. God, now you couldn't even come close to a tract of land around here. Couldn't even get a sidewalk for that.

KATHERINE: For our generation to get a house, you have to have parents who have [extra] money. Only way you can buy something around here.

Often enough, Pleasanton's postwar parents share the MacDowells' outrage and join the younger generation in pointing the finger at inept politicians, unfairly advantaged classes or nationalities, undeserving minorities, or chronically overpaid workers who got more than their share and left the country holding the bag. At the same time, however, there is the nagging, barely articulated fear of postwar parents that they are at least partially responsible for their children's frustration. With only the best of intentions, these children of the Great Depression showered upon their own children all the benefits of the postwar years. They wanted to do more for their kids than their own parents had been able to do for them. Yet now they are left wondering whether their generosity did not create false expectations, a misplaced sense of entitlement, an "I want it all *now*" attitude.

Why Can't They Wait Their Turn?

From the perspective of postwar parents, one of life's most important lessons revolves around the need to "pay your dues," a morality of deferred gratification acquired the hard way in the Great Depression. Since the 1930s gave way to the boom years of World War II and its aftermath, it is easy enough to see how that generation came to conclude that all good things come to those who wait.

For Pleasanton's postwar parents, good times came just as they were ready to put the war behind them and establish their families: the rebound gave them the necessary resources to do so in relative comfort. The lessons of the depression were permanently engraved on their souls, however. Fear of economic insecurity never waned, despite the upward mobility. Saving for a rainy day was second nature. They were leery of credit, critical of those who lived beyond their means, and convinced that their good fortune in the 1950s was a reward for all the suffering they had weathered in the 1930s and 1940s. Hence, even as Pleasanton's World War II veterans traded up into larger houses, joined the town's swim club, and gave their children ballet lessons, they continued to see themselves as practicing the art of survival. Having been denied and denied again in their youth, they had learned the real value of money and security.

Circumstances would create a completely different environment for the next cohort. The children of the boom years were children of plenty. They took it for granted and never saw themselves as overindulged or especially privileged. "Everyone"—that is, everyone in Pleasanton—lived in a single-family house. Everyone got to take an occasional vacation of some sort. No one in the community was threadbare. In the 1950s and 1960s unemployment was a rarity for the white middle class.[1] In short, the two generations could not have had more different histories in terms of childhood standard of living.

This conclusion may make good sociological sense, but it is largely irrelevant in the moral lives of the people of Pleasanton. The two generations do not understand themselves as the products of divergent economic epochs and different historical conditions. Their generational "personalities" are, from their point of view, their own creations. Depression survivors define themselves as pragmatic people, inclined to sacrifice—certainly not neutral descriptions. The generation of the depression esteems these characteristics and tends to think less of those who seem not to have learned these fundamental lessons. When they confront their children, whom they raised in the midst of plenty, only to find themselves downwardly mobile, these parents cannot help but think that the next generation is seriously flawed.

Diagnosing the disease is a complex matter, for it necessarily implicates postwar parents as unwitting agents in the transmission of a culturally contagious virus: the affluence bug. If their adult children are too demanding, unwilling to pay their dues, have too low a frustration threshold, or are simply shallowly materialistic, who else is responsible? There are other players who can be blamed: the media or the unholy revolution of the 1960s that laid waste to the plans of postwar parents to shape their children in their own image. But when it comes down to it, the child-rearing industry to which we are all subject tells us that parents are primarily responsible for transmitting basic values.

The generation steeped in the experience of the depression cannot help but see its (now adult) children as spoiled, even as it assumes responsibility for the spoilage. Barbara Cazera, who raised three kids in Pleasanton, believes her thirty-year-old daughter, Andrea, just does not understand the sacrifice it took to provide her with a middle-class life:

Andrea and her husband both come from the same type of backgrounds. Both [sets of parents] have homes. They see that as a nice way to live. They don't realize how much we struggled to get there. We threw out all the frills along the way to get where we wanted to go. They want [everything]. It's a different way of thinking. We never went to the movies, to restaurants, never anywhere. We did without a lot and I don't regret it. I was thrifty because I knew what I wanted. I still am cheap.

The Cazeras' neighbors—the Neilsen family—could not agree more. Modest people of modest ambitions, the Neilsens have lived in Pleasanton for forty years. They moved into their two-story brick house and slowly began to add on rooms to make it big enough for their family. Mr. Neilsen worked nearly all his life in a middle-management position at General Motors, until the factory closed, forcing him to retire on his pension and benefits. Mrs. Neilsen worked in clerical jobs before and after Anna, their only child, was born. The Neilsens are hardworking people who never indulge themselves. Hence, when they hear about baby boomers (Anna and her friends) who are not satisfied with their lot in life, they can only respond with mild disgust. "Anna has a better life, financially," notes Mr. Nielsen. "We were struggling!"

> Anna doesn't have to struggle. I think that's why their attitude on life is so much different. We had to struggle for everything that we got and we appreciate it. They have the money. Don't bother taking care of [what they have]. They'll just buy a new one. That's their attitude today, like most kids. Money is no object. In our day, money was the only object. You had to work hard for it. If it didn't come in [as fast as you needed it], well you learned to stretch it.

From the Neilsens' viewpoint, Anna and her age-mates around the country have no experience with or appreciation for budgeting. They have no sense of limits and moderation. While necessity drove the Neilsens to accept the limitations of an ordinary life, Anna's lack of experience with necessity has left her a flawed individual. In the long run, it will be her Achilles' heel. She will be unable to cope with the frustrations of a limited income and escalating costs. From the tone of the Neilsens' remarks, one might almost conclude that they look forward to the day when this reality hits. Not that they wish their daughter ill; they simply want her to acknowledge the truth of their own generational experience, something that will not happen until reality forces her hand.

Mr. and Mrs. MacDowell—Oran's parents—second the opinion that only hardship will teach their son and his wife to lower their expectations and wait. It is, they believe, a lesson that runs against the grain of their children's generational culture. The MacDowells know how hard it was to achieve the standard of living they have today; they can't understand why this point never registered with Oran. Their struggles are invisible to their children, as if the boomers subtracted the depression, subtracted the war, and somehow assumed that all this good fortune came along without sacrifice. What is worse, according to the MacDowells, is that Oran does not realize that if he just starts small, he and Katherine will ultimately end up where they want to be. They simply have to wait their turn. According to Oran's father:

> If they want to live in [Pleasanton], they may have to live in Oshkosh for a year and have a house there, sell that, and then come back. They might not be able to make [my] house their first house. That's where the me generation has to learn to say, "I'm not going to be able to satisfy this goal tomorrow. But I can satisfy it next year by doing this and that." But they get to a level of frustration when they can't get what they want when they want it.

Yet the MacDowells think Oran's attitude is not all that surprising. After all, he picked it up right there in Pleasanton:

> It's our fault. What they wanted, we got [for them]. It's our generation's fault, not the children's fault. Our children got more than we ever had, and their children will probably get even more.

Richard and Sharon Wozniak think along the same lines about the attitudes of their children now in their late twenties. Unlike the native-born MacDowells, however, they grew up in Europe and emigrated after the war, Richard from Poland and Sharon from Germany. Although they were not poor in their youth, their exposure to the devastation of war made them pragmatic, realistic, and intolerant of people in this country who complain about their circumstances without ever having confronted real desperation. The Wozniaks believe that the boomers expectations are cushioned by the knowledge that they can rely upon a support structure in the form of loving parents that was never available in the past:

SHARON: Everything was more difficult for us. Our children started out much better. For one thing, they know if something goes wrong, Mom and Dad are there as a cushion. We [Europeans] didn't have that. Even Americans of our generation didn't have that. We have all achieved. We all have a nest egg. Our children, no matter who they are, can always come back to Mom and Dad. Look at how many have moved home! We couldn't do that.

RICHARD: Our children don't see it this way because their expectations are so much higher. People feel entitled to a job, they expect to be able to marry, buy a home, two cars, and a snowmobile. If our son doesn't have those things, he feels deprived. They may have to wait a little bit longer before they buy a home, so they feel deprived.

SHARON: Our children go on vacation several times a year. We didn't go on any vacation for about ten years after we were married. . . . We were never poor or hungry but we didn't have all the things that our children take for granted.

Neither the MacDowells nor the Wozniaks are sure where their children's unrealistic expectations came from. Even though they worry about their own complicity in creating boomer culture, their louder impulse is to indict the kids for character flaws and pre-scribe a comeuppance as a remedy. They don't *really* want their boomer children to hit the skids, but they do want them to assimi-late the lessons of the depression era without having to experience such hardship.

Not all postwar parents blame their children for failing to hold their expectations to a reasonable level. Indeed, some Pleasanton parents find their children's expectations completely understand-able and are outraged on their children's behalf that they have not come to pass. They argue that they too expected their children to surpass them—this is a national credo after all. The Oldman family sees this inflated sense of entitlement as the natural result of cul-tural pressures that have been building in America for the past thirty years. The Oldmans believe that their children could not help but absorb the omnipresent images of affluence that typified America:

Our children who have grown up with the material life-style, expect to have that life-style now. There were different expecta-tions when we got married. We didn't expect to have it all. There are many things that contribute to that [expectation]. Our soci-ety's instant gratification, capitalistic way of looking at things, having possessions as proof of one's self-worth. Television too.

Exposure to a barrage of advertising, images, this is what an important person is all about. Designer clothes, cars. I can't see how [our kids] wouldn't be affected by that constant input.

When postwar parents criticize their offspring for being too materialistic, they are often thinking of the yuppie, the spiritual progeny of the Reagan presidency, which encouraged the pursuit of self-interest to the exclusion of all other values as a moral enterprise, the highest expression of the American way. Despite the fact that yuppies never constituted more than a small fraction of the boomer population, their presence as culture heroes and villains—to be alternately cheered and condemned—reinforced in the minds of many in the postwar generation the unbearable feeling that their kids were part of an organized generational conspiracy to overturn the old standards and values. Yuppies symbolized that most unfortunate tendency to accumulate for the sheer pleasure of self-indulgence and for this a hailstorm of unfavorable press rained down upon them. Moreover, this tiny privileged minority tainted a whole generation of boomers, particularly those who came of age in the 1980s, as conspicuous consumers.

Ironically, Pleasanton's boomers are just as critical as their parents are of the yuppie phenomenon and go to great lengths to disassociate themselves from it. "We are not looking to make money for ourselves, to buy houses to satisfy our egos," they say with a frown and a tone of exasperation. Apart from the constraints it imposes on their own lives, what distresses boomers the most about not having the standard of living they define as normal is the inability to provide *their* children with the kind of life their parents gave them. "We are not selfish, we just want to do right by our own kids"—this is the refrain of the boomer generation.

For many boomers, however, it has proved either impossible to meet this standard at all or difficult to reach it by the time they want to begin a family. The pressure to have everything in place—a home, a solid job, a schedule that leaves room for a baby's needs—collides head-on with the high cost of housing, the increasing insecurity of the marketplace, and the relentless demands of the work world on both men and women. The contradiction seems irreconcilable: boomers simply cannot accept the idea, so familiar to their parents, that children can be born into struggling young families and not be any the worse for it.

Having set this requirement for themselves, boomers set about planning in minute detail exactly how they are going to acquire what they need. Hypercalculation thus replaces the casual, unplanned style of pregnancy of the postwar parents. Boomers ruminate for years about how to sequence their decisions in order to be sure that when they do have children, all is in order. Conflicting demands often appear irreconcilable, as Bob Fieland, a twenty-seven-year-old insurance broker, explains:

> One kid . . . I don't even know if we can afford having one child. There were two in my family, three in Jane's, and that would be the range [we'd like]. I wouldn't want to have any more than that, but certainly let's say two. But two is going to be a tremendous, tremendous financial burden and drain. Not that you want to think of it in those terms, but right now I can't afford one child, no less two children. Especially when you think about the expenses . . . and then you combine that with the loss of the second income, right? Because you can't have Jane working. Well you're gonna lose, I figure a year or two [of her income]. And its just a double whammy that cannot be overcome.

Bob just cannot figure out how to balance what he thinks he and Jane must provide for their children-to-be. Bob's classmate at Pleasanton High School, Oran MacDowell, and his wife are just as worried. Katherine MacDowell has very definite ideas about how their private lives must be organized before they can start a family, but she is not really confident that it can be done:

> I'd like to have kids before I'm thirty. I'm twenty-five now. So we have five more years to get a house, get settled, so that we're comfortable. Comfortable means you have the coffee table, you have the lamps. The drapes match. Just little things like that. And then be able to start. Thirty isn't late now, but I want to make sure that we do it by then. But can we do it in five years? Which means that you'd really like to live in the house for two years before you have kids.

Oran's parents, who still live in Pleasanton, cannot fathom this approach. Why is it so important to Katherine and Oran to have every last detail of life in order before they start a family? Their eyebrows lift and their voices rise when they compare their own generation's casual attitude with their son's programmatics:

MRS. MACDOWELL: Our generation didn't do that. That was the culture of
the times. This generation has certain goals set. They're not going to
have children until they have a down payment for a house, until
they've traveled as much as they want. They're already planning to
go back to work after they have a child because they're used to a
certain life-style. . . . That's the world today.

MR. MACDOWELL: When we got married the expectation was that as
soon as she got pregnant, she'd spend the rest of her life at home
watching kids.

Oran's parents can understand to a degree this desire to be
secure before starting a family, but there are two things they cannot
really accept. First, their own definition of a minimum standard of
living for "affording" children is far below the threshold Oran and
Katherine have set for themselves. Second, they cringe at the calculating orientation of these boomers. "Babies just happened in our
day!" the parents claim. "They don't get planned." In fact, as the
MacDowells (senior) see it, the only reason for all this organization
is Katherine and Oran's unrealistic expectations and unnecessary
material ambitions. Sure, people have to plan carefully if they must
have all this stuff to make a decent life for their kids. But if all that
stuff is deemed superfluous, babies can come into the world as
soon as the wife can get pregnant.

Not only do the MacDowells fail to understand why their kids are
stuck on hypercalculation, but they also cannot figure out where
their inflated standards come from. Keith James's mother thinks she
knows. Where the MacDowell parents look at Oran and see an
unrealistic, overly materialistic young man, Mrs. James looks at
Keith and sees a boomer who emerged from Pleasanton having
learned from his parents' comfortable example. She cannot fault
Keith or Oran for believing that boomers owe their own children a
middle-class life or for assuming the burden of making good that
promise before they bring kids into the world. Indeed, she reserves
her wrath for those members of her *own* generation who rail at the
boomers. How dare they suggest now that their children's expectations are inflated? she wants to know. The source is clear: the postwar generation's own experience of upward mobility and their confidence that more of the same was in store for their own children. It
is hypocritical, in Mrs. James's view, for parents to turn around now
and level accusations at their children:

Well, come on! This is the first generation in the history of the United States that can expect to live less well than their parents lived! Every last one of us, up until this point in time, has lived better than our parents. Our parents came, made a better life for their children, who made a better life for their children . . . and now all of a sudden we've peaked. And this generation is not living as well as their parents. But they have a right to expect more!

I don't think it's unreasonable for kids to expect to do well. They've seen material excess and I do think that has caused them to suffer from wanting too much. But I don't think that's necessarily their fault. If they're materialistic, it's because they saw it at home. . . . I mean, what should a child whose mother drives a BMW convertible think? Where did her mother get the notion that her child should learn values of not owning a car or having a house? We've taught our children those things are important by our example. And I don't think it's realistic for us to [blame them] or say they are spoiled. If they're spoiled, we did it!

Mrs. James is in the minority. The old-fashioned recipe of hard work and deferred gratification is gospel for most postwar residents of Pleasanton. The Oldmans, however, are skeptical. They are beginning to think that even those boomers who adopt a more realistic posture toward their standard of living may not see a payoff. Times may have changed for the worse, and uncertainty may be the new rule. As Mr. Oldman sees it:

In the 1950s things were more stable economically. You knew that if you worked for a few years and saved some money you could put a down payment on a house, 10–20 percent down. But today someone out of college can't save that kind of money in order to do it. And the cost of housing keeps going up, moving away from you. For every dollar you save, the house goes up two. . . . Before you knew that if you wait a bit, plan for [what you want], then it would come. Today things change so quickly, you're not sure.

Deferred gratification made sense in the postwar world, but today's economic trends, discussed in chapter 2, would seem to indicate that the causal connection between waiting and succeeding was, in fact, a historical accident. Those who have to "wait their turn" in today's economy could end up waiting forever.

Contrary to their parent's view, most Pleasanton boomers have long since given up the notion that they will ever surpass their parents' standard of living. They *do* abide by the principle that they must pay their dues if they expect to equal the life-style their parents have enjoyed. The two generations are in fundamental agreement on this. They diverge sharply over the efficacy of "waiting one's turn." Whereas postwar mothers and fathers are confident that time is on their children's side, as it was on theirs, boomers believe that this prophecy has *already* failed to materialize. Time is not bringing any improvement: housing is still out of reach, even with the slumping prices of the early 1990s; cars are not getting any cheaper; the expense of raising children seems to grow exponentially. If anything they see the economy softening, with more layoffs in the offing, more foreclosures, and one industry after another developing anemia. At what age, boomers want to know, is the future already here? Boomers cresting into their early forties believe that their future has arrived, and it is not what they had in mind.

Some boomers respond with a kind of self-criticism that essentially concedes that they are spoiled. This does not mean that they lower their horizons or find it easy to do without. It simply means that they recognize the impact their past experience of affluence has had on their tastes in the present. Donna Yengoyan is one of the most adventurous members of the Pleasanton High class of 1970. After kicking around New York City in various journalism programs, she decided some overseas experience was in order. Donna accepted a position teaching English in Tokyo where the waning power of the Yankee dollar teaches a quick lesson in frugality, but at least Donna had long ago learned to be careful with her money. For her as a single woman, it never stretched very far. She recognizes that her desires for more are directly traceable to the childhood experience of having plenty. Knowing this does not make the downward adjustment any easier, however:

> Occasionally I think, God it must be nice to be able to go into a store and buy whatever you want. I can't remember the last time—I must have been a kid on my father's payroll the last time I did that. I'm always looking at price tags and evaluating brand names and how much to buy. And there are times when I put the dessert back on the shelf because it's the dessert or the main meal and you can't afford both, and that's just—and I accept that now

most of the time. But there are times when I get so tired of scrimping and saving and then you just blow it because you can't contain yourself all the time.

. . . Most of the time I think I do this because I grew up with opulence. My parents are very frugal, but growing up I had a sense that there was always money if we needed it. Money was just so visible that you felt that it was always there.

Donna often feels as frustrated about her expectations as her immigrant parents do. She accepts their view that her generation is spoiled. Unfortunately, she cannot turn the clock back and remake her sense of a normal standard of living. The damage is done; all she can do is struggle to get what she wants or force herself to make do with less.

Among the sons and daughters of Pleasanton's blue-collar families, one finds a different perspective, one that is quite congruent with the condemnatory attitude of many a middle-class postwar parent.[2] Martin O'Rourke, the commercial artist born of a construction worker father we met in chapter 3, shares his age-mates' frustration with the high cost of living and the difficulty of supporting a family. Sure, he'd like to do even better, but when it comes down to it, Martin defines himself as someone who has really worked hard to sustain his life-style. He loses patience with people of his generation who seem unable to apply themselves and stand around all day complaining about their inadequate standard of living:

I think my generation's a very selfish [one]. We want it all. We want every damn thing. And we want it now. We want a BMW, we want a house in Pleasanton, we want everything Mommy and Daddy had, plus we want more and we want it now. We're not going to save for it, we're not going to work for it. No one wants to work. Everything's just expected to come. That's why we're going to suffer. . . .

I see a lot of the people that I went to college with, people of my generation, who are very spoiled, and although I don't know why, I can venture a guess. Because they did grow up in [Pleasanton]. Their parents were either Republicans or Democrats. They went to church on Sunday. They didn't do anything wrong. Kids went to summer camp, they had nice clothes. When they turned seventeen they were given a car. "Here, use my expense account, use my Mobil card, go fill up the car with gas." That's what I saw. . . . Permissive attitudes, not having to work for what they

got, and expecting that it's just got to come. "I went to college,"
they thought, "my daddy made it. I should make it." Why, why
should you make it? What's so good about you? What are you
doing? Why do you deserve better?

Martin rejects the notion that simply having been born in Pleasanton
entitles one to that kind of life. He believes that being middle class is
not an entitlement but is a privilege that must be earned anew by
each generation. It annoys him that his generational brethren have
set their material standards so high that they will never be satisfied.
Shaking his head in dismay, he marvels at acquaintances who feel
that a car is not good enough unless it is a Volvo. Even though he
does not entirely approve, Martin can tolerate the idea that people
his age *aspire* to these material goals. What he cannot accept is the
notion that they *deserve* to attain these heights of conspicuous consumption simply by virtue of birthright. Like his blue-collar father
before him, Martin agrees that only those individuals who are willing to work damn hard to secure a Pleasanton standard of living can
lay a legitimate claim to it.

There is no unanimity over the question of entitlement in Pleasanton. Some held that the derailment occurred because a moral
flaw was unwittingly allowed to develop within the boomer camp.
Boomers, say these elders, lack the work ethic, have unrealistic
expectations, and are unwilling to pay the necessary dues to realize
these ambitions. To put the matter bluntly—they are acting like
spoiled brats.

This attitude infuriates many a boomer. "We *are* working hard,"
they fume. "But our hard work isn't getting us anywhere and it
doesn't look like it ever will." The accusation is a thorn in the side of
a good number of postwar parents as well, for the critique implicates
parents too. These postwar parents wring their hands over every
depressing headline in the *Wall Street Journal.* Even the most driven
of their children are paddling harder just to stay afloat. Every generation is *supposed* to do better than the one that came before, but this
one will not. For these citizens of Pleasanton, the flaw lies not with
their children. If this is not the locus of the problem, then what is?

America's Cultural Revolution

In recent years we have been treated to a host of personal accounts
and biographical excursions into the meaning of the tumultuous era

that has come to be known as "the sixties."[3] Most of these books focus on the lives and experiences of the culture heroes of the time—the radicals, hippies, flower children, philosophers for the common man. Few consider how the 1960s appeared to or affected ordinary people, the bystanders who hugged the sidelines and absorbed the messages secondhand. We will return to the general subject of America's homegrown cultural revolution in later chapters, for the experience of that era permeates the meaning of downward mobility for the boomers. For the moment, however, it is important to understand how the sixties informs the thinking of postwar parents.

The search for the answer to the question, Why are these kids so different from me? is an odyssey of exploration in generational culture that would appear to have little to do with the tumult of the antiwar period. How could an era known for its antimaterialism and nonconformity serve as a foundation for understanding a generation that is obsessed with homeownership? For postwar parents, the importance of the 1960s lies less in the specific values that it inspired and more in the way it symbolized or catalyzed a breakdown in the certainty of the American "program." Men and women who settled down in the aftermath of World War II never felt they had much choice in how to establish an adult life for themselves. The Ozzies knew that their task was to go out and find a job—not necessarily a rewarding one—that would pay the bills. The Harriets defined themselves as mothers-to-be from the moment they slipped on their wedding rings. Conventionality was the order of the day, and it governed everything from what one could wear to how the sex roles should be organized in the privacy of one's home.

The advent of the 1960s shook this certain, defined, and constraining structure right down to its foundation. More than any other facet of the period, this defines the difference between the postwar generation and its children. Chroniclers of the decade devoted most of their attention to the cultural excess—the drugs, music, and sexuality—of the time. To be sure, these flamboyant elements color the national memory of the age of abandon. But its legacy is more than a bundle of experiments in the art of living; the era bequeathed to the boomer generation a sense of possibility, the belief that they could define a new set of rules for themselves—or live without rules at all. They need not accept their parents' perspectives as givens. They could, and did, live together before marrying, choose unorthodox careers, reject the materialism of their suburban upbringing, turn their backs on the religious traditions in which they were raised, and construct a wholly new set of blueprints for life.

As the boomers grew up and rediscovered (to their own amazement) the virtues of settled family life and their attachment to the trappings of a middle-class existence, their parents heaved a sigh of relief. But even they knew that this did not signal a recognition of the perennial validity of Ozzie and Harriet's one true path to a moral life. Even the "great return" to conventionality had to be cast as the boomers' own voyage of discovery, their own reinvention of the nuclear family. From their own point of view, it would be anathema to embrace an inherited set of rules and regulations for adulthood. Over time, similarities have emerged between the boomers and their postwar parents in what they want out of life: these consistencies are particularly striking when one compares the postwar traditionalists with those sons and daughters who came of age in the Reagan years. Nevertheless, intergenerational consistency is not part of the story they tell about themselves, nor is it part of their parents' understanding of how their children unfolded in adulthood. The watershed that separates the certainty of the "American program" from the age of experimentation was the sixties, and it is to that era that postwar parents often turn to explain why their efforts to socialize their kids in their own image failed to take hold.

Yvonne and Ed Winnow are a case in point. Ed's career as a commercial artist had its ups and downs, but he was able to make a go of it in advertising. Their daughter, Joanne, was born in the early 1950s and soon displayed evidence of her own artistic talent. She is now a fine artist and college-level art teacher. She is also happily married and has a little girl of her own. She has come full circle as her parents see it, arriving "back" at the only sensible life-style they can imagine—but only after a series of personal experiments that had terrified the Winnows. In the world they knew, there was only one way to live and few choices to be made. For Joanne, by contrast, there was no program; it was all up to her:

ED: When we met and got engaged and married we were living under the old rules. You had a long engagement to save money. Marriage from our point of view was "for keeps." What a shockeroony it was to raise these kids through the sixties. The different values. They've change so drastically in our little short lives. My head is still spinning from it.

YVONNE: The change in values is earthshaking. I know that the kind of family life I came from was strictly Victorian. Prim and proper. It's unbelievable. It's like black and white today.

ED: Joanne was rebellious. She went off to San Francisco to be part of the Haight-Ashbury scene. I wanted to go to California to work as an artist for Walt Disney in 1938. My father said, "No, you're not going to go out to California. You're going to finish high school and you're going to college." Dad said I couldn't go, so I couldn't. I was very obedient.

YVONNE: Joanne felt she was wealthy. She had $1,000. So she went. When she came back from San Francisco and said she knew that family was all that mattered, you could have picked me up with a straw off the kitchen floor.

Joanne does not think of herself as one who sold out to tradition. What she discovered when she arrived in San Francisco in the early 1970s was that it's no fun to "slum it," that the sexual revolution had its drawbacks (particularly for women), and that she needed to come back East if she was ever going to get serious about her art. But this was Joanne's own search for self, not an instant replay of her parents' lives. She never even dreamed of applying her talents to a commercial field; she preferred the life of a "real" (read starving) artist, living in a closet-size apartment, to the conventional suburban milieu in which she was raised. Joanne considers herself to be her own pilot in the world, charting new waters as have her friends.

Joanne embraces freedom and delights in making choices. Her parents' certainty, their undeviating attachment to tradition and authority, represents a drastically different way of thinking. In many respects the two generations look at each other as if they were born on different planets.[4] Joanne's experience of freedom was not shared by everyone she knew in the high school class of 1970. While her age-mates all understand what she means by the sense that rules were to be questioned, some found the laissez-faire culture of the 1960s bewildering. Ron Rittenberg was one of those kids who feared the thought of being the architect of his own life:

Kids from my generation were loaded with choices; our parents' generation was not, at least in their perception. When you don't have choices, the question is, Is it easier or harder [to live]? I don't know. Sometimes when you don't have choices, in some ways I think it's a lot easier, because you pursue something relentlessly when you don't really have a choice. Whereas people in my generation . . . were so loaded with options that it becomes harder to know what the heck to do. You know, my generation has been characterized as "trying to find themselves." Well, for me, that was a very difficult thing.

The 1960s imposed a great divide between the postwar parents—the Eisenhower generation—and their boomer children, who, while far from a uniform group, share a common view of themselves as questioning received wisdom about life. Regardless of whether this has proved to be inspiring or unsettling, boomers nonetheless evaluate themselves in this light. From their parents' point of view, however, all this freedom was not good news. It created cleavages between old-school parents and their experimenting children. As Martin O'Rourke reminds us, the generation gap catalyzed screaming matches and deep divides that have never really healed:

The fights that happened in Pleasanton families were frightening. Not that there weren't fights in the forties and fifties. But those were arguments about who could have the car on Saturday night. I'm talking about real political arguments. . . . Fathers wanted their sons to go to Vietnam because it was the right thing to do and "It's your country and you're a chicken for not going." Those kinds of things changed the whole way in which families dealt with each other. They caused rifts that still haven't healed.

The 1960s disrupted the messages postwar parents wanted to send to (or impose upon) their children. Were it not for this cultural revolution, they say shaking their collective head, they would have succeeded in socializing their kids into our value system. Instead, their charter as chief influence in their children's lives was revoked, replaced by political radicals or visions of VW vans headed for California.

Explaining why boomers cannot adopt their parents' patience and wait for their turn in the sun turns then upon the cleavage that divides the two generations, a cleavage born of the social upheavals that gripped the nation in the late 1960s and early 1970s. For the epoch did more than capture the imagination of the young, drawing them to new fads and exposing them to political ideas that had never had a presence in middle America before. It created in the boomers the idea that they could set their own agenda.

6

Illegitimate Elites and the Parasitic Underclass

I understand some of the factors that have been involved in [the changes we see in Pleasanton]. There's been a lot of foreign investment. People are moving into the community that were never there before. My brother works in the school system, and a quarter of his students are Oriental. Half of them are very, very wealthy Orientals. People who buy homes for $500,000 in cash. Walking into a strange land with bags of money. It's bound to affect the local economy! It inflates the prices of homes all around. I have a friend who's a real estate broker in the area and the stories he tells about the Asian families. . . . He just says, "It's ridiculous!"

—Martin O'Rourke, age 40

The welfare system is absurd. There are guys in New York sitting on curbs smoking joints today. Six-foot-two, 190-pound guys with other 200-pound guys. That's how it works. Second- and third-generation welfare people, that's absurd. Nobody should receive welfare unless they're at least willing to work. It's draining our country; making it third world.

—George McDermott, age 62

Neither Martin O'Rourke nor George McDermott considers himself to be a racist; they bridle with indignation when they hear people with opinions like theirs described as bigots. Yet the melting-pot theory to which they subscribe at some level posits only one acceptable path of entry, only one way of making a claim to the good life that lies at the end of the American rainbow. Newcomers must start at the bottom and work their way up.[1] This maxim applies both to new immigrants and to minorities who have long been here but want something better for themselves and their children.

When Martin examines his world critically, however, he does not see an orderly progression of ethnic communities and new immigrants lining up to claim their fair share, with evidence of their hard work in hand. Above himself, Martin sees a group of elites who have exploited the present weakness of the U.S. economy. The price has been paid by hardworking Americans who have forfeited the opportunity to live in their own communities to these interlopers. Casting an eye to the bottom of the social structure, he sees the dangerous classes who inhabit the inner city or segregated suburbs nearby. Chronic welfare dependents, criminals, addicts, women who cannot control themselves, and men who have no attachment to family—these are the denizens of the underclass. They may as well live a million miles from Pleasanton, for all the immediate connection between the two strata.

But the underclass and the politicians who want to do something about poverty in the United States want Martin's tax dollars; they want the people of Pleasanton to support single-parent families; they want to take money from his kids' school and throw it at urban schools in the name of equality. In the best of all possible worlds, Martin might be inclined to help the deserving poor,[2] for he does believe that the disadvantaged deserve some help. But Martin is feeling the pinch; his resources will not stretch to care for his own family the way he thought he would be able to. He wonders whether the middle class, sandwiched in between illegitimate elites and parasitic underclasses, is being played for the fool.

The stresses and strains of raising a family in tight economic times are leading boomers like Martin to push the argument over what has gone wrong with the country beyond the internal conversation over the legitimacy of his generation's expectations. They are looking to place the blame elsewhere, and their gaze reaches above and below. What they find at the end of this exercise is a disturbing departure from traditional virtues and an Alice in Wonderland inversion of the rules that are supposed to lead from the work ethic to the good life.

Apple Pie versus Sushi

When Martin was growing up in Pleasanton, the community was almost entirely composed of white ethnics and WASPs. Though they could trace their origins to different nations, the commonalities that bound these suburban-bound refugees from the inner city were more important than the differences. They were all seeking the same thing and were all doing it the same way: from the sweat of their own brows, or so they see the matter with hindsight. There were people in the community who were rich by Martin's standards, kids whose fathers were doctors or lawyers. Yet even the privileged residents of Pleasanton were people who "made it" by virtue of their own brains. Everyone in Pleasanton—whether the well-heeled doctor or the self-made blue-collar craftsman—looked with satisfaction upon his material accomplishments because these comforts came by virtue of his own efforts,[3] that is, according to the rules of mobility in America.

These moral preconditions for personal accomplishment leave little room in Martin's mind for outsiders to march into his community, or his country, and reorder the traditional route to upward mobility. He believes that natives have to work hard if they are to lay legitimate claim to comfort. Foreigners should be held to the same strictures:

> These are the new Americans. But the difference between the way my parents came to this country and these people is that my grandfather and his kids came with just the clothes on their backs. They had nothing except a few relatives who set them up with work. The Asians that are coming here now come from rich backgrounds. I met one gentlemen from Korea whose kids go to school with my kids and his father owned a big textile business. He's opening up a distribution center in the city, and they moved to New Jersey and plunked down a huge amount of money for a beautiful, expensive home in our town.

In essence, Martin believes that the Asians who have leapfrogged their way to the top are as illegitimate in their claims to this comfortable life as his spoiled classmates who expect to be (and sometimes are) set up by Mom and Dad. Neither group has done it the hard way; hence, neither deserves what it has. Success gained that way is not morally justifiable because it fails to express the core values of American culture. Martin's voice betrays his frustration when he reflects on the lack of moral purpose in the Asian ascent of the American class structure. "They have no real reason behind their efforts to push for better," by which he means they are not trying to prove themselves and point to their houses and cars as evidence of their inner worth. By starting at the top, they have no real proving to do. Rewards are going to the undeserving too easily, he figures. The "overprivileged" rich are benefiting at Martin's expense:[4]

> They come into this country with a lot of money and I can't help but think that it's inflating the real estate prices tremendously. This has got to calm down, but I don't know when or how. There are a lot of [native-born] people who are very upset that they can't live in Pleasanton or anywhere nearby. A lot of my friends think that it's absolutely ridiculous that they can't buy houses around here.

Martin knows who is to blame, who has derailed the natural progression from parents to children in the community: the new Asian neighbors.

If Pleasanton were Detroit, the intensity of these sentiments would hardly come as a surprise.[5] We are accustomed to hearing that our manufacturing industries have been battered by competition from overseas. Autoworkers who have the bad sense to leave their Toyotas in GM parking lots are asking for slashed tires. While we may not condone violence, we surely understand the sentiments of blue-collar folk who have seen their livelihoods destroyed through competition with Japanese and Korean car manufacturers. But Pleasanton is nowhere near Detroit. The boomers who grew up in Pleasanton are generally a well-educated lot; most are white-collar employees. They are supposed to be above crude expressions of nativism. But it is testimony to how deeply they feel the sting of eviction from their community that they focus as much energy as they do on the Asian invader as the source of their problems.

Displacement of this kind is particularly evident among the boomers who were born in the 1960s, graduating from high school in the midst of the recession of the early 1980s. These people, who represent the tail end of the baby-boom phenomenon, have seen the most pronounced ethnic shift in the composition of their town, and they (along with their parents) are most prone to defining this shift, not as a gradual change in the nature of Pleasanton, but as a sharp departure from what Pleasanton should really be. It was supposed to be the kind of place where each generation naturally took the place of the one that came before it. It was supposed to be a place where "real" Americans—descendants of immigrant stock, children of depression survivors—could keep the extended family together by moving in around the corner.[6] If there was room left over after continuity was assured, then they would be happy enough to welcome faces of another color. But as Oran MacDowell sees it, Pleasanton has become a community closed off to its own progeny:

> Every house on my mother's block has been sold to an Oriental. That's a little depressing at times. It's not that they're second-class citizens. But now you're being alienated from your own town. You're not given a chance to move into your town.

Even more galling to Katherine, his wife, is the fact that these families can afford to do exactly what she would like to pull off, but cannot:

> These people are able to move into those houses with one person working. Mom staying home with the kids. For them it's just like back when our parents were growing up. One supporting person. That's all out of the question for us and it's frustrating.

Katherine and Oran cannot imagine having the luxury to buy a house, even one far from Pleasanton. If they are lucky enough to manage that feat someday, it will take both of their earnings to do so. Katherine will not be able to follow her mother's example—or the Japanese example—and stay home with her babies.

Postwar parents did not themselves experience the displacement their children are complaining about. Most stayed put in Pleasanton unless their jobs required a transfer, or they decided to leave for a retirement haven where the taxes are lower. Yet the Pleasanton they have remained in is not the Pleasanton they raised their children in, as they see it. The grandsons of Italy, Ireland, Germany, and France—who came to Pleasanton via the Bronx, Brooklyn, and the less desirable parts of Manhattan—believe the last of their kind have come to this suburban community. All around them houses vacated by these "real" Americans have been bought up by families from

India, Korea, and Japan. And though the "natives" of Pleasanton are themselves only one generation removed from the immigrant experience of the early twentieth century, many find they cannot accept these newcomers as today's example of those who follow a familiar pathway from the old country to the new.

The Fieland family is a particularly vocal example of this new nativism.[7] George, the machinist who worked in aerospace, and his wife, Julie (a longtime sales assistant in local department stores), believe that Pleasanton should be a quintessential American town. Its people ought to express the values that made the country great. They should articulate these values in the English language. Only newcomers who visibly aspire to these marks of assimilation should be welcomed with open arms. Until then, the Fielands argue, immigrants should be regarded with suspicion:

JULIE: I can understand why people come here. This is what this country was all about. After all, our own parents were immigrants.

GEORGE: But if you come here you come for a reason, right? You come here for a better life. So why drag all the bad stuff with you? Maybe bad is the wrong word. But if you're so interested in your background and culture, don't leave [the place you come from]. Stay where you are!

The Orientals move in and right away they put up their own signs. I can't read those signs. Business signs, the church down here. Not that I go to that church, but what's the difference. . . . I should be able to read a sign in this country, but they're all kinds of Chinese signs, or Korean, or whatever. . . . You go into any of these stores and it's either Indian or Oriental. If they want to come into this country and make all their money . . . there's no reason why they can't at least have the sign so I understand it. People with money that are leaving their own country and coming here to make [more of it].

The Fielands believe that there can be only one motivation for coming to Pleasanton and that is to become as American as apple pie, to leave the old ways behind and adopt the superior culture of the United States. This is as true, they tell us, for rich immigrants like the East Asians as it is for the poorer ones.

The Fielands are especially fearful of the Asian "invaders" who have come to Pleasanton. These newcomers are not the meek, dependent, immigrants looking for acceptance. They hold power. The financial resources they control have already shifted the balance in Pleasanton against the Fielands' son, Bob, who will never be able to live there or anywhere like it. This, however, is but the tip of the iceberg. Asian money has undermined American independence, say the Fielands: it has invaded the institutional real estate market, U.S. corporations, the stock market, and the political arena. These, they say, should be immune to foreign influence:

> I don't really understand how foreigners are allowed to own that much of this country. I can see allowing people to invest in the U.S. In most countries, I believe, you cannot own more than a certain percent—say 50 percent. These people, actually, as far as I'm concerned, control [our] money. If they pulled all the foreign money out of this country, within a month it would be worse than a war. You couldn't fight them.

At some level, the Fielands (and their many neighbors who agree with them) realize that these nativist sentiments are not acceptable in polite company, that they run against the grain of the American tradition of tolerance. The unholy attitudes that breed today's anti-Asian fury are the result of racial antagonism, immigrant hysteria, and residual hatred of our enemies from the Second World War. But the rejection of Asian neighbors must also be understood as reflecting the dismay and confusion that postwar parents and their children are experiencing as they bear witness to the breakdown of upward mobility in this country. There would be plenty of room for newcomers—even newcomers of a different culture—if the boomers who expected to follow their parents to Pleasanton (or places like Pleasanton) could still make that journey. Seeing the children sent out into the unknown—or worse, the known and unacceptable—fate of downward mobility, the "natives" react by looking around for the nearest visible agent of this misfortune.

When they begin to read this personal fate as symptomatic of something much, much bigger—the erosion of American independence and affluence—they magnify their firsthand observations into a national nightmare. We are being taken over, they say. We are trapped by our dependence upon alien nations, a dependence from which we cannot extricate ourselves. For Americans accustomed to thinking of themselves as the dominant nation in the Western

World, this is a hard pill to swallow. For veterans of World War II it is nearly unthinkable that the United States would allow itself to become a poor stepchild of Japan.

There is a certain irony in all of this. Pleasanton's senior generation, those who were lucky enough to buy when homes were cheap, have been able to sit back and watch the value of their assets skyrocket. Indeed, many of them can look forward to a comfortable retirement because of a near-miraculous increase in their equity, an unexpected windfall. (It is certainly folly to think this came about simply because of foreign investment in towns like Pleasanton.) Hence, as much as they would like to see a drop in property prices so that their children can get into the market, many postwar parents are depending upon this very windfall, sustained in part by foreign investment, to bankroll their twilight years.

How then are we to understand their anger at their neighbors, their sympathy for their own children? Sociological insights into class identity are of little value here.[8] The traditional perspective tells us that class position is a matter of individual occupation, individual income, individual interests. On these grounds, the "Asian invasion" has been nothing but a blessing for Pleasanton's postwar parents. To the extent that it contributed to the inflation of housing prices, it has dropped a great financial benefit in the laps of those "natives" who were already in place when the great escalation began.

The reaction of these parents to the displacement of their children signals the folly of defining identity even in a capitalist society according to an individual's position. In fact, our sense of position in the class hierarchy of our society is a matter of family trajectory, a corporate identity that cannot be defined by any given individual in a family. An acceptable sense of position can be achieved only by lineages acting through individuals who form a long chain from father to son, and increasingly to daughters as well. Kinship is the key: only when each member has achieved what the lineage defines as an appropriate economic or occupational standing can its members feel a sense of closure on the question of class.

This is particularly the case for the great chain that links today's boomers back to their grandparents, who as adults had suffered through the Great Depression. The postwar boom was of great importance to these working-class immigrants. Men and women who arrived at Ellis Island with nothing, only to suffer through the ravages of the depression, could look with pride upon the accomplishments of their sons and daughters who established Pleasanton, accomplishments that reflected back upon the parents and defined the positive identity for the entire family line.

Yet just as the success stories of the postwar cohorts transformed the parents' self-images for the better, so the interrupted trajectory of their own children—the boomers—reflects back upon the prosperous postwar generation for the worse. This inability to replicate an appropriate standard of living casts doubt on their own identity, on the durability of their own achievements. It suggests that something has gone dreadfully amiss with the normal process of transmitting social standing in America, with the result that frustration rises, scapegoats emerge, and the politics of "mine first, theirs last" takes hold.

The arrival of well-to-do immigrants and sojourners from Asia, in combination with other forces that have boosted real estate prices around the country, has brought that much more affluence to Pleasanton. But because the Oran and Katherine MacDowells were displaced in the process, their parents were left feeling that their own identities as members of the middle class were under assault. Oran is upset because he feels robbed of his birthright, and his parents are angry as well, for they see their new Asian neighbors as the proximate cause of Oran's displacement.

Anger and resentment are hot emotions that surface in the "native" parents and boomer children from Pleasanton.[9] Yet their overall attitudes toward the new Americans is more mixed than these vignettes from the housing wars might suggest. Steeped in the work ethic themselves, Pleasanton's postwar parents cannot help but admire the remarkable industry, seriousness of purpose, and high standards that their new neighbors have brought to the community. This is nowhere more evident than in the local schools, where children of Japanese and Korean descent now account for nearly 50 percent of the younger classes. Teachers and parents alike remark upon how well behaved, intelligent, and hardworking these children are. Old-timers in Pleasanton are proud to note that one of the reasons their community is deemed so desirable by foreign families is that its school system has a good reputation. As Mrs. James put the matter:

> Now that the Japanese have moved to town, the [school] system is really terrific. Because they value a good educational system

and they're willing to put the time and effort into it. . . . The high school has always been good, but the elementary school system has come a long way and I think the Asian population is responsible for it. Some things about the Asian community drive me up the wall, but as far as their caring about the educational system, you can't beat them. They really care about what happens with their children. And if some of these folks [who complain about Asians] would stop and think about it, a good school system is the equivalent of a good neighborhood.

Nevertheless, underlying this sentiment lurks a fear of intellectual domination by the Asian community. Schools are the proving ground for future success. Those who fail in school or who do not do well enough to make it into a good college pay the price for the rest of their lives. Not that the presence of hardworking Asian students will foreclose further opportunities for longtime Pleasanton residents, but the competition underlines a more general feeling that Americans are falling behind in the international contest for market dominance. If we are surpassed in the schools, say Pleasanton's old-timers, can our downfall in other arenas—jobs, standard of living, industrial clout—be far behind? How do we maintain our advantage in technical fields if our children are unable to compete against foreign brain power? It is bad enough, they say, that this specter haunts us in the international arena: it is worse when that sad fact is the reality in your neighborhood schools.

But what is most galling about the local competition between ethnic groups is that old-timers feel they are being bested at their own game. They want to know the secret of this success. Are Japanese children so much smarter than American children? Are Korean kids constitutionally better at mathematics than their U.S. counterparts? The most frightening and perhaps damning answer Pleasanton parents can come up with is the possibility that Asian families exert the kind of discipline over their children that middle-class Americans long ago yielded. Defensive at the very idea, they turn around and indict their neighbors for preventing children from just being children.

The Krasdales have thought long and hard about this issue. Joan Krasdale's job as a local real estate agent provides a vantage point from which to view the changes in the community. She knows that Asian families have come to this pleasant suburb because they want their children to be well educated. The results are obvious:

We were talking to a mother who lives in an adjoining town. She mentioned that her son's elementary class is 50 percent Oriental. I was rather shocked or surprised, but I shouldn't have been. If you read the local paper, you read about these kids that are on the high honor roll. They all excel; you'll see all Oriental names. . . . They're very serious. No nonsense.

All to the good, one might imagine. But as Joan and her husband, Norman, continue the conversation, we find that this is not what she thinks of as normal or good for a child:

JOAN: I think there's no balance in their lives. That tends to make them totally stressed out. They have the drive to be achievers because their parents have put this into their culture. I was reading some statistics about high suicide rates in Japan because they can't face their parents if they don't do well in school. . . . They go crazy if they don't win the prize or don't get into high honors programs.

NORMAN: I'd hate to see my kids run up against them.

JOAN: Our son was a merit scholar in high school, but he was a jock. That was his prime concern, although fortunately for him he scored well [on standardized tests] . . . but if he had had to bear down and compete [in the classroom] like he did in the sports arena, I don't know what would have happened.

NORMAN: I don't think I like what has happened around here. I think that there are too many of them. It doesn't come from prejudice. It just comes because of numbers. We're overloaded now.

As the Krasdales see it, Asian children are not allowed to be kids; their parents push them to be intellectual robots grabbing up honors at every turn. The Krasdales find this approach unnatural, and feel alienated from their Asian neighbors. Japanese and Korean families are defined as "the other," "the foreign," who by some mystical force manage to achieve a discipline that only an alien could want.

What really unnerves Americans is the possibility that the Japanese know precisely what it takes to succeed in the modern, high-tech world and that garden-variety white Americans have somehow lost their touch and the spirit of their immigrant forebears or the depression survivors. Joining the middle class has made Americans soft. Of course, removing our noses from the grindstone is part of what upwardly mobile Americans were striving for in working their way toward Pleasanton. Little did they realize that unrelenting discipline would be required in the late twentieth century. Ironically, then, Pleasanton parents who bemoan the fact that their boomer children are spoiled turn around and indict their Japanese neighbors for pushing their children to compete.

Nativism is not a pretty sentiment. It is a selfish and fearful streak in American culture that belies the ideal of welcoming tolerance and diminishes the benefits the United States reaps from including new groups into the fold. Pleasanton's postwar parents do not want to think of themselves in this light and would reject this characterization. Indeed, most consider themselves to be open, unbiased, and sincere in their desire to be inclusive. From their perspective, the Japanese and Koreans would be most welcome if they wanted to join the mainstream. Unfortunately, the signals they see are just the opposite: their Asian neighbors seem to want to keep to themselves. The community institutions that used to guarantee a sense of participation and inclusion have faded away and the old-timers attribute this sad fact to the presence of an alien element that has no interest in block parties, Girl Scout clubs, or the PTA.

Evelyn Maguire is a widow. She moved to Pleasanton forty years ago with her husband and raised her five children there. Evelyn grew up in the Bronx, one of seven Irish Catholic children raised by a widowed mother. She wanted something better for her own kids, so with some regrets she moved out of the city and into a friendly suburban town. Evelyn's husband was a cab driver when they met, but eventually he moved into the security field and ended up as the head of security in a local manufacturing firm. He died in 1974, but while he was alive, Evelyn's husband devoted his weekends to the volunteer fire department and their sons' softball league. These were the kinds of activities that made the Maguires feel a part of the community. As Evelyn sees it, those symbols of community no longer exist because the newcomers refuse to participate:

> We're getting a lot of Orientals in town and it's changed everything. Before the people worked together. We have a volunteer ambulance and a volunteer fire department, and it was terrific. But we can't get anybody to join. The Orientals won't join. They keep to themselves. The woman who lives across the street, I guess in two years I spoke to her once and she looked at me incomprehensible. If their house burned down, the fire depart-

ment would have to fight it anyway. So they should [do their share] . . . well, anyway, they don't. They're not pulling their weight and they don't get involved. And I think in a small community, people should get involved.

As Lou Campagna, Evelyn's neighbor down the road, sees it, these new people not only fail to involve themselves in these participatory institutions, but are also unfriendly in more casual circumstances:

> They're kinda unsociable. Don't get me wrong, I got nothing against Orientals. But I got nothing but Orientals livin' around me. They seem to stay on their own. You'll be outside doin' something and they'll walk by. You say hello, but it's changed.

Intimacy, neighborliness, friendship, participation—these are the elements of community that the old-timers in Pleasanton value. Their young married years were defined by them, and they are sorely missed. Much has changed in the town since the postwar years, but the ethnic mix is often singled out as the prime mover in the destruction of that sense of belonging.

In truth, most of the clubs and activities that made postwar families feel so much a part of Pleasanton were organized around the children: block parties, Scouts, the PTA. An aging community, where children are no longer around to serve as the social glue, is one in which old-timers are bound to feel a sense of decline or alienation. Without the child-driven voluntary organizations, they have few institutional connections to bring them into sustained contact either with other empty-nested adults or younger families preoccupied with raising children. For all they know, the new Asian families may be active in the very organizations they rarely participate in now that their own children are grown.

Add the social distance that language differences create to the changing demography and you get a recipe for ethnic conflict. Overlaid with a visceral fury over the displacement of the baby-boom generation, the recipe shifts from sub-rosa conflict to out-and-out nativism. "The community belongs to us," they thunder. "Our children are the ones who really belong here. They would be the backbone of the volunteer fire department, the PTA, the Cub Scouts. They would preserve the town as it was." From many an old-timer's perspective, the invasion of a wealthy, secretly superior, and aloof Asian population ruined their community.

Robert Bellah and his colleagues wrote at some length about the importance of civic involvement for sustaining a national sense of community in their tour de force, *Habits of the Heart*.[10] The yearning for commitment, the confidence of purpose that we seem to lack in the contemporary United States, they argue, can only be satisfied by local participation. Individuals must invest themselves in community institutions in order to generate a sense of bondedness to each other and in turn to the nation as a whole. Bellah and his colleagues have in mind here primarily political institutions that exercise some kind of decision-making authority in localities, but the argument can be extended as well to the more informal, nonpolitical organizations.

The problem with this vision is that it presumes a kind of commonalty that can override demographic, class, gender, and ethnic differences in places like Pleasanton. Of course these divisions always created barriers to the kind of egalitarian *gemeinschaft* that *Habits of the Heart*—and a good many Americans—long for. In recent years, however, these lines that divide have grown into trenches that continue to widen. The old-timers view the prosperity of the newcomers as illegitimate, a form of international robbery. And the victims are the baby boomers who no longer are able to settle in Pleasanton. Surely the people who have taken their place must be responsible—so the thinking goes. Can a community be forged out of this kind of resentment? Pessimism would seem to be the order of the day.

Behind the personal experience of generational displacement lies the specter of something much larger: the declining fortunes of the boomers is interpreted as symptomatic of the end of American dominance in international commerce. Pleasanton's boomers and the parents who raised them are convinced that they have been denied an entitlement. They are also certain that their own experience is but a smaller version of a more profound problem: the United States is losing its power, ceding its autonomy, endangering its status as a preeminent nation. "Asian countries," it is asserted with dismay, "are taking over and we are doing nothing to stop it!" We have allowed ourselves to be driven into a corner. Our labor is overpriced, our competition prone to taking unfair advantage of our markets, our government unable or unwilling to stop unhealthy foreign ownership of our productive resources. This can only spell one thing for Americans: the end of affluence.

The Fielands argue that immigrants should drop their foreign ways and foreign tongues in favor of American culture and the English language. But their insistence that immigrants blend in masks a deep concern about the vulnerability of the U.S. economy. George figures that the country is so dependent upon the capital of Japanese nationals that any move to reverse the situation would cause widespread chaos. George blames politicians for being too weak-willed or corrupt to do anything about this unholy state of affairs:

> It seems to me that they got no guts, the politicians. They're always bowing to somebody; they're always trying to please the majority. But the Japanese firms are influencing votes in Congress!

George is worried that the United States has lost the capacity to order its own affairs by allowing foreign penetration of our banking system, our real estate, and our industrial economy. We can no longer even put up much of a fight.

The Fielands may be extreme, but even their less conservative neighbors worry about America's decline. Jim Leary lives in an area of Pleasanton that could almost be declared rural: his road is unpaved, and his home is in the woods. Sitting on his front stoop, one can watch the dusk fall across the woods and picture Pleasanton as a frontier town far, far from the city. Jim is a plumber, as was his father. Like his father, he is proud of the skill he brings to the craft. Colleen Leary, his wife of thirty years, is a vivacious, no-nonsense woman, with a quick laugh and a serious smoking habit. The Learys both grew up in midtown Manhattan, part of the Irish community that once surrounded what has become the Lincoln Center for the Performing Arts. They met in church, the institution that bound their kinsmen together and instilled in them a sense of ethnic identity that has survived the adventurous move to Pleasanton.

Jim's sense of being American is a very important part of his identity. To him this means that individuals must submerge those parts of themselves that would set them apart, that highlight differences. Jim does not believe his Japanese neighbors are willing to do this, and it bothers him. But what worries the Learys most is the feeling that the United States has lost its way, lost its preeminence as the "leader of the free world." He moves easily from a fear of economic subordination to anger at political impotence—neither of which is consonant with his understanding of our national heritage or purpose:

> The country scares me, the shape it's in. We import so much! Look at the farmers, losing their land and equipment. I worked in Pittsburgh years ago. . . . We don't have the steel industry anymore. We're donating all this money to foreign countries. Hostages. I don't say, "Go and bomb [Iran]," but they need to know we won't put up with that.

The economic disarray of the past ten years has threatened the security of people like Jim Leary, though not in the traditional economic sense. He is an established homeowner, with little debt, relatively comfortable in his job. But his son, Jim Junior, has not been able to follow in his footsteps where life-style is concerned. Jim Junior went into the military and then joined the police force in a lower-income town nearby. He works seven days a week in order to afford his home. Junior counts himself lucky on this score; many of his close friends from his high school days in Pleasanton are far from this goal and do not see it coming any closer. On his more exhausting days, he wonders if all this struggle is really worth it. His Dad is sure the uphill climb his son endures is the only way to go. But he feels uncomfortable at the prospect that everything could go up in flames at the national level. He knows that his personal prosperity and the goals his son is working toward depend upon a kind of national security that he believes has been thoroughly undermined.

Johnny Carson, former king of late-night television, captured the fears and furies of Pleasanton's native whites well the night his monologue focused on America's disintegrating economy. "If we'd let the Japanese win the war," said Carson impishly, "maybe we'd still own the Rockefeller Center."[11] The sale of the Rockefeller building was followed in short order by other symbols of the great American sellout. Sony bought the AT&T building. The largest communications companies in Hollywood are acquired by their Japanese counterparts. One after another, the icons of American business deliver themselves into foreign hands. Business may be business, but the transfer of these national symbols is emblematic of our commercial decline, and sends an unwelcome message to the average citizen: we no longer control our destiny.

People who live in communities far from Pleasanton, who may never see a prosperous immigrant population in their midst, follow these events closely. They would agree with suburban soul mates in Pleasanton that the country is on the road to ruin if it sacrifices its most precious resources to other (unscrupulous) nations. Someday, they imagine, we will need to rely upon ourselves again. What will be there for us to depend upon when that day comes? Who else can we really trust? For most Americans, the answer is, No one else is really trustworthy. In Pleasanton, signs of this posture abound: in comments about the superiority of the English language and the denigration of Asian neighbors as unfriendly or as alien types who push their children to succeed where "real Americans" are failing.

Little assistance can be expected from the native-born elites who run the power machine in Washington. This is not because they are somehow uniquely insular, unable to see what has happened to the heartland. Their myopia has more sinister origins, at least in the eyes of some of Pleasanton's more conservative residents. Politicians who are not working on behalf of special interest groups concerned with the poor are on the bandwagon of the homegrown wealthy. Some Pleasanton old-timers are turning to populist candidates who promise to do something about privilege, something to force the rich to do their part. It is to people like Ralph Anderson that the populism of the 1990s is directed, for he is as angry at the rich (and those in Washington who have done their bidding) as he is at the poor:

> Political corruption [is rampant]. Take tax reform . . . it made the rich richer and the poor poorer. The poor get away with almost nothing and the middle guy, like I am, pays the brunt, because the rich people don't pay anything. Leona Helmsley, she says only poor people pay taxes. She was right! She was telling the truth! Now they're talking about reducing the capital gains tax . . . to eliminate any disadvantage to the so-called rich people. It's absurd![12]

Ralph remembers that when he first moved to Pleasanton his property taxes amounted to a modest $400 a year, a manageable burden, particularly for a suburb like Pleasanton, which has no industrial base from which to draw additional revenues.[13] These days the same house costs $4,000 a year in taxes, a sum that falls hard on the shoulders of people like the Andersons who see their retirement prospects compromised by these voracious demands for their dollars.

Parasites in the City

As the economy tightened up in the late 1980s, a cry went up across the United States to reform the welfare system. In some states this took the form of cutting off or cutting back on benefits for women who continue having children after being placed on welfare rolls.[14] Some reforms imposed work requirements on welfare recipients. Local initiatives followed on the heels of federal legislation, spearheaded by the chief social scientist on capital hill, Daniel Patrick Moynihan, the Democratic senator from New York and a longtime student of the welfare system. The timing of these amendments was no accident and was, in most respects, unrelated to the financial burden that welfare imposes on state and federal budgets—a cost dwarfed by the cost of the more middle-class entitlement programs, social security and Medicare.[15] Welfare reform got a shot in the arm because it served as a focus for the wrath of people in communities like Pleasanton who have felt increasingly frustrated about their own declining fortunes.

Statistics on teenage pregnancy, high school dropouts, and soaring crime are the daily media diet in households full of people who fled to suburbia to find their own patch of blue sky and green lawn but also to put the problems of the cities behind them. Now, it seems, one cannot escape these problems: the urban underclasses look to be on the verge of exploding, with the Los Angeles riots of 1992 only the beginning.[16] Liberals argue that large-scale disturbances are the inevitable fallout of a decade of deliberate neglect, the erosion of employment opportunities in the nation's cities now bereft of factories that once employed inner-city minorities, and the progressive deterioration of urban school systems.[17] But the liberal argument has had only a limited appeal with the American middle class that supports civil rights but remains too attached to traditional norms of family life and the work ethic to buy the argument that the problems of the urban underclass rest on anyone's shoulders but its own. They were once willing to look the other way and let the War on Poverty go forward because it cost them little; the economy was fat, taxes were relatively low, and the fortunes of the middle class were secure.

In the less favorable climate of the 1980s and 1990s, the conservative posture has won the day: what we need, say the right-wing critics, is to stop coddling people by making it easy to be poor in the United States.[18] We must make welfare more difficult to access and thereby encourage the underclass to get back on its own feet and off the backs of the rest of us. They do not favor draconian measures that leave women and children without food or shelter. But they do believe that the traditional virtues of family integrity and the work ethic have disappeared in the nation's cities, and they insist upon personal responsibility as the cornerstone of individual worth, whatever the origins of contemporary poverty may be. And until these values actively reassert themselves among tax-hungry minorities, Pleasanton will be skeptical, even angry, about the demands of the inner-city underclass.

George McDermott has worked for the past twenty years as a commissioned sales representative for a company that makes home appliances. He has never lived in a big city, having come originally from a suburban community in Pennsylvania. George married his high school sweetheart and together they steadily worked their way up from a small garden apartment in southern New Jersey to a house on Long Island. With a promotion in hand, George and his wife, Jenny, finally had the wherewithal to buy their dream house in Pleasanton, where they subsequently raised three children. By his own admission, George is one of the old-timers in Pleasanton, an Irish Catholic by descent who settled in thirty years ago as one of the postwar upwardly mobiles. George knows he has been fortunate, but he attributes his success to traditional virtues, which he has tried to communicate to his own children:

> I taught my children to be hard workers. . . . My boys started working when they were twelve. They were paperboys. And my next-door neighbor has a cleaning business that my kids worked in when they were fourteen or fifteen. . . . So even through high school they worked. They learned the value of money, they learned to apply themselves. At one point—my sons were runners—they would go out in the morning and run seven miles, then

come home, eat, go to school, come home, go to work, then come home, eat their dinner, then study and go to bed.

George believes that discipline of this kind is the key to his children's success in life, and he points with pride to their flourishing careers as pilots and teachers. However, in his view, these virtues are dying everywhere else in American society. We are fast becoming a country that, in George's words, is "deteriorating, sociologically and graphically." He rails against crime, crowded jails, early parole, and the short-sighted rejection of the death penalty in a society more inclined to mollycoddle criminals than deal with them in the no-nonsense fashion they deserve. From his perspective, however, crime is merely the tip of the iceberg. Next on the list is our misguided generosity toward the able-bodied poor:

> I believe in morality; I believe in ethics; I believe in hard work; I believe in all the old values. I don't believe in free handouts. . . . So that whole welfare system falls into that [category]. . . . The idea of fourteen-year-old kids getting pregnant and then having five children by the time they're twenty is absurd! It's ridiculous! And that's what's causing this country to go downhill.

George does not see himself as a racist. Publicly he would subscribe to the principle everyone in this society deserves a fair shake.[19] But he does not see welfare or its twin policy—affirmative action—as legitimate redress for these historic wrongs, particularly since they are likely to hit him in the pocketbook or his children in the sweepstakes for job opportunities.[20] What George sees is a loaded deck: minorities that cannot really compete claim jobs, all sorts of federal programs, and general social sympathy while the rest of the country is left to struggle on its own. Under these circumstances, the disorganized but virtuous many are likely to lose out to well-organized, powerful, nameless special-interest groups.

George's neighbors up the street, the Lanackers, do not fully accept his brand of conservatism. Jane Lanacker's family fled Europe during the war, and her own experience of refugee life, of the difficulty of making one's way in an unfamiliar society, has left its mark in the form of a more benevolent spirit. Jane believes that the government does have a responsibility to assist the less fortunate to get back on their feet and is discouraged by the resistance of the White House to take initiatives that would help people help themselves. Her more Republican, American-grown husband, Walter, accepts her point but believes that while immigrants do dedicate themselves to a life of hard work and deserved rewards, native-born Americans have forgotten how to do so:

> I had a client who was an immigrant who made good. Hardly spoke English but he worked sixteen hours a day, built up a nice pizza shop in Plainview. I had gotten some insurance for him. One day he put a big sign in the window, "Help Wanted." He ran adds in the papers. He couldn't get anybody who wanted to learn to make pizzas. Five-fifty an hour was pretty decent pay. Nobody wanted to take the job. . . . A carpenter who didn't have a job would rather accept welfare benefits than do some honest work because he felt it was demeaning. I think there's something wrong with that. Before I accepted a penny of welfare, I would sweep floors just to stand on my own two feet.[21]

The appeal of outsider political candidates like H. Ross Perot lies in the rough seas that seem to envelop "middle guys" like George McDermott: squeezed between the demanding poor and the favored rich, with no one to defend their interests, no one to look out for their well-being.[22] And while life has been pretty good to George and to most of the postwar generation who joined him in Pleasanton, it is dealing a bad hand to their kids. What George sees in protest candidates are people willing to stand up to this system that privileges those at the top and those at the bottom—people willing to challenge the status quo in the name of the hardworking middle class. George longs for the "good old days" when hard work ruled and was properly rewarded, when poor people did what they could to better their lot without asking anything from anyone else, and the rich were at least minimally responsible. Populist politicians who promise to turn the clock back and take no nonsense from anyone are enormously appealing to the George McDermotts of the country. The major parties simply have not been able to convince him that they are challenging the influence that the parasitic underclass and the undeserving rich have brought to bear on public policy.

Living with Contradiction

It is always tempting to seek coherence in culture. Anthropologists are confused by contradictions and devote many hours and countless pages to the task of reconciling mutually incompatible beliefs, usually by demonstrating that they are not as contradictory as they appear.[23] We like to think that people try to make sense, if not to the scholars they speak to, then at least to themselves. But it is in the nature of our culture, and no doubt of most cultures, to live with incoherence and contradiction. This is not a particularly troublesome feature of social life; it bothers social scientists much more than it bothers people.

When postwar parents and their boomer children knit their brows over what has gone wrong for the younger generation, they focus in on a complex set of problems for which they have few solutions. Kids are spoiled; they expect too much too soon; they aren't willing to work as hard as was the generation hardened by the depression; and they cannot seem to get it through their heads that rewards will come in the fullness of time. At the same time, parents shake their heads, wring their hands, and proclaim that their children are working like maniacs and getting nowhere, that the country is "going to hell in a hand basket," that our politicians cannot rescue us because they are hopelessly corrupt or incompetent.

In the next breath, the same people rail against their neighbors, arguing that they are the frontline troops in an international effort to rob the United States of its economic independence. We can see it happen right in our own backyard, say the elders of Pleasanton. These wealthy foreigners are evicting our children from their own hometown, and there seems to be nothing we can do about it. The international economy becomes visible at the local level, where declining opportunities in the job market (relative to the spectacular upward mobility of postwar parents) and the rising cost of housing have combined to create sharp differences between the generations in their personal experiences of economic well-being. However inconsistent the explanations offered for this unwelcome state of affairs, there is no mistaking the frustration these problems cause. Nor can there be much doubt about the destructive potential of nativist or racially charged explanations themselves. Generations who point fingers at each other, ethnic groups who look with envy upon the accomplishments and possessions of their neighbors, comfortable "middle guys" who flare up at the demands placed upon them to support the less fortunate through their tax dollars— these are the flash points that flare into strained relations, reactionary politics, and violent confrontation.

7

The Fractured Generation

When we were in school, relationships, politics, the Grateful Dead, partying, and sex were on our minds. The idea of getting a job was the furthest thing from your mind. Kids in the eighties went to school and they thought, Job and job and job. They were more mature in that way. And in other ways we were more responsible because they'll stay home with the creature comforts until they can afford their own creature comforts. What will my salary be—what if I can't be what I want to be? Who thought of that in the seventies? Money! You lived with four people in four different apartments and that is just what you lived with. They want to create what they grew up with. We were still rejecting all of that. We didn't want a house in the suburbs with two kids and a station wagon. We wanted the bus across country.

—Mary Castan, age 40

There is no escape from the baby-boom generation. Its sheer size has forced American society to remake its institutions. When the boomers were infants, maternity wards were overflowing and hospitals responded by building new wards at a frantic pace. Entering the public schools, their numbers meant double sessions, classes in trailers. As they worked their way into adolescence, their impact on popular culture grew to a crescendo and paved the way for the enormous and persistent popularity of rock music. Without the boomers, we might never have seen the phenomenon of the Beatles, the Stones, and the Grateful Dead, with their legions of followers now turning gray.

The impact of this cohort has been so profound that we have a tendency to think of the baby-boom generation as a uniform subculture with almost anthropomorphic qualities. We speak of what the generation "wants," "feels," "thinks." Newsmagazines analyze every boomer problem or craze.[1] In this the media merely reflects the common belief: that the boomers are a unique, bounded, and internally coherent group within our society.

While the Americans born between 1947 and 1964 share many common problems and experiences, they are far from a uniform subculture. It would be more accurate to say that the two segments of the boomer group are locked in cultural combat. Americans like Mary Castan, who came of age during the heady days of America's flirtation with radical counterculture, bear little resemblance to those who entered adolescence during the Reagan revolution. Both groups are bona fide members of the baby-boom cohort, yet in many respects they are different generations that embrace different versions of American culture. The social and political climate that defined their young-adult lives diverged so dramatically that they may as well have been fifty years apart.

Why does this matter when it comes to understanding the problem of downward mobility in America today? The answer is simple: the reactions of different generations to changes in their economic fortunes depend upon the values they subscribe to and the expectations these values generate. Both the generation of the 1960s and their younger brethren in the baby-boom group have had to confront declining fortunes. Only the most privileged of either group are likely to realize the promise of their suburban upbringing. Yet the significance of that brutal assessment, the extent to which it dominates their lives, depends on the cultural baggage they have brought with them into adulthood. And here the two generations within the boomer group could not be farther apart. There are few values that they hold in common: their vision of the country, their understanding of the relationship between their own lives and the fates of others less privileged (or more so), their attitudes toward work, toward family life—all of these bedrock elements of middle-class culture are fundamentally at odds.

To claim that the "sixties generation" was party to a different social climate than the Reagan generation is so self-evident it need hardly be argued. What is important, however, is how the historical experiences of these two generations followed them through time. For long after the flower-power era faded, the impact of the 1960s remained embedded in the character of the young adults who lived through the tumult of the antiwar crusade, the awakening of feminism, the birth of the black-power movement—even if only as observers on the sidelines. And when the ruckus of the social movements subsided, to be replaced by an insistent conservatism, a new group of boomers was on hand to absorb a completely different message about what is important in life, about where the United States was headed, and what the role of the individual should be.

It is important to move away from models that portray culture as static to think instead about the importance of history—of change in carving out the multiple generational cultures that live side by side in the United States—or any other society at any given moment in time.[2] For while it is comforting and even politically useful to some to conceive of the nation as a unified entity based upon a single culture or even as a pluralistic society that binds different ethnic, religious, and racial groups into a common enterprise, we are in fact a fractured, divided people. And among the many lines of division that define the subcultures within our boundaries, generation is one of the most powerful though one of the least studied.

Any analysis of the long-term meaning of declining fortunes in the lives of the boomers must turn upon the ways in which divergent generational cultures have defined conflicting perspectives of economic slippage, relative disadvantage, competition, and above all the importance of attaining a middle-class station in life. The two groups of boomers are sharply divided in their assessment of these problems. They do not seek the same satisfactions in life, do not place the same priorities on material achievement, and do not agree about what a person should seek from education, work, or civic involvement.

The Sixties Generation

Mollie Duke has been an office worker since she left college in the early 1970s. Little in her appearance today signals the free spirit that was Mollie back in those wild and woolly days. But appearance is deceiving in this case, for Mollie remembers all too well how she was made to feel unwelcome:

> I remember walking into a store and having people look at me. I was called dirty hippie many times, even though I never looked dirty. My clothes were always clean, but I just remember how

I was criticized, how my friends were criticized. I was called names just for the way I looked, the long straight hair, the little band I had around my forehead like everyone else.

People were so livid with us for the way we looked. One of my boyfriends rode a motorcycle, his friend had a chopper, they had the long hair, the beards, and peace signs all over them. They dressed in scruffy jeans and one guy laced them up the side. We looked like God knows what and it scared a lot of people. The older generation didn't even know why it was happening. All they knew was that their kids had long hair and were being rebellious.

Mollie was neither a wild-eyed radical nor a genuine tie-dyed hippie. She was just a teenager who dressed like her friends and indulged modestly in the drugs that were commonly available at the time. Indeed, from Mollie's viewpoint, the brief occasions when she altered her consciousness were fewer in number and significance than the recreational drinking so common to her parents' generation. But her most vivid memories are not of cultural experimentation; they are of rejection. It stuck in her craw that she was labeled and looked down upon by her elders, the people in the office typing pool, the neighbors in Pleasanton, who did not like her style, her friends, her whole generation.

In the beginning Mollie's rebellion was little more than stylistic. Over time, though, her defensive response to adult criticism began to harden into anger. She started thinking about why people around her were trying to force their own ideas about hair, life-style, and music down her throat. Mollie started to take another look at the more worldly people of her own generation, the ones who were storming the barricades and writing Port Huron statements, the ones who seemed to know the real reasons for cultural rebellion, reasons not easy to grasp from behind the high hedges of Pleasanton. Mollie would be the first to admit that she never did fully understand the subtlety of these political ideas. But the rejection she met in her own hometown pushed her to defend her generational culture. In the course of this exploration, Mollie become more aware of the social movements developing around her, gradually identifying her own mild attempts at fitting in with the hippie crowd as something more important:

People were angry and upset with the younger generation. We really weren't doing anything. All we were doing was looking like the way you looked in those days, just like kids are doing now with their half-shaved heads in different colors. . . . But in those days people were really upset about it. There was a divide and you felt it everywhere. People my age were going through whatever we were doing at the time which was just growing up and being a part of what was around us.

But I started to feel that the force that started this [change] was something stronger than any one person's [rebellion]. I believe that women's lib started by a group of women who were a much stronger force than the kids in school were, the neighborhood kids, people in town. I always felt it was coming from someplace else and I remember saying to my friends, "You know, I realize that this women's lib is happening now and a lot of changes are coming. I never started any of this protest business. But I think I'd like to be a part of it."

The ideas Mollie drew out of her arm's-length encounter with the women's movement and the antiwar movement were only weakly connected to a specific political agenda. She never became a feminist per se, and apart from some general antiwar sentiments, Mollie did not take an ardent, committed position on the Vietnam conflict. What she did come to understand was that it was up to her generation both as a group and as individuals to break with the conformity of their elders and define their own collective and personal ideals. She realized then that they had not been trained for this mission. On the contrary, Pleasanton society taught the lessons of conformity. Her generation's burden was to blaze new trails, often in face of overt hostility.

Mollie came to believe that she did not need adult approval. Her generation could learn to stand for something they had never been socialized to represent. To this day, Mollie sees this as a laudable quality in herself and her age-mates:

I didn't go to Woodstock, but I understood what they were doing. I was very proud. Even though I thought the mud was yuck, don't get me wrong, I was proud. I felt that the individuals were standing up for something. I may have not even understood what each one was standing up for, but I felt, Good for them.

You know, my parents brought me up in such a way that I was not my own person. I had to obey my elders, always look to my elders as figures of respect. I was always brought up by rules versus brought up as an individual. I was always afraid to express what I felt when I was little because I thought I was doing something wrong. But that changed when the movements came along.

What Mollie learned was that she had to break the mold her parents and her community had constructed for her, most particularly, the part that dictated unquestioning acceptance of the rules and values of others. This, more than the specific content of the social movements that swirled around her, was the import of being a member of the sixties generation for Mollie. She realized that she would have to find a way to become her own person:

> The values that I had changed because of what was happening around me. I realized that I had to find values within myself and not be misdirected by someone because they were in charge or had the authority. I'm not trying to say that I'm a saint or that I'm so special or honest. I just decided that I had to stick to what I believed in from within myself and not get distracted.

Mollie's high school classmate, Kathy Hayes, realized that finding that independent voice sent her into a head-on collision with suburban culture. The more the world outside intruded into her high school years, the more she realized the shortcomings of a place like Pleasanton:

> We felt really rebellious against the feeling that we had grown up in a vacuum. We had this contrast [before us] of New York City. Pleasanton was like a sterile, Republican sort of unreal society, where everybody had everything they needed and they tuned into their TVs at night and there was no overt evidence of community and working for social change in our parents' generation.
> My senior class had a peace march. We were singing "Give Peace a Chance.". . . John Lennon had come out with it. We had candles and we were marching through that whole area around the high school. The summer of my junior year was Woodstock. Suddenly we were all dressing differently. It was really all about self-loathing. We thought, Hey, what have we been doing here? We've been cheerleaders [for the high school and for the country], saying America, America, rah, rah, rah! [We suddenly realized] we'd been such stupid conformists here in our little sheltered world. Well, wait a second, down in Greenwich Village, you have this whole other world! It was if we suddenly woke up to see that . . . the country wasn't all so rosy and safe; there were

a lot of people out there with problems we were blind to in Pleasanton. We were ashamed of our ignorance and wanted to make a lot of changes.

A steady stream of books and films has come out in recent years celebrating the days of psychedelic bands, free-flowing drugs, and radical politics. The period is, by these lights, best understood through biographies of cult figures who had their heyday in the 1960s. Timothy Leary encouraged young people to "turn on, tune in, and drop out," to reject the upward-striving materialistic society of their parents and seek instead some kind of spiritual fulfillment. More political-minded icons of the period—ranging from Eldridge Cleaver and the Black Panthers to the Berrigan brothers and the Chicago Seven—urged their audience to reject the establishment and form a new politics. Above all, these public figures urged young people to reverse the catechism of their postwar parents: the belief that the United States is the most powerful, rewarding, and morally correct society on the globe. In its place was to grow a powerful skepticism about American foreign policy and a deep resentment of our domestic arrangements.

These sentiments clearly appealed to millions of college students. Berkeley, Columbia, Kent State, the University of Michigan—one after another they exploded with energy and rage. The leadership of the student movements, from Mark Rudd in the East to Mario Savio in the West, articulated this boiling resentment, this urgent desire for change, and in so doing defined the voice of a generation.

Much of the nostalgic, retrospective treatment of the 1960s comes to us through portraits of these activists.[3] The people who leaped to the barricades to define a new politics have come to stand for the whole, including the bystanders. And though their ideas and intentions are worthy subjects, they cannot tell us all there is to know about what the 1960s meant (and still means) to people like Mollie Duke and Kathy Hayes, who saw Woodstock on the evening news or stood at the edge of the crowd as the tear gas swirled around Berkeley's Sproul Plaza. How did being there—rather than participating actively—come to matter to the sixties generation who lived in Pleasanton? And how does it matter still?

Over the past decade the American economy has been so turbulent that it is hard to remember how stable the position of the middle class appeared to be, how optimistic people were about their futures, in the expansive years when the sixties generation entered the universities and the labor market. Unemployment was so low it was a nonissue. Inflation, too, was negligible. The economy was growing so fast in the long and glorious period that followed the end of World War II that opportunity appeared to be everywhere.

Yet serious trouble in the international arena marred the domestic picture. The war in Vietnam was becoming a tangled nightmare, its bloodshed brought nightly into the living rooms of America. And while it was a war fought overwhelmingly by the poor, by minorities, and the white working class, the military draft virtually ensured that Vietnam would be an issue for the middle class as well. Indeed, one of the most vivid memories of Pleasanton High School's class of 1970 was the night the draft lottery numbers were announced—numbers that would determine who would go and who would stay, the year that college deferments for military service were abolished.[4] Judy Resnick, a self-described member of the hippie/intellectual/foreign-film set in the high school, remembered the tension of the draft twenty years after the fact:

> A lot of the guys, including my boyfriend, were scared they were going to get drafted. They were very strongly opposed to the Vietnam War. Some of them left for Canada. Even a close girlfriend of mine went to Canada [with her boyfriend].

For many of America's young people, including President Clinton, Vietnam represented a conflict so far from our shores that no argument for self-interest or national security made sense. Domino theories, cold warrior anticommunism, containment theory—none of it compelled their allegiance or convinced young people in the middle class that a jungle war ten thousand miles away was worth dying for. Few were sold on the argument of the far Left, that the conflict was a nationalist struggle the North Vietnamese deserved to win. They simply looked upon Vietnam as a war with no identifiable purpose, a war the United States had no business participating in.[5] Their parents, veterans of World War II, were often aghast at this attitude, at the refusal to follow the dictates of the authorities. Few fathers were enthusiastic about shipping their sons off to the jungles of Southeast Asia, but they drew the line at the refusal to register with the local draft board. Yet as John Ellwood, Pleasanton class of 1970, saw it, the days of acquiescence were fast coming to an end. Where the older generation accepted the notion that they were duty bound to fight when called upon, John's generation questioned not only Vietnam but the very concept of obedience:

> My father, despite all of his democratic leanings, was a product of the World War II mentality. For him that was the greatest collective endeavor the world has ever seen, as far as the Allies were concerned. He totally embraces the military mind; in desperate situations, one surrenders one's individuality and does what one is told. He put a very strong emphasis on that, and I grew up thinking that was right. At the same time, I was very puzzled about this attitude; my artistic inclinations and my civil rights inclinations and my basic hatred of Pleasanton led me to sympathize with the Left, the flower children, and the student demonstrations.

When Pleasanton High School's class of 1970 arrived on college campuses around the country, the antiwar movement had already been gathering strength for several years. Its predecessors, the civil rights movements and the Free Speech Movement (in California), had galvanized older students into believing they could change the course of American politics. Students from the North had journeyed South to spearhead voter registration drives in the heartland of segregation; students in Berkeley had journeyed but ten miles west to San Francisco, where they forced major hotels to open the ranks of their work force to blacks. As this activism gathered strength on one campus after another, administrations reacted sharply and tried to head off the politicization of their once tranquil islands of contemplation.[6]

Suburban kids like the contingent from Pleasanton walked into this heady climate and barely had time to figure out who the players were before they were faced with police barricades, older students occupying the dean's office, and marches to the draft induction center. Most kept to the sidelines and watched the confusing scene unfold. As the rhetoric of the student protests escalated into profanity and strident opposition to adult authority, Pleasanton's young adults hung back and tried to figure out which side they were on. The sum total of their prior experience with protest had been a fairly mild rebellion against the high school dress code.[7] Blockading buildings, dodging the blows of police nightsticks, and boycotting classes was not part of their repertoire. As John Ellwood remembers the period, activists seemed to have positions on the big issues all worked out; he was just trying to get a handle on the basics:

> When I came to Columbia College in the fall of 1970, all the anti-war stuff was going on. Flakes running around the campus shouting out all these slogans. I kept trying to find the wisdom. They seemed so confident. They seemed to know what they were talking about. And they're calling everybody and his brother a fascist. I didn't quite know what a fascist was. I was trying to make sense of this. I had friends who were somehow connecting behaviorism with Maoism and Kant and Kierkegaard. I had never heard of Kant or Kirkegaard when I came to Columbia. I would listen to all these arguments and they would talk in shorthand. . . . I didn't know what was going on.

For many on the larger college campuses, a major turning point arrived with the bombing of Cambodia in 1972. The war threatened to spread and escalate into previously uninvolved areas of Southeast Asia; President Nixon's actions evoked an immediate, angry response from student protesters. By now, Pleasanton's neophytes had a better grip on what was at stake, and a few of the less intimidated joined in.

Antiwar protests blossomed into more general rejections of authority.[8] The sixties generation rejected the notion that those in power should channel and control the expression of ideas or the style of political conflict spilling over the ivy walls. Terry Morrison, Pleasanton High class of 1970, is now a businessman in the computer industry. Terry remembers this atmosphere as a radical departure from the status quo:

> I was always raised not to question authority. But the saying during the sixties was the opposite: question everything, don't take anything as gospel. Everyone has the right to shape their own reality, you don't have to accept somebody else's. I thought it was important to develop a social conscience. I grew up in a community where there were no blacks, but I thought desegregation was very important. Marches on Washington, the protest against the bombing of Cambodia. These events made a very big impression on me. The period had a very small impact on the populace at large, but for me it was absolutely the essence of life. It made me see that if everybody shared some kind of concern then maybe something important could happen, things could change.

Rejecting authority did not come easily; it was not a natural meta-morphosis for kids from Pleasanton to set aside convention and pro-claim themselves independent spirits. The tumult of the period pried people like Donna Yengoyan away from a disposition to con-form to adult expectations:

> The social movements of the sixties were like blasts of air. I was much in tune with the idea of authority figures before that. You do what they say because they're an authority, not because they're right. And the idea that you think for yourself, you take risks . . . this was a revelation. Civil disobedience was a wonderful idea. It gave me the courage to say no or yes, where I might not have otherwise have learned to take that step.

Change was a goal shared by all, but there were internal differences that distinguished the minority who were willing to be arrested and the majority who stood in silent support. Real radicals urged complete disavowal of mainstream higher education, mainstream jobs, mainstream marriage and family life, and above all mainstream politics. People like Terry and Donna were committed to the pursuit of an independent pathway *inside* of society's institutions.[9] The baby-boom majority flirted with the counterculture but were genuinely afraid of its excesses. The four or five kids from Pleasanton who took off for California in the symbolic transportation of the time—the VW bus—came back after a short time hungry for a decent meal, a real bed, and some limits to acceptable behavior. The drug culture scared them and with good reason: they had seen living examples, usually among the working-class kids in the high school, of kids who seemed to be losing their grip on reality altogether. Rural communes were attractive to a very small group and beside the point for the majority. The separatist agenda of the Black Power movement bewildered liberal students accustomed to thinking of themselves as proponents of racial integration, and it drove a partic-ularly painful wedge between Jewish students and African Ameri-cans.[10] The wilder dimensions of radical politics—the bombing of the mathematics building at the University of Wisconsin, the Sym-bionese Liberation Army kidnappings and armed robberies, the trashing of university campuses—were taken as evidence of insanity within the radical fringe, even by most college students of the period.

Rejection of the louder, more colorful aspects of the protest and counterculture movements did not, however, imply a romance with the status quo. Pleasanton's young people clearly conceived of themselves as standing at a major watershed in their cultural and personal history. As Paul Cornell, president of the senior class of 1970, put it:

> What I loved about the whole period was the fact that it was politically more radical than it had been or has been since. I was very glad about that. The music was wonderful. The change, the excitement. There was a sense that things might change and that even if they didn't there were lots of people who wanted it to change. We finally had people who cared about something other than their football uniforms. This gave us a tremendous sense of freedom, casting off the past like some old oppressive shroud that had just hung over everything. Everything in the past seemed like some bizarre nightmare: the fifties, the cars, the fashion, the way everyone was expected to behave. It seemed like such a horrible tyranny. The sixties offered an alternative. You didn't have to grease back your hair . . . in order to be popular. It allowed a number of misfits—and I see myself as being one of them—to get together and inspire one another to challenge things like racism.

Paul's friend Chuck Peterson went to college in Pennsylvania. Chuck hung back from the more violent protests of his time, but he threw his support to the antiwar effort in his own way:

> I was never on the frontlines. I never went to any of the moratoriums in Washington although I was very much interested in them. I didn't want to devote my whole life to the cause. . ., but I did whatever I could and am still trying to do whatever I can to combat what I see as the forces of evil. I never threw bricks through anybody's window, although I often wish I had. I went on a couple of marches . . . in Teaneck, Trenton. There were hunger marches and marches against the war when I was in high school and my first two years of college. . . . I was an ardent supporter of such causes and still am; I just didn't jump on the bandwagon. Instead, I did whatever I could on a smaller scale.

Paul and Chuck were not going to follow in their parents' conventional footsteps: they rejected the war, they were not about to yoke themselves to unrewarding careers for the sake of upward mobility, they were not going to accept outdated strictures on their sexuality, and above all, they were going to decide for themselves how to live their lives.

For the most part, however, these personal ruminations did not result in wholesale abandonment of "the system." Pleasanton's sixties generation wanted to straddle the fence and pursue rewarding, even transformative, activities *within* the institutional framework of American society. Whatever vision the more radical proponents of the women's movement had, Pleasanton's young women fully expected to marry and raise children—they just wanted to do it their way, in their own good time, and in many cases in combination with other pursuits, rather than blindly following the unquestioning ways of their mothers.[11] Men in the sixties generation had every intention of pursuing careers but were not inclined to put on the gray flannel suits their fathers had worn and march off to the command centers of corporate America.

Even to middle-class young people who sat on the sidelines the 1960s bequeathed the conviction that "committed individualism" was the best way to structure a moral life in America. People had to make their own rules for their education, their sexuality, their careers, and their politics; they could not blindly follow the herd. Terry Morrison captured the sense of the times:

> People made a real effort to put off everything that had been taught to them and just try to appreciate things for what they were and take it from there. Everything they had been told was good and bad, things you should and shouldn't do they set aside. Let's do what *we* think we should do or shouldn't do.

The political atmosphere of the period schooled the sixties generation in the notion that their individual pathways should be chosen in accordance with some, often ill-defined, notion of the social good. But for most people from Pleasanton, the path led to jobs within "the system," and the social good was to be delivered by working from the inside.

Radical politics has such a bad name that it has become impossible for many Americans to understand, much less embrace, the idealism that lies below.[12] But the underlying message of the 1960s— the one that older baby boomers carried with them into adulthood—was the possibility of social change and the responsibility of individuals to order their lives toward that end. It was enough for their postwar mothers and fathers to "take care of business" by earning a good living and raising their children. The antiwar generation charged itself with a higher calling, a commitment to nudge America toward a more just, less inequitable, and less militaristic society.

I am not suggesting here that Pollyannas emerged by the thousands, ready to dedicate their lives to the transformation of civil society. Indeed, teasing out precisely what "committed individualism" has meant in the lives of the sixties generation is not so simple. For some, it has come to stand most centrally for their desire to craft their lives around meaningful, personally satisfying work even at the cost of a comfortable standard of living. The sense of commitment this expresses derives more from a rejection of what these people perceive as the more normative instrumental or pecuniary interest that drives others—most notably their parents—to work. It is not enough, the sixties generation tells us, to work for money or for prestige. As Mary Castan explains, one must look upon work as a calling:

> I'm very motivated towards growing in my work . . . expanding my knowledge in general about people. . . . I always see myself as contributing at least 50 percent in terms of supporting our family financially. But at the same time . . . [I am] motivated by a drive inside of myself just to widen my consciousness. When I look back at my life as an old person, I want to feel that I always tried to reach toward understanding people better in my work.

Don Hillard, who now works as a salesman for a manufacturing firm, does not have the kind of job that would inspire such feelings. But even people like Don, who have made their lives in the business world rather than in the realm of the arts or teaching, feel that work should express something deeper than a means to a material end:

> People in my generation can find a job and survive, but that's not what we're looking for. More than the desire for material wealth, they want something more than that. Our parents might have been satisfied by just having a job which would give them a certain standard of living. I think we take it for granted that there's a certain standard of living we are entitled to. But you want more

out of life. You want a kind of inner happiness beyond the material. Life and work should have some meaning to it. You're not just
here to work and make money and buy a car and have a house.
This is hard, because it's not always easy to find meaning in a job,
but this is the difference between my generation and the one
before me.

For the writers and artists among Pleasanton's class of 1970—and
there are surprisingly many of them—the expressive arts are just
such a calling. And to the extent that they beautify the world,
reshape our culture, or offer a critical perspective on American culture, the artists exemplify the ideal of meaningful work. Men and
women who became teachers, when teaching was (as it still is)
financially unrewarding and prone to frequent layoffs, understand
their careers in a similar light. They turned their back upon more
lucrative career tracks because they wanted to dedicate themselves
to the improvement of others.

Donna Yengoyan finished a master's degree in education after
leaving Pleasanton. Her first job was in West Africa, where she lived
in poverty-stricken villages and taught reading to children. She now
teaches in an American school in Japan. Her piddling salary barely
covers necessities in Tokyo. But teaching is her calling:

> You feel like you make a difference in some kid's life. Making him
> feel better about himself, making him try harder, strengthening
> his potential, what he can do in the future—these are the real
> rewards of my job. Making my students curious, making them
> think. When a kid makes the connection between something you
> taught in October and something you are teaching in April, it's
> wonderful. It's a real thrill when you see them get excited about
> learning.

Selfless devotion to others might be expected of someone who
chooses teaching as a profession. But even Donna's classmate John
Riordan, who became a policeman (easily the most conservative of
career trajectories among the graduating class of 1970) was motivated by a desire to help kids:

> I have always had a rapport with kids, and always cared for peo-
> ple that had less than me. . . . When I switched to psychology, I
> wanted to work with runaway kids. Kids with problems at home,

maybe physical problems. The kids out on the street who really can't get along. That's really what I geared up for. When I came home from college, I applied for jobs and found out that the best one I could get was with the police department.

And when John thinks about the highlights of his career as a cop thus far, he does not think about gun battles. What he remembers with pride is the day he rescued a four-year-old boy who nearly drowned in a backyard pool a block from the house where he grew up:

I got the child out of the pool and gave him mouth to mouth and CPR. He was blue; he was dead; no heartbeat, no breath, nothing. . . . I worked on him for twenty minutes. I picked him up and he cried and I threw him to the paramedics and raced to the hospital. When the doctor came out and said he was fine I broke down. I was on my knees crying.

This incident epitomizes John's view of what work is all about: an opportunity to serve, to contribute, to right something that has gone wrong.

Robert Bellah and his fellow authors of *Habits of the Heart* have contrasted American individualism with the kind of commitment to community that they believe characterized the United States in its infancy.[13] Indeed, it has become fashionable to rail against individualism, to equate a desire to seek a personal pathway with the abandonment of any kind of collective commitment to society and its institutions. In the generation of the 1960s, however, a constellation of cultural forces came together to produce an amalgamation of individualism and social commitment that has proved particularly powerful and durable. The single most consistent strand of that generation's cultural experience revolves around ideas of social justice, personal contributions to the greater good, and a belief (that has been shaken many times) that the long-standing social problems of the country can be attacked and changed through the activities of individuals.

Yet in responding to their generational culture, with its twin emphasis on antimaterialism and meaningful work, the older boomers inadvertently boxed themselves into downward mobility. For it remains an unfortunate truism that good works do not pay well. As long as the easy-living days of the 1960s and early 1970s were upon us, this unhappy fact had few consequences. Moreover, in advance of settling down to raise families, the cold realities of rising housing prices, flattening job pyramids, and the low wages accorded "socially responsible" jobs imposed few constraints on the sixties generation. As the economy went sour, however, the choices made by older boomers in pursuit of soul-satisfying but not terribly remunerative employment began to cut deeply into their standard of living and more importantly, into their capacity to provide for their own children. Pleasanton's writers and teachers began to realize that the pursuits they treasured for their intrinsic worth might well end up penalizing the next generation. They began to worry that responding to their own calling could have serious ramifications for their children.

Reaching this conclusion has brought a painful confrontation with the limitations of the sixties revolution as a blueprint for life in a competitive society. This point became even clearer with time as the sixties generation moved into mainstream jobs. As Carl Anderson, now nearly forty, put it:

> I think that Woodstock and all that was a real neat rebellion against society and structure and rules and parents. That's the free spirit that came out then. Cut loose. It's a shame, though, 'cause I think it didn't work. It turns out that generations later realize that that life-style and those philosophies were wonderful but they don't pay the bills. They don't make careers happen. They way to make it in society is to work hard, go to school, pay your dues, brownnose, play politics. That's what kids are doing today. They're conforming to the rules.

It was easy enough for the sixties generation to be antimaterialist in their countercultural youth. They accepted responsibility for the fact that their own occupational choices translated into a lower standard of living. It has become harder for them to live with the notion that their personal choices have unfortunate ramifications for their own children: for the quality of the communities they can afford to raise them in or the schools they can afford to send them to. For in the past of many a former flower child lies a comfortable, suburban, Pleasanton childhood, with its spacious house, wooded backyard, well-appointed school, and local swimming club. And while they may once have rejected the suburban dream, some version of this rather privileged way of life still resonates for them when they consider what a child "needs" to grow up properly.

This is an especially stark problem in the context of what appear to be ever declining prospects for social mobility. No one is more aware than the professionals and managers of the baby-boom generation of how critical educational excellence and cultural capital are in determining a child's future. Educated boomers may not be doing as well as they would like, but they are infinitely better off than their age-mates who didn't finish college, went the blue-collar route, or "turned on, tuned in, and dropped out." This knowledge fuels their anxieties about their capacity to boost their own kids to anything approximating their own class.

These vexing choices have fueled the anger and frustration of older boomers. But it is important to distinguish their views, the particular "spin" they put on downward mobility, from the views of other, equally disappointed and displaced members of the middle class. The sixties generation continues to be committed to the vision, however vague, of alternatives. They have not invested themselves in questions of material well-being to the same extent that other, particularly younger, baby boomers have. When all is not well, when they feel disappointed, they can still point with pride and satisfaction to their accomplishments in other realms. They continue to believe in the moral wisdom of their choices. Their worries about the well-being of their own children is tempered by a generational culture that values a trade-off between socially rewarding work and affluence.

Children of the Reagan Revolution

In the class of 1970 . . . kids went into the Peace Corps. There were probably more kids in my class who went to work for Dean Witter.
—Mark Eden, age 29

Conservatives would like the 1980s to be remembered as the period that saw the United States enjoy the "longest economic expansion" in postwar history. But by the time the Pleasanton High class of 1980 was ready to move on to college or into the work world, the United States had become a far different place from what it had been for the preceding generation. The shock waves first ignited by the oil embargoes of the 1970s, sent the economy into a tailspin that reached into the ranks of the white-collar middle class, right into the heart of Pleasanton. People with impressive credentials, years of professional experience, high-ranking management careers discovered that they were nearly as vulnerable as blue-collar workers caught in plant shutdowns.[14] It was a decade with some spectacular success stories—the Donald Trumps—and some equally spectacular failures, including most of the nation's savings-and-loan industry.

Up until the recession of the early 1980s, no one had anticipated trouble ahead for the suburban children of America's middle class: they had been promised only sunshine and good times but were greeted instead by double-digit unemployment. While the wealthy indulged in the stunning speculative boom that fueled the economic expansion of the 1980s, ordinary people, particularly the young, started looking for a haven from the gathering economic storm. Risk taking was fine for the well-off; regular folks felt the rising tide of insecurity in the gut and took the most pragmatic route possible.

Nowhere was the new conservative spirit more evident than in the decisions these younger boomers made over the kind of education to pursue after high school. Their older siblings had eagerly left Pleasanton in search of self-understanding and education for its own liberalizing sake, symbolized by their pursuit of art, philosophy, or psychology. The new pragmatic spirit of the 1980s led in a different direction: to accounting, finance, stock brokerage, real estate. These were the jobs most likely to yield good money and a decent life-style in the post-Aquarius age.

Joseph Belli is of Irish-Italian Catholic extraction, one of two sons. When he graduated from Pleasanton High School in 1980, Joseph enrolled in a small state college in southern New Jersey. He planned to study accounting, a field he had already pursued during the last two years of high school. His parents did not have enough money to put him through college, so he took out loans and set out to graduate as soon as possible. He remembers being irritated by any course requirements that did not pertain directly to accounting, courses designed to broaden his intellectual horizons:

> I was frustrated because I saw the loan I took out building up for courses I didn't want to take in the first two years. I paid for things that I'll never ever use in my life. I could have bought the book for $30 instead of spending money on a course where the guy said, "Read this." To me that was horrible. Knowing that

when I got out of college I would have $10,000 in loans and knowing that that money was mine and being wasted. . . . A lot of my money went down the tubes.

Joe's attitude toward education is purely instrumental. He appreciated having the chance to go to college to "see what real life is really like without really being part of it yet," but after one year he became impatient with what he considered to be the irrelevant aspects of education. His goals were set, and everything that got in the way just cost him money when there was little money to spare. He never felt he had the flexibility to pursue other possibilities in life, but this did not bother him, because he was looking for a steady job, not an opportunity to expand his psychic horizons.

Much of what journalists wrote about young people in the 1980s focused on the yuppies: the young, childless, urban professionals whose high spending fueled the spread of boutiques, designer labels, and urban gentrification. The yuppie phenomenon was vastly oversold, at least as a description of America's youth, the majority of whom could only dream about that sort of material excess. What *was* true of the 1980s generation was that unlike their antimaterialist predecessors, they did hunger for financial well-being and social stability. Their backs were up against a fiscal wall; they would have to buckle down if they were to have any chance of replicating a Pleasanton life-style. Hence, the dawn of the 1980s found the nation's younger boomers in no mood to experiment. They needed practical skills that would translate into safe, secure jobs. This was the only motivation that made sense in an era in which the expansive possibilities of the past were just that: past. Clinging to tried-and-true blueprints with fairly traditional parents shouting encouragement from the sidelines, the Reagan generation eagerly sought protection from the ill winds of economic change in the form of practical, credential-oriented higher education.

These younger boomers were not looking for high adventure when they ventured out of Pleasanton. Going on to college did not mean stepping out into the great big world; it did not even translate into going across the Hudson River into New York City, a path many of their older siblings had willingly traveled in search of new horizons. What the Reagan boomers wanted was to stick to their old horizons, to stay close to home and old friends while they prepared for future careers.

The homebody orientation was born of financial necessity: as more and more Pleasanton parents began to feel the brunt of high unemployment in the early 1980s, fewer could afford to lash out on their children's education. As Pleasanton parents faced those astronomical tuition charges, they began to ask themselves whether the payoff was worth it. But more than finance was involved in the desire of the younger boomers to stick close to their roots. The expansive, experimental attitude toward the world characteristic of the sixties generation was replaced by a more cautious spirit, a fear of the unknown, a desire for the familiar. With the economy in disarray and the future so hard to predict, it simply seemed a safer route. Indeed, in keeping with national trends, a record number of Pleasanton's younger boomers stayed home with Mom and Dad, enrolled in a local college, and took a part-time job to cover the car payments.[15]

Their older siblings were aghast. For the sixties generation, moving out, defining oneself, was perhaps the most important challenge. Older boomers were willing, even happy, to forfeit creature comforts to "finance" this life free of adults.

By 1980 the situation had reversed itself. With unemployment high and secure careers hard to find, the symbolic character of American culture, particularly youth culture, changed in dramatic ways. No longer was independence and freedom from adult control the central goal of every adolescent: security was what mattered. In a sense, the generation of the 1980s bears a cultural resemblance to postwar Americans born during the depression. Certainly, the country's economic woes in no way approached those of the 1930s, but nevertheless the unsettling sense of impending disaster was spreading among the white-collar middle classes.[16] The response of Pleasanton's high school graduates of 1980 was predictable: they wanted their share of the pie and cared far more about that than autonomy from their parents.

For the boomers who came of age in the Reagan years, there was no cultural divide between parent and child. There was no reason to run from postwar parents when the two generations had so much in common. George McDermott, who spoke with such conviction about the follies of welfare in chapter 6, has a twenty-nine-year-old son named Jimmy. For the past few years Jimmy has been stationed with the Air Force in Texas. But he has high hopes of being able to move back to New York or New Jersey so that he can spend more time with his parents:

I've only been able to see my folks once a year since I've been in Texas. But if we move back to New Jersey, we'll want to see them a whole bunch more. We talk on the phone about once a week. I discuss everything with them, especially about job changes. My parents are a very good influence on me. I really respect them and listen to them. I confide in my dad all the time.

As Jimmy sees it, he has grown up in a time that bears some resemblance to the unsettling depression years that shaped his father:

My parents grew up around the depression time, and maybe some of that carried over to me, some of that thinking that you've got to save and you gotta prepare for the future and stuff like that. I see eye to eye with my parents on a lot of things because this is a pretty difficult time too.

The boomers of the sixties felt a profound distance between themselves and their parents. Their younger counterparts saw the reverse, a remarkable convergence of views. Postwar parents believed in conservative sexual mores, stay-at-home motherhood, the importance of financial security and upward mobility, and the central symbolic and material significance of homeownership. Their 1980s progeny saw the world in very similar terms, even as they lack the financial means to realize these aspirations.

Pleasanton's younger boomers were not about to accept the notion that there is nothing they can do to outrun the downward economic trends. Educational credentials in hand, they set out to establish careers that they hoped (and still hope) would put a financial floor under them and offer the prospect of a reasonable future. For many of Pleasanton's younger boomers this has meant taking low-level managerial jobs in financial service industries of one kind or another. The money they make is fairly good and certainly would have been sufficient in their parents' youth to underwrite a middle-class life. Today it is enough to rent a reasonable apartment but not enough to save for a down payment, enough for an occasional weekend trip but not an elaborate vacation, enough to buy a used car not a new one. In short, they can fund a modest life-style if they are extraordinarily careful about their pennies and nothing major goes wrong.

One way they endeavor to make sure nothing goes wrong is to shun risk. From the beginning of their educational preparation through the development of their careers, they have seen themselves on a treadmill: they cannot afford to step off, to deviate, to experiment, a perspective Andrew Lerner knows all too well:

> When I went to college my attitude was that I wanted something practical. I wasn't going to major in philosophy. I decided that I would go into advertising or public relations. Diverse communications activities. There was something powerful working inside me. I could not deal with uncertainty. I had to have direction. I had to know what my purpose was, my objective, my goal. I had to latch on to something and have it definable. I couldn't live with ambiguity.

Andrew's generation cannot afford to do what the generation before it did with such abandon: search this way and that way for satisfaction in career and life-style. Getting off the treadmill is too much of a risk.

America's youngest boomers may accept this as their lot for now, but they worry a great deal about the future, for the dreary present appears to stretch on endlessly toward the horizon like a Kansas wheat field. Their jobs promise no glamour, hold out little in the way of challenge, and are unlikely to yield dramatic promotions that will catapult them into higher tax brackets. Indeed, with the economic calamities of the 1990s now upon them, this generation will be lucky just to hold on even to these positions in the middling levels of white-collar management. Steven Krassman is an artist whose talent was apparent early on. He would love to make his living as an artist, but the economic climate of the times has locked him into a career in commercial real estate. He has lowered his expectations:

> The job I have now is a means to an end and I pay for that attitude; there are personal satisfactions that I have to forgo to gain some security. I am not really doing what I want to do; my job just allows me to live the way I want to live. I don't think I could support a family on painting. That would be too precarious. The most important thing is to be financially stable; if I can ever get there, I'll be able to pursue my interests, as more of a hobby situation. So I'm sacrificing my enjoyment, my happiness now, in order to do something pragmatic for the future.

This would be a frustrating situation for anyone who shared the values of the sixties generation and saw work as the locus of self-development. But the Reagan generation has a more instrumental approach: one's occupation is not an expression of the inner self, nor is it a means of contributing to the greater social good. The purpose of work is rather to purchase a degree of freedom, freedom to consume, freedom to build a privatized life. Their sense of social conscience extends to the members of what Herbert Gans has called the "micro social world," where family and friends are the center of the individual's universe and social commitments beyond these boundaries are of far less importance.[17] Gans has argued that this insularity is characteristic of America's lower middle classes whose economic insecurity places a premium on "taking care of one's own." The privatization Gans describes has spread, in part because the financial instability that was once largely confined to the working class has moved up the ranks.

Richard Sennett and Jonathan Cobb pointed out years ago that for many upwardly mobile children of the working class, the transition into the white-collar world produced a sense of "hidden injury."[18] For the hopes that drove parents to encourage the move—the desire to see their children free from oppressive supervision, the hope that the next generation would validate the sacrifices of its elders by doing better—often went unrealized. Low-level white-collar jobs, Sennett and Cobb argued, often provided no greater sense of autonomy than working on an assembly line and lacked the reward that comes from seeing the outcome of one's labor—a car, a bridge, a house.

In quiet, reserved and almost resigned voices, these very sentiments are often echoed by Pleasanton's younger boomers who chose to become accountants or managers in the service industry. The young men, in particular, often feel like paper pushers stuck at the bottom of the status ladder. There are no intrinsic rewards for their efforts; they are on an assembly line of another kind. The ties they wear to work often feel more like choke collars.

Oran MacDowell, now nearly thirty, found that steady job in 1986, as an accountant in a manufacturing firm. It gives him a decent, though not spectacular, income but consigns him to the role of an invisible man. Few people in the firm appreciate the quality of his work, there are not many challenges to be had, and his whole division is generally sidelined from the important parts of the firm's hierarchy:

Accountants have to clean up the rest of the financial world's . . . crap. We're the guys who have to do all the crap. The higher you go up the company, the more they overlook [accountants]. We'll bring problems to the VP for Finance and he'll push them aside. Everybody calls this man "Smiley" or "Mr. Sunshine," but he barely even recognizes that you're alive. Accounting is boring. It's tough for me to be stuck at a desk all day. I'd rather be outside. I never figured what sitting in an office was like.

Between the anonymity of his work and his dissatisfaction with his salary, Oran has begun to dream about other pathways in life. If he could have any job in the world, he would like to own his own company, a woodworking shop. It is not so much that he wants to be his own boss, although that is part of it. He just wants to be out of the white-collar world. But he is not hopeful about the prospects:

This job is my purgatory. If I just go to another accounting firm, maybe that's the wrong direction. I'm just going to end up in another bad place. That's the problem. I know my place and my work environment isn't the best, but there are a lot worse. What am I going to do then? I'm not in the same position as I was before I got married where I would say, Well, if they fire me, they fire me. Now I have to have a job. We won't have an apartment if I don't work.

Oran's friend and former classmate at Pleasanton High School, Charles Kruger, took exactly the same route, to accounting, and finds himself in the same unfulfilling but relatively secure position. If he had his druthers, he would spend his life in the woods:

If I could have any job in the world it would have something to do with the outdoors or animals. Outdoors particularly because I hate to be indoors . . . even if I was cutting lawns. Gardening or working in a forest. I had a neighbor who was working in a forest and I used to go down there to see what he was doing. Right now, though, I'd have to practically win the lottery to take a risk like that.

Neither Charles nor Oran sees any improvement on the horizon. Some of their age-mates have been spared this disappointment because they never thought of work as the locus of self-satisfaction or an avenue for contributing to their community. For Ron Christopher, now nearly thirty, work is nothing more than a means of putting bread on the table:

> My parents very much see the job so as you can eat, provide for your kids. It's just work. I never saw it as having to have any bigger meaning than that. Work is a substitution for not growing your own food. That's all any job really is. I never looked at it as much more than that. I never saw it in the sense that you should also have to seek part of your like as being responsible to the community overall—that the work you do should have an altruistic undercurrent. I'm not sure where that idea cropped up in people's minds.

These limitations would be bearable for younger boomers if they yielded the appropriate rewards. They thought they were parties to a bargain: trading adventure or self-satisfaction for job security and financial comfort. Instead, however, they kept their part of the bargain only to have the rewards compromised by the U.S. economic slide. Job security has been threatened by persistent recessionary downturns, and key aspects of middle-class comfort are beyond their reach. Hence, many have come to question the wisdom of a pragmatism that has bought them so little.

Of course, the jury is still out in on this matter, and few of Pleasanton's younger boomers are prepared to give up their standard of living. They recognize, with bitterness to be sure, that if they are ultimately fortunate enough to re-create a middle-class life as independent adults, this will come later in life than it did for their parents. In the meantime, they have adopted strategies of financial management that draw upon their parents' resources to preserve their own class identities. Where older siblings were "slumming it" to gain their freedom, younger boomers have stuck close to home in order to maintain a standard of living that is consonant with a core sense of who they are. Remaining home through their college years or returning home when their studies are finished, they can afford to buy the status symbols that would devour their incomes if they were financially independent. Not having to pay rent or buy food enabled the younger boomers to afford clothes, cars, and vacations that would otherwise have been beyond their reach. This boomerang pattern represents a major cultural adjustment of our definition of adolescence and adulthood, a sea change that has intensified with the deepening economic doldrums of the 1990s.

Some murky "in-between" category of quasi adulthood is emerging. These "psychologically middle-class" children cannot remain middle class without major financial infusions from their parent.[19]

Redefining the limits of adolescence is a process fraught with hidden tension and distress as befits a limbo identity. The twentysomething dependent is neither fish nor fowl, neither child nor adult, but an identity in the process of unfolding. Americans chafe at these new arrangements because our ideal cultural time clocks are generation specific. History may take us through ups and downs that determine the timing of the transition to adulthood, but our internal cultural gyroscopes do not adjust so easily. Instead, we tend to judge the behavior of adjacent (particularly immediately younger) generations by our own standards. When we find them wanting, we do not leap to the sociological conclusion that times and opportunities have changed; instead, we take out our moral yardsticks and argue that the youth lack ambition (if they are too long in their natal homes) or lack respect for their elders (when they are too quick to depart).

Parents know that being independent in these times would impose harsh economic penalties on their children. They do not want to see Johnny or Mary "slum it"—their children's identities are too much a part of their own self-image to let them do that. For the sake of their own parental self-respect, they need to be able to point to their children as success stories or at least not as failures. The solution in this economy seems to be to sit and stew: they let their children return to the family fold, support them for many years beyond what they believe is "good for them," and hope against hope that they will manage to strike out on their own before they cross another dreaded age-defined Rubicon.

What do the young boomers themselves make of this enforced dependency? They reject the negative characterizations, arguing that they are doing their best in a terrible job market. They have had to face choices that neither their parents nor their older siblings had to worry about: enormous bills for higher education, with no guarantee that the credentials will pay off in the form of a job that will even enable them to make good on their massive student loans. They realize that they cannot compete in the housing market. What else would anyone have them do? Live in a flophouse in order to be the independent adult that everyone seems to want them to become?

The Divided Generation

"Downward mobility" captures the economic experience of the baby boomers relative to their secure and affluent postwar parents, but it is hardly a uniform cultural experience. No one greets the prospect of a slump in their life-style with enthusiasm. But the degree to which the slide represents a catastrophe, a blow to all the hopes and dreams of a generation, depends to some extent on one's life-style expectations. For the sixties generation, downward mobility began almost as an elective enterprise. Their generational culture led them in the direction of careers they deemed socially and personally rewarding that were often not terribly remunerative. The sons and daughters of Pleasanton's postwar doctors, lawyers, and skilled blue-collar workers went off to become creative-writing teachers, artists, legal-aid lawyers, or social workers. They were never destined to equal their parents' standard of living, nor was this their objective. In seeking a more soul-satisfying life, they turned their backs on money, on security, on the trappings of a middle-class life.

By the time they had settled down and begun to raise families, the consequences of these decisions had caught up with them. Landing on the wrong side of the booming real estate market, many discovered that they were locked out by high prices and low wages. Their jobs simply did not pay enough to foot a middle-class bill by the time they decided it was important to provide one for their own children—and this is a constant source of worry. Nevertheless, these veterans of America's culture wars do have other values and commitments that can at least validate the meaning of their lives. They can point with pride to the novels they have written, the children they have taught in classrooms around the world, the paintings they have created, or the juvenile delinquents they have tried to help.

For the younger boomers, by contrast, this sense of alternative values has never loomed large. Indeed, they see themselves as a very conventional, conservative generation whose aims differed little from the desires and goals of their own suburban parents. They never set out to change the world, and they are not about to upset the cultural applecart now. They simply wanted their share of the pie. They did not bargain on an extended lesson in economic insecurity and relative deprivation: this, however, is the hand history has dealt them, and it perplexes them.

This experience of downward mobility is terrifying. The economic experience of the late 1980s and early 1990s is a recipe for frustration, envy, fury, and a growing sense of helplessness. No amount of waiting, no amount of deferred gratification, no amount of hard work is going to make it possible for these young boomers to lay claim to their birthright.

There are aspects of history that connect all baby boomers. The sheer size of the generation has preoccupied the country, as its schools, job markets, housing markets, maternity wards, and advertisers reacted to its movement through the life cycle. To a certain extent, this has exposed most members of the baby-boom generation to common experiences of competition for scarce resources and the sense of hierarchy or moral judgement regarding who deserves the best that this entails.

Yet beyond these structural similarities, the differences that separate the cohorts within the boomer group are deep and persistent. They do not remember the same music, they treasure different films, their experience of politics is as distinct as one could imagine, their occupational pathways express divergent interests, and their social values are at odds with each other. They are different kinds of Americans. They may have grown up in the same households, gone to the same high schools, and shared a community life in places like Pleasanton, but they are forever marked by the years in which they came of age.

8

The Politics of
Generational Division

The baby-boom generation could become the most powerful political interest group ever seen in the United States. As a collectivity, its members now constitute some two-thirds of the American labor market; they are entering the prime voting age years; they are a massive consumer group whose likes and dislikes are critical in defining the mass market; and as they age, they will become the repository of the nation's wealth, as holders of whatever savings, earnings, and taxpaying potential the country possesses. If they were ever to organize as an interest group, if they were ever to follow the lead of the postwar generation now in retirement, it would be political suicide for anyone in Washington to ignore them. Gary Hart, the ill-fated senator from Colorado, is the only politician in the country ever to attempt to build support on the basis of this reality. Bill Clinton and Al Gore sent mixed signals over their generational identities, wanting to court the boomer vote but wary of sounding a divisive note.[1] But the fact is, the boomers have yet to band together: despite the fact that they continue to fall farther and farther behind their own parents economically, they have not yet raised their voices in collective protest or demanded that politicians pay special attention to their needs. Why are they not a major political force in the United States? What is it about their generational cultures that makes it so difficult for them to find the common ground?

Unlike the postwar generation that did so well in claiming its share of the public and private pie, its children have not stepped forward to demand their own fair share. As student loans replaced the free ride of the GI Bill and declined sharply for middle-income kids, they did not articulate their fury in terms of generational fairness. The idea of tampering with social security cost-of-living increases terrifies Congress, while little or nothing is done to assist first-time homebuyers.[2]

The great "giveaway" of the postwar years was, of course, never understood or particularly intended as a gift to a particular generation of Americans. It was a political program made possible by economic circumstances that followed the war. Pent-up consumer demand was ready to explode, as the shortages of the war years gave way to pockets bursting with money to spend on new cars, new refrigerators, new houses, and above all new families. Government spending on education and housing, though of greatest benefit to the postwar generation, merely provided an infrastructure that would enhance business expansion. The high-tech revolution in manufacturing demanded engineers; the expansion of the service sector required new managers. All of these people had to be trained, and the nation's universities were the venue within which this was to be done. Housing was in terribly short supply during the war, and the returning soldiers needed to put roofs over their heads, which dovetailed nicely with the growing appetites of real estate developers like Levitt and Eichler.

What made this largesse a generationally specific endowment was that the whole period of expansion came to an abrupt halt before the succeeding generation could claim its share. The U.S. economy first slowed, then faltered badly in the late 1970s, and finally came to a crashing halt in key sectors in the early 1980s. Industry after industry contracted and failed thereafter. Spiraling debt ensured that the investment in America's middle class that began in the postwar period would ultimately benefit only the one generation.

Of course, such an outcome is not written in stone. Politicians respond to organized interest groups that articulate their demands with clarity and force. The postwar generation realized this truth some time ago and has lobbyists to prove it. America's elderly are heard loud and clear: from the Gray Panthers to the American Association of Retired People to the indefatigable attention of the late senator Claude Pepper, nothing escapes the watchful eye of the country's senior citizens. The baby-boom generation has yet to learn this valuable lesson; as a result, its interests go unrecognized.

Why is this the case? Some pundits argue that this is because the boomer generation has outgrown its youthful preoccupations with social justice or outsider politics, that its interests are now indistinguishable from other, older generations. Indeed, on this account boomers are portrayed as having become so affluent that they turned their back on the liberal ideals of the past and joined the conservative groundswell of the 1980s. The opposite view is also offered: that boomers remained true to their liberal leanings but were "locked out" of the circles of power throughout these years of conservative domination and have been unable to find a mainstream vehicle for their politics.[3] These portraits of boomers are rarely based on any firsthand acquaintance with real people, drawn as they are from opinion polls, income surveys, and the like. When we look closely at communities like Pleasanton, we see a more complex picture of generational politics.

One of the few means of defining ourselves that is consistently used by ordinary people (and only rarely invoked by professional analysts of the social scene) has to do with generational identity.[4] There are well-known studies of generations—Glen Elder's *Children of the Great Depression,* Robert Wohl's *Generation of 1914*—but for the most part the strength of generations as sources of community, of connectedness, of identity formation in our culture has been only weakly recognized. It is as if the very idea of a generation is easily understood and constantly invoked by the layperson, but thorny and troublesome to the academic.[5]

The coherence of a generation, the extent to which it exists in the social imagination, is generated by cataclysmic events: wars, depressions, revolutions, dramatic social change. These are the conditions that create the stuff of memory, and memory, as well as experience, is critical to the social process of creating a generation. For the real meaning of belonging to a generation is often fully recognized only on reflection. Ask people who lived through the London blitz and the evacuation of children to the countryside, and they will tell you that these memories marked them for life. At the time, they were merely trying to survive, but eventually the struggles of everyday life under wartime conditions took on a larger significance. They then bind together people who do not know each other personally, to create a consciousness of shared experience of despair or elation, heroism and treachery.

Two important points follow from these observations. First, while everyone in this society is in a sense part of a generation (defined in terms of the period in which they came of age) all generations are not of equal salience. The strength of generational identity varies enormously along a continuum that stretches from those individuals whose self-understanding is entirely defined by their generational membership to those for whom it is barely relevant.

Second, generational identity can become so powerful a source of social solidarity that those on the inside of a generational culture may come to see themselves as special and distinct from the communities all around them. They may, for example, define themselves more as members of the depression generation than as part of the cultural mass called "Americans." Generational culture can become a reference point that challenges those values, cultural precepts, and experiences that tell us we are all part of one nation, one culture, one people. When this happens, generational culture becomes a catalyst for long-term division that springs, paradoxically, from its equally powerful ability to create psychological bonds between age-mates.[6]

When the boomers of the 1960s are asked to describe their youth, to reflect upon the meaning of their generational identity, they have no trouble resurrecting dozens of images, each instantly recognizable to their fellow travelers. Younger boomers find it much harder to distill the experience of coming of age in the 1980s. Oran MacDowell, Pleasanton class of 1980, finds it hard to "see myself as part of a generation."

> I can see my friends from high school, but a larger group is tough for me to see. The sixties/seventies generation had all this action that labeled them, but we didn't have anything to get us to that point. In essence, we were born in the sixties, grew up in the seventies, and matured in the eighties. So which generation do we belong to? There just wasn't any binding point.

In the dim recesses of his childhood, Oran remembers Watergate, the spectacle of the White House cover-up, and the resignation of Richard Nixon. The scandal broke when the youth of his generation were in grammar school, and although the details are obscure in their minds, it cast a long shadow over their faith in government. But because Watergate never catalyzed a social movement that enveloped young boomers, it had no lasting force as a rallying point for their generational identity, and nothing else more dramatic came their way.

America's younger boomers do not lack for anchors to their personal identities, but the quiescent politics of the 1980s has meant that they do lack a sense of tightly bounded *group* identity. They do not think of themselves as a generation in the sense that their postwar parents or their siblings from the sixties generation do. The younger boomers look at the sixties generation as out of step with the mainstream, while they understand themselves as committed to the traditional center of American culture. Ironically, it is their very integration into the mainstream that underlines the absence of a strong generational identity.

Pleasanton's children of the Reagan revolution have mixed feelings about this void. Confronted by the example of the sixties generation, they feel somewhat adrift, unable to consolidate an identity that works in the public sphere where the press, at least, often labels interest groups in terms of generations or groups defined by age. They express admiration for the dynamic energy that motivated the flower-power Americans who came before them and often wonder what it would have been like had they been adolescents during those heady days. Joe Cornblum's older brother came of age in the 1960s. Joe believes his brother has a place in history but that his own generation lacks the fire that comes from being alive in earthshaking times:

I grew up after the sixties and after the Vietnam War. It was a noneventful period. We inherited a certain amount of their political energy but had nowhere to go with it. America was trying to get its shit back together after the crises of the sixties and we had all this energy, but nothing we could do with it. My brother's friends were involved in a lot of group activities—huge parties, marches. We were just sort of there and had a disco. But there weren't any major problems going on that we were aware of. My friends were goody-two-shoes compared to my brother's, where everyone was a rebel. It was like my group was coming on the backswing of the pendulum; we lacked the anger and venom. It had been exorcised out of society, so we just went along with what was being handed to us. Those of us who had older brothers and sisters had something to compare this to and we thought, What's wrong here? Where is the energy they knew? Parents were glad their kids were back to just being good, but I thought the apathy was sort of depressing.

These wistful comments betray a recognition that the Reagan years failed to capture the imagination of Joe's generation, failed to craft them into a meaningful group and therefore left them betwixt and between, an inchoate group standing in the shadow of their more culturally powerful predecessors.

The strength of generational identity has a great deal to do with the sense individuals have of their capacity to affect the political process. As the events that catalyze strong generations recede into the background, their members feel the residue in the form of a conviction that their presence matters, that they are influential in their numbers, that they have moved the world. Under certain conditions, such a feeling can metamorphose into a political movement in which generations become effective interest groups. Even when these conditions do not materialize, a strong generation remains so in part because people who are central to it continue to see themselves as party to an identity that counts. By contrast, weak generations, whose members do not feel bonded to one another by virtue of common experience, do not define themselves as actors on the political or historical stage. They are more likely to take a more passive role, responding to the trends and events rather than seizing the opportunity to impose their own interests on the historical landscape.

The older boomers made their way from Pleasanton High School into the stormy world of protest marches, counterculture, and the much discussed "generation gap." That world stamped their political attitudes. Paul Cornell, president of Pleasanton High's student body in 1970, describes his present-day politics in words that could well have been voiced in his youth:

I think the way things are now is just wretched. Everybody should be entitled to the necessities of life; you shouldn't have to pay for education or medicine or anything to do with human needs. I think our society is a barbaric one; it has systematically stripped away any benefits to humans and it is getting worse all the time. The people who suffer the most are minorities or women, especially single mothers, old people. This is just the result of greedy people who should not be allowed to be in positions of power. . . . I'm in favor of any government that will help humans to live a life where they're free from nagging anxieties about their materials needs. No old person should ever have to worry about their care. Young people should be able to go to school. What we have now is simply a widening gap between the rich and the poor, like a continental drift.

Whatever its long-term performance as a political pressure group, the sixties generation can look back and see the myriad ways in which its presence, its actions, and outlooks changed the popular culture, the political language, and the historical course of the United States. They were the women and men whose street protests brought the war in Vietnam to a close; they were the generation that fought the sexual revolution and made the feminist movement an enduring reality hovering over the lives of men and women alike decades after it began. They gave political voice to the long ignored demands of minorities and for a time held the nation captive before television sets trained on violent confrontations.

America's younger boomers, descendants of Richard Nixon's silent majority, never had their own generational identity. They stand in the shadow of both their postwar parents and their counterculture siblings, unable to say that their actions made a difference. Indeed, they never aspired to make a difference *as a group*. Nor do they believe they are in a position now to articulate their needs, their views, their desires. As a generation, they are invisible.

These very differences cause the two generations of the baby boomers to view each other warily, at best. The sixties generation looks upon the younger boomers as hopelessly materialistic, politically retrograde, and utterly lacking in commitment or identity. As John Ellwood put it:

> The best thing about the sixties, transient as it may have been, wrongheaded as it often had been, was that there was a concern for other people. It wasn't the age of greed. There also was an idealism then which I think is very important and which has now been rejected. The generation that followed rejected idealism. Their attitude is that the world sucks, so I'll just take what I want. I have a lot of nostalgia for that more idealistic and ethical period.

Janet Osgood, a classmate of John's from Pleasanton High, believes that these qualities were important in her generation and that the loss of them in those that followed represented a retreat into apathy:

> My sister is eight years younger. She is typical of the eighties generation. She is not interested in social issues and problems at all. She doesn't feel she has to solve them. I see a lot more shallowness in younger people. They accept authority more and more. There isn't much of a sense of skepticism, which was very important to us. We marched about it, yelled about it, wrote about it, we advertised it. I don't get the impression that these people stayed up all night talking about issues, politics, religion, you name it, as we did. I don't have the sense that they see any value to sharing.

Paul Cornell, the high school class president in 1970, refuses to take this difference lying down. He utilizes his platform as a writing teacher in New Mexico to get the message of his generation to young people for whom the 1960s is history:

> These eighteen-year-olds, just trying to get them to believe that just because our side did it doesn't make it right! Oliver North is not a hero because he has a uniform on. Ronald Reagan was not a great president because he made it seem that we were back in the old days. You just can't sit by the fire and talk on the radio when at the same moment you're trying to overthrow governments and throw toxic waste in the water. . . . We can't go back in time to the sixties, but we have to hold on to what was good about it. . . . We have to stop thinking so damn much about what movie we're going to rent tonight.

Boomers of the 1980s often look over their shoulders at the flower-power generation as failed revolutionaries or as people whose attitudes were fine for their own time but out of step with today's realities. A new set of concerns is needed now, one that keeps a person's feet on the ground and is not so lofty or abstract. As Joe Cornblum sees it:

> The sixties generation was very idealistic. We're more pragmatic, I guess. More of a realist. I'm more concerned with paying the bills and future-type stuff, and they are more concerned about man's oppression of man or whatever. I'm not overly selfish, but I want to have a comfortable home and a comfortable life-style. I

don't want to be rich, I just want to be independent and not heavily in debt. They didn't seem too worried about these things; they were busy saving the world.

Different dilemmas confront these two groups as they face the problems of adulthood. For the sixties generation, the task is to salvage the worthy parts of tradition. As Martin O'Rourke sees it, people from his generation must make their way through this moral maze:

> The sixties produced a lot of free-thinking people, people who openly questioned power and authority. But a lot of people were destroyed by that freedom; they were given enough rope to hang themselves and they did, with drugs especially. We can't turn back the clock; we are all products of those times. And it is good that we questioned authority. What was bad was that we threw away a lot of good things in the middle of that turmoil. We threw away values like the family or respect for certain institutions. Now we have to figure out what we respect. I don't mean respect in a blind way. I mean truly respect.

People in Martin's generation are trying to figure out how to back away from the excesses of their youth without becoming the boring materialists they once criticized. They want to find ways to place the family in the center, but without a return to the subordination of women.

The boomers of the 1980s offer a sharp contrast: they look upon the choices they have made as necessary evils—utilitarian, pragmatic attempts to achieve financial security. They feel both trapped and scared: trapped in jobs that are not terribly rewarding, scared at having made this sacrifice, only to find that the rewards are not forthcoming. They have not been able to insulate themselves against downward mobility simply by pursuing a B.A. in accounting rather than philosophy or by going into real estate rather than becoming a teacher. All their hardheaded realism yielded little advancement at all, and they have no cultural alternatives, no sense of inner satisfaction, to salve the distress of economic displacement.

The boomers of the sixties—though they moved history and have a powerful sense of generational identity—are nevertheless not without an Achilles' heel: the ascendance of conservative politics in the last decade has left them with the nagging sense that their impact was short-lived. Not only were their liberal leanings not embraced by the nation, but their politics catalyzed political divisions that delivered a serious blow to the Left. The Democratic party, the only mainstream representative of this agenda for change, has lost many of the elections in which this generation has been able to vote. Right-wing populism, whether in the form of David Duke or Patrick Buchanan, has emerged as a credible possibility in many states. Backlash movements against abortion rights and affirmative action are widespread. Ku Klux Klansmen have been legitimate candidates for public office. In the eyes of many, the advances of an earlier age are in jeopardy. The most pessimistic among the sixties generation would argue that nothing was accomplished, that all was lost in the swing toward conservativism.

For all the disappointment, the sixties generation can still articulate its ideals, its demands, its hopes for the future. The memory of the past lives on in the way that this generation monitors the political life of the nation, consumes the news, supports challenges to conservative nominees to the Supreme Court, marches for abortion rights, and discusses endlessly the importance of pressing for social justice. If there are signs of insecurity, it is because that generation sees past advances rolled back, even vilified by so many Americans older and younger than themselves, or because they sometimes wonder whether adult responsibilities will deter them from the values of their youth. As Karen Rosen, now working as a legal aid lawyer in the Midwest, put it:

> For my generation, the most pressing problem involves our capacity to hold to our own vision. When we finally become the generation to hold power in this country, will we have the strength or the generational self-esteem to be strong and not reject the ideals we fought for? Can we adhere to the values that were so important to us then? I mean giving people opportunities, affirmative action, the right to a legal abortion. I just hope that when we become leaders we can continue to be . . . what we were.

Her former classmate John Ellwood, who teaches writing to inner-city elementary school kids, believes that these values do live on:

> The writing program I work in came right out of the sixties and I think it's great. I think that the orientation towards helping peo-

ple, being politically involved and caring about other things besides your own immediate success is also very important. My friends who were political then are political now. There hasn't been any "Big Chill" among my friends and that's good.

E. J. Dionne, author of *Why Americans Hate Politics,* argues that real debate over the most serious issues facing the United States has been made almost impossible by an artificial division between the political ideals of the liberal 1960s and the conservative climate of the roaring 1980s.[7] He suggests that voters have turned their backs on the system because they do not accept this polarization; instead they embrace a more unified vision, a consensus that politicians have refused to recognize because they benefit from oppositional party politics. Dionne moves back and forth between the extremes of conservatism and liberalism, with the idea of generation nowhere in the discussion. When we look beyond the opinion polls that purport to tell us what Americans believe, to the experience of ordinary people, we find less consensus and more division on some fundamental questions of modern politics. This is largely because the social experience of the various generational groups divides them from one another. The sixties versus eighties "false dichotomy" is quite real, quite durable, and difficult to broker.

The country rejected the sixties generation's vision of the nation, which placed this huge cohort outside the mainstream. Nevertheless, for those boomers, the core set of values retains its internal validity even in the face of external rejection. They know that they are different and that only among their age-mates will they find kindred spirits and a common sense of purpose.

Despite the strength of this cultural identification, the sixties cohort has thus far not articulated its worldview as a set of generational *interests*. Their support for liberal political figures is steadfast—they are an important part of Jesse Jackson's rainbow coalition, the backbone of support for the failed candidacy of California's Jerry Brown, State Senator Tom Hayden of former SDS fame, and the diehard supporters of Congressmen Ron Dellums and Senator Ted Kennedy, for example. But they have not pushed forward with a generational agenda that combines a liberal vision with the demand that the nation pay attention to their concerns now that they are parents of school-age children, downwardly mobile taxpayers, and struggling consumers. They have not been able to do what their parents did with apparent ease—claim their share of the nation's wealth and direct it toward social policies that would improve their own standard of living. Their political energy is instead diffused into general liberal causes.

The generation of the 1980s is far less organized and far more fearful. It was that generation, the Reagan generation, that foundered most severely on the shoals of recession. Their intense attachment to the ties of friendship, parents, and the old hometown has been most sorely taxed by their economic exile from Pleasanton. America's younger boomers have found themselves with no voice at the very time when they have the most to scream about. America's youngest boomers appear not to recognize themselves at all as a group capable of claiming the nation's attention. In this regard, other generational groups are better off.

Claude Pepper, for example, the late senator from Florida, built his career by championing the interests of retired people who relied upon evocative symbols of respect, obligation toward the elderly, and the sanctity of age to make inviolable their claims to the nation's medical and financial resources. The sixties generation has a long way to go before it can match this track record, but at least it has that potential based on prior experience in the political arena.

Because the two subcultures within the boomer group came of age in different historical moments, they appear bound to accentuate their differences and remain blind to their common interests. Hence, even though their interests are the same in many respects, they are at loggerheads with one another and unable to see past their cultural divergence to the economic problems that should, in theory, draw them together as an interest group unity. The two generations of boomers inhabit a house divided, indeed so divided that no politician has yet had to respond seriously to the demands of this, the largest potential voting block in the nation's history.[8]

The End of the Social Contract?

It is an article of faith among middle-class Americans that every generation will do better than the one that preceded it and that upward mobility is a birthright for those who work hard. By the same token, nothing is due those who slack off and expect a handout. Indeed, the promise of economic success defines our national identity, but it is a cultural premise built upon shifting sands. Our economy has grown increasingly more fragile, buffeted by forces we barely understand and cannot seem to control. With every day that goes by, these unseen hands seem to interfere more and more in our most intimate decisions: when to marry, when to have children, where to live, how easily we can remain close to our extended families, whether we will be able to enjoy our sunset years or will have to fret over every dime. And on all of these counts, the largest living generation of Americans is doing worse, enjoying less of the good life than those who came before, most notably its own parents.

The baby-boom generation feels strangled by this decline. Decisions that were once left to the vagaries of emotion are now calculated down to the last nickel; risks that could once be taken in education or career are now out of the question. If being careful could cure the disease of downward mobility, baby boomers would at least have a strategy for overcoming the obstacles the economy has placed in their way. But in truth, being careful and making all the right choices is no guarantee that the future will work out well. Indeed, for many of the nation's youngest boomers who put aside risks and dreams in favor of the pragmatic course, economic history has been unkind in the extreme. No amount of deferred gratification will buy them the gratification they want: skyrocketing prices, stagnating wages, dissipating promotion prospects, and the relentless pressure of an economy that just does not seem to work any more—these are the forces and trends that are choking them.

At the very least, sympathy would seem to be in order. After fifty years of sustained expansion in the United States, the bandwagon has come to a screeching halt. The brunt of the slowdown has been born by the baby boomers, with more to come as their own children mature into an economy characterized by fits and starts, weak recoveries, and industrial decline. Surely the country must realize that they are deserving of some concern, some recognition of the price they have had to pay for maturing in the wrong place at the wrong time.

Postwar parents, perhaps more than anyone else, know how steep this slide has been: it is after all their flesh and blood that has been exiled from the places where they were born and raised. Long-awaited grandchildren are growing up many miles away because the boomers in between cannot afford to live near their hometowns. The Ozzies and Harriets of the 1950s would like to be able to point with pride to the material accomplishments of their adult children as a natural extension of their own talents and drive. Instead, they confront boomerang kids who cannot seem to break free and forty-year-old progeny whose life-styles cannot hold a candle to their own, even if they are managers or professionals. The whole program they so believe in seems to have gone sour and no one really knows why. They take some solace, pointing the finger at elites, often those from other countries but some homegrown as well, who have taken unfair advantage and "jumped the line." Expressions of disgust at the urban "other," the underclass that demands tax dollars and affirmative action, creates a sense of moral superiority and a mandate for rejectionist "throw the bums out" politics. In the end, however, postwar parents believe that the boomers themselves are to blame for wanting it all too soon. They need to "get a new culture," divest themselves of their overblown expectations, and learn to wait their turn.

The problem is, of course, that waiting does not seem to work anymore. Postwar parents who had to wait because their young lives were tangled up in the depression and the war found the pot of gold at the end of the rainbow more by historical chance than anything else. Not that they did not work for it, but their children are working equally hard and are not likely to see the same rewards. They will pay the price for this misfortune for the rest of their lives: delayed entry into the housing market, among other things, will put them at a serious disadvantage from which they are unlikely to recover.

The United States is mired in an economic transformation that may turn out to be as profound as the industrial revolution itself, with consequences that are only vaguely understood by those of us whose lives will be shaped by them. But the decisions we make at this juncture, particularly those that govern the use of federal, state, and local budgets, will shape the very soul of the society we will pass on to the generations yet to come. Will America be a country in which we are our brother's keeper? Or will it be a culture where "every man for himself" summarizes our sense of social responsibility? Will the generations reach across the divides that time and history have placed between them, or will they turn inward and demand their share first, and others be damned? Will our suburban citizens—rapidly becoming the majority—turn their backs on the cities and define the nation's urban problems as someone else's responsibility? There are philosophical questions at issue here that go the heart of the country's national character. But underlying every moral question lies the simple, irreducible, problem of money: who is going to be allowed to lead the good life to which all middle-class Americans believe they are entitled, and who is going to be shut out.

Jim Florio, the ill-fated governor of New Jersey, knows this changing mood all too well. His state budget has been drowning in a sea of red ink, and his every effort to restore solvency through tax increases has met with resounding rejection. Angry middle-class taxpayers have marched on Trenton in protests that looked like the old days of the antiwar movement, save for the Brooks Brothers suits and the silver hair dotting the crowd. Lowell Weicker, independent governor of Connecticut, discovered the same fury in his constituency when he attempted to introduce a state income tax for the first time in order to preserve the public services the budget could no longer cover. All across the nation, starting with the new-age tax revolt in California (Proposition 13) to its companion measure in Massachusetts (Proposition 2-1/2), voters have thrown local government out of their pocketbooks and issued ultimatums to politicians of all persuasions: find the money somewhere else. Not on my back, Jack.

For a nation that professes a firm belief in education as the proving ground for young people, we have been surprisingly mean in our support of public schools throughout the 1980s and early 1990s. School bond issues that passed without a second thought in the expansive years of the 1950s now fail regularly, leaving local school districts no choice but to fire teachers, cut back on extracurricular activities, skimp on supplies, eliminate enrichment courses, and bear down hard in order to meet prefabricated objectives in standardized test scores, hoping to shield themselves against the criticism that they are wasteful. In 1990, 48 percent of the school budgets in the state of New Jersey were rejected by taxpayers,[9] continuing a trend that had been on the upswing since the mid-1980s.

New Jersey residents were hardly alone: school bond failures have become epidemic throughout the nation.[10] Voters charge that there is altogether too much fat in the public schools, and they have served notice that they are not about to pick up the tab. School officials, however, see their districts as skeletal, their mission threatened, and their very value as educators under the gun. Since they make little money to begin with, teachers are beginning to ask themselves whether some other way of making a living might be preferable to the beating they are taking at the hands of the public.

If this were merely a matter of squeezing the funds out of the citizens of Pleasanton to educate their own children, this would be bad enough; in fact, it might be regarded as self-destructive. But the political conflict over school expenditures is everywhere crisscrossed by generational and racial turmoil, by the demands of equity and fairness to distribute whatever resources we have to all comers. Retirees whose own children benefited from public education when they moved to towns like Pleasanton, now turn their backs on the needs of today's young families. And while they often do so in the name of elusive standards of efficiency in public education, underlying their rejection of school budgets is the cold fact that they do not want to pay for services they no longer use. The exile of their own progeny from Pleasanton, fueled by ridiculous real estate prices, has exacerbated the tendency to pull out of the social contract at the local level. After all, what's in it for them?[11] If the same logic were ever applied to social security or Medicare, we would surely see the contract that binds the generations fall apart.

The fiercest debates over school funding have come in states like New Jersey and California, where equalization is the issue. Rich districts fight tooth and nail to prevent their coffers from being tapped in favor of communities with far fewer options for funding the public schools. Supreme Court decisions notwithstanding, the well-to-do have made it clear that they are loath to see their money distributed to those less fortunate, particularly when they are of a different skin color or speak a foreign tongue. Jonathan Kozol's searing account of the nation's inner-city school districts, *Savage Inequalities,* stands as a moral indictment of the consequences: poor kids everywhere attend schools without books, without pencils, and with roofs that are caving in and windows that are broken.

We could chalk these inequities up to racism, and many minority advocates as well as their constituents readily draw this conclusion. There can be little doubt that the fortunate residents of Pleasanton are uncomfortable with minorities who live far away, who come to them through media images of crime and unrest. But racism is far too simplistic a diagnosis of the revolts that have blocked the distribution of middle-class tax dollars to the working poor in the cities and suburbs. It is the sharp edge of declining fortunes, the hoarding mentality that derives from the sense that there is not enough to go around, much less extra to fund the demands of the dispossessed.

The business community is also party to the hue and cry over schools and taxes. It is up in arms over the declining quality of public education, worried about the literacy and numeracy problems of a work force it argues is only marginally able to handle entry-level jobs in banks, stores, insurance companies, and fast-food restaurants. Business leaders bemoan the sliding competence of high school graduates and argue that we have yielded our international economic position to the Japanese and the Germans in part because we have abandoned high standards. Hence, the captains of industry promote highly visible schemes to resurrect the educational enterprise, by adopting schools, promoting voucher systems to stimulate competition, and pushing for more resources to be put in the hands of the educational system.

Yet the business community is caught in the same web of contradictory impulses as the average taxpayer: its market position has eroded, income has plummeted. Hence, business is on the lookout for any means of cutting expenses, including business taxes. Communities hungry for economic stability have traded corporate tax breaks for jobs and in the process have left themselves short of the funds they need to operate the public sector. In Florida $32 million went to public education in 1991, a sizable sum. But the amount is trivial compared with the $500 million claimed by Florida businesses as concessions in sales taxes, machinery, and fuel costs.[12] In Cleveland, Ohio, where the public school system was $34 million in the red for the 1991–92 school year, administrators filed a lawsuit arguing that tax breaks for business have seriously eroded the resource base of public schools. Teachers in Washington State walked off the job in protest against corporate tax breaks, singling out the case of the Boeing Company, which, they charge, was exempted from more than $900 million in sales taxes that could have been used to support public education. In Kansas, Texas, and Minnesota, among other places, legislators have pushed to eliminate property-tax concessions for businesses, since this is the revenue source most directly tied to education.

Businesses themselves point to their losing battle with overseas competitors and argue that their performance will only get worse if they are forced to absorb additional tax burdens. Besides, they argue, the schools should be pushed toward greater efficiencies in the name of accountability. As Forrest Coffey, corporate vice president for government affairs at the Boeing Company in Seattle, put the matter: "First they say, 'Give us more money.' Why should I give [the schools] more money? What do I get?" A powerful rhetoric of efficiency has found a great deal of support in a country skeptical of government and of public sector services: school teachers find themselves having to justify their calling in terms more appropriate for the assembly line. How many widgets were turned out per hour; how high are the reading test scores per hour of invested instruction? Educators lament the increased reliance on these stultifying forms of educational processing, though they have little choice but to prove their merit according to this yardstick. Next to the consumer price index, annual statistics on reading scores have become a major benchmark of mayoral efficacy. Meanwhile, the business world and state governments square off against each other in a fight for resources, while municipalities stand by and pray that they will not have to withstand more plant closings, more defections of firms who can always find other states where the economy is bad enough to extract new concessions.

The nation's colleges and universities have been similarly trapped. Federal contributions toward financial aid declined precipitously throughout the 1980s, leaving just enough for the poorest would-be students and relatively little for the struggling middle-income kids. State budgets for higher education have been slashed, a reflection of the weakened political clout of the education industry. University officials have had no choice but to begin stripping the universities first of their support staff and then of their faculty. No one is going to cry themselves to sleep over these problems, except perhaps the students who will be denied access to a college education, a sheepskin that is irreplaceable in this increasingly credential-oriented climate.[13] Because middle-class children know just how important higher education is for job opportunity, the issue of access has become politicized and, on occasion, ugly. The University of California at Berkeley, the nation's premier public university, has been in the spotlight in recent years because of its admissions policies.[14] High-achieving Asian high school students have squared off against African-American students long denied their turn at the elite schools; affirmative action has been embraced and then reversed as the politics of access heats up. Economic constraints on higher edu-

cation are turning into blocked opportunities, and when this tran-
spires, conflict inevitably intensifies among those critical credentials.

Private universities, including Brown and Columbia, have seen
student protests swell over financial-aid policies that threaten to
exclude those who cannot afford to pay the astronomical tuition
charges of the Ivy League. On both fronts—the public and the private universities—we are seeing a wrenching end to the period of
expansion in higher education that began in earnest in the 1960s,
democratizing access to the scientific and humanistic knowledge
that is the hallmark of a great nation. The country that bestowed
the GI Bill on its deserving soldiers and provided generous student-
loan programs to the older boomers is about to let higher education
become the province of those to the manor born and the poorest of
the poor, leaving everyone else standing at the door.

The 1990s are returning us to an earlier era in which birthright
determined one's fortunes. Those who can afford the better things
in life will have them from the beginning, and those who do not will
find it much harder to lay their hands on a middle-class identity. The
issue of schools and taxes makes the cleavage between haves and
have nots abundantly clear. Other sources of division are less obvious but have the same destructive potential for undermining the
social contract. Generational differences are among the least recognized but most important of these "hidden" conflicts.[15] Richard
Lamm, the outspoken former governor of Colorado, now a professor
of public policy at the University of Denver, recently spoke out
about the age-based inequalities in the way we spend our federal
budget:

> Congress . . . has just passed a budget that gives approximately 60
> percent of our federal social spending to just 12 percent of our
> citizens: Americans over sixty-five. Yet the elderly have the high-
> est disposable income and the lowest rates of poverty . . . in
> America. . . . There is little question that the elderly are the most
> politically powerful group in America. It's highly questionable
> whether they are the most deserving.[16]

Lamm goes on to explain that Medicare pays for the health costs
of thousands of elderly millionaires, while 20 percent of the nation's
children go unvaccinated.[17] We allow Medicare to pay for heart
transplants, while thirty-one million Americans lack health insurance

of any kind. "We have created an excessive sense of entitlement in the elderly," laments the former governor, "and they are vociferous in defending and enlarging their benefits."[18]

Lamm's warning is the first volley in a generational conflict that is not yet full-blown. His voice is not the only one raised against generational privilege. In the early 1990s the *New York Times* began an opinion series entitled "Voices from a New Generation," a periodic column in which young Americans at least one generation removed from the boomers have the opportunity to speak up. One particularly angry column was written by Mark Featherman, a young man who works in the library of the Jewish Theological Seminary. Mark complained about the colossal national debt racked up in the 1980s by a nation unwilling to live within its means, noting that his generation would end up having to pay for this binge:

> America had a party in the 1980's and we—the "twentysomething generation"—weren't invited. While high-flying S & L robber barons were making millions with other people's money, while men of bad conscience were constructing investment houses of paper, we were making our way through college and graduate school, taking out loans to finance our educations. Odd, then, that now that the party's over, we should get stuck with the bill.
>
> People are now speaking of the "new austerity." . . . Those doing most of the talking, of course, are those who can afford to be austere; their income is safely tucked away in tax shelters and investments. But for those of us just entering the work force, austerity is not something we have chosen; it was chosen for us. . . . The baby boomers have a long-term lock on the upper levels of the marketplace, and we face increased competition for entry-level jobs. Who will be made to pay for the good times of the last decade? It doesn't take a genius to figure out that it will be us, the youngest and rawest members of the labor force.[19]

Mark is not a happy camper; his age-mates are likely to be just as upset if their prospects continue to decline and they come to identify the source of their problems as older, more privileged generations of Americans.

The disparate fortunes of these generations may well become so blatant that they will catalyze a new kind of political dialogue. As the stresses and strains evident in the boomer generation become clearer, they may well turn around and ask their politicians (not to mention their own parents) why the country seems so uninterested in their problems. They may well want to know why so little attention has been paid to their concerns, particularly in light of how much attention is given to the problems of other groups: the elderly, the poor, the cities. Boomers are likely to open a generational conversation on the subject of equity and it will not be a pleasant one, for their complaints already evoke countercharges that they are a spoiled generation with inflated expectations, a critique they sometimes level at themselves. If the economic prospects of the boomers continue to sag, the country may hear the sound and fury of promises unfulfilled and hard work gone unrewarded. And this will be just the beginning of the generational debate: in time, the "baby-bust" generation will surely ask why they should have to bear the burden of supporting the boomer generation in retirement.[20]

Until that time, we are left with pressing questions of public policy that cannot wait. Who will pay for the national debt? How are we going to compete in the international arena if we refuse to pay for the school bond issues that will fund quality education? The skyrocketing cost of health care threatens to bankrupt workers and employers, and there appears to be no end in sight. The nation's inner cities are suffering from massive neglect, severe unemployment, and persistent poverty. Where will the resources come from to speak to these critical issues?

If the experience of the generations of Pleasanton is any guide, the country is in for a rough ride indeed. Even the generation of the 1960s, with its liberal political history, feels economically vulnerable. Their younger counterparts, the boomers of the Reagan era, are that much less inclined to be sympathetic toward the need to be their brother's keeper. Postwar parents who were lucky enough to be in the right country at the right time are now faced with escalating tax bills that are driving them out of towns like Pleasanton. Their need to marshal their resources in order to support themselves through a long retirement, leaves little to help their boomer progeny. The social concerns that no country can afford to ignore, the problems that festered and then exploded in south central Los Angeles in the spring of 1992, flicker on their TV sets and then dissolve into the great beyond of the increasingly distant cities. Suburban dwellers are too preoccupied and too worried about their own problems and those of their children to leave much room for the demands of the inner city. They want someone else to handle that headache, someone else's resources to pay for it.

This does not augur well for the soul of the country in the twenty-first century. Every great nation draws its strength from a social contract, an unspoken agreement to provide for one another, to reach across the narrow self-interests of generations, ethnic groups, races, classes, and genders toward some vision of the common good. Taxes and budgets—the mundane preoccupations of city hall—express this commitment, or lack of it, in the bluntest fashion. Through these mechanistic devices, we are forced to confront some of the most searching philosophical questions that face any country: what do we owe one another as members of a society? Can we sustain a collective sense of purpose in the face of the declining fortunes that are tearing us apart, leaving those who are able to scramble for advantage and those who are not to suffer out of sight?

There will be little left of the nation if we withdraw into our own little corners and refuse to "pay" for anyone else's needs. If the fortunes of the generations diverge to the point where they cannot see each other's legitimate claims and heartfelt dilemmas, we may well see the development of warring interest groups competing for politically sacred identities: the inviolable elderly, the deserving children, the baby boomers holding IOUs because they have yet to claim their fair share, the burdened baby-bust generation that did not get to "come to the party" in the 1980s. This is a nightmare vision of American politics that we cannot afford to entertain. We cannot allow public policy debates to descend to the level of squabbles over who is spoiled, about which ethnic groups deserve the good life and which should be excluded, about who is really deserving of a decent retirement or adequate medical care. The social contract upon which we all depend requires some recognition of the common rights and legitimate aspirations of all Americans for a share of the good life.

In explaining our fate, American culture tends to subtract large forces from our lives—economic trends, historical moments, and even government policies that privilege one group over another—and looks instead to the individual's character traits or values for answers. Ask members of the postwar generation about their extraordinary experience of upward mobility and you are likely to hear a sermon on the importance of hard work and "your own bootstraps." The GI Bill, low-interest mortgages, and the booming economy of the 1950s and 1960s will barely rate a mention in this tale of upward mobility. But the truth is that the hard work paid off only because economic conditions over which no individual had control made it possible and because government policies provided a helping hand.

In the legacy of the GI Bill, the WPA, and a host of other government initiatives lies the kind of active program for recovery we sorely need today. These programs created confidence that we lack at present that there are measures we can take, investments in the well-being of all Americans that will actually make a difference.[21] The Great Depression was a far worse economic calamity than anything we have seen since, and we found our way out of it. It is true that part of that trajectory of success came about because the United States was arming itself for World War II, a catalyst for government spending that few would want to see repeated. But the lesson we might take from the experience of the nation's recovery from the blight of the 1930s is that we need not assume that nothing can be done to move the economy and the generations that depend upon it out of the current malaise. We can ask and should ask what government can do as well as what private industry can do. And when we have finished that agenda, we must ask as well what we must do for one another if the present generations and those that follow are to claim their own share of the American dream.

Notes

I: The End of Entitlement

1. Glen Elder discusses the fate of this generation in his important book *Children of the Great Depression: Social Change in Life Experience* (Chicago: University of Chicago Press, 1974).

2. The research for this book is drawn from life history interviews of two cohorts of high school graduates who attended the only public high school in Pleasanton, a real community (with a fictitious name) in northern New Jersey. Graduates of the class of 1970, the class of 1980, and their parents were interviewed between 1988 and 1990. Some 160 people were interviewed in all, representing 60 families whose children fell into the two cohorts. All the names and some of the biographical details of my informants' lives have been changed in order to protect their privacy. At the same time, the specific identity of individuals is largely irrelevant. Pleasanton is presented here as an example of a national phenomenon of escalating land values and housing prices that is typical of most of the suburban communities surrounding major cities in the United States.

3. In fact, the farms of Pleasanton did supply the troops of the revolutionary armies with food and lodging. The area is studded with old battle sites that reflect the central preoccupation of both British and U.S. troops with the Hudson River as a strategic asset.

4. In 1956 the Interstate Highway Act allotted federal money for 41,000 miles of new public highways. For a historical analysis of the connections between transportation technology and suburban growth in the United States see Kenneth T. Jackson, *Crabgrass Frontier: The Suburbanization of the United States* (New York: Oxford University Press, 1985).

5. Pleasanton has resisted pressure, including pressure from within, to build denser housing (apartment buildings, town-house develop-

ments, and so forth) to accommodate less affluent sons and daughters.

6. Herbert Gans argues that the common factor in the suburbs is a relatively equitable distribution of income and status; thus, his Levittowners were able to reject ethnocentrism and trust their neighbors not because of an increase in ethnic tolerance but because of an increase in wealth. See Gans, *The Levittowners: Ways of Life and Politics in a New Suburban Community* (New York: Vintage Books, 1967). See also Micaela di Leonardo's *The Varieties of Ethnic Experience: Kinship, Class, and Gender among California Italian-Americans* (Ithaca, N.Y.: Cornell University Press, 1984) for a discussion of ethnicity in the suburbs. She takes issue with the common assumption that only urban residents enjoy ethnic culture and examines the role of women in the continuation of ethnic identity.

7. Everyone who was white. Blacks were cutting the ties with the rural South and filling the urban spaces that the white working class and middle class left behind. The black middle class that did exist encountered racial barriers in trying to escape the ghetto. Just after World War II, suburbs were economically and racially homogeneous. Jackson, in *Crabgrass Frontier,* points out that only in the 1970s, when more minorities were entering the middle class and overt racial discrimination was declining, did black suburbanization become a major phenomenon. In 1980, 23.3 percent of all U.S. blacks were suburban, compared with 40 percent of the total population.

8. In a very real sense Pleasanton was never a true melting pot. African Americans never lived in the community; neither did Hispanics. The population did include a large variety of white ethnics, the classic ingredient of the "melting pot."

9. As of August 1992 the average list price for a home in Pleasanton was $330,0000. The median sale price was $260,000. These averages remain even after the considerable slump in the real estate market that commenced in the late 1980s.

10. For an ethnographic study of workers' views of American industry, see Katherine S. Newman, *Falling from Grace: The Experience of Downward Mobility in the American Middle Class* (New York: Free Press, 1988), chap. 6; and idem, "Turning Your Back on Tradition: Symbolic Analysis and Moral Critique in a Plant Shutdown," *Urban Anthropology* 14:1–3 (1985): 109–50.

11. "Workers Must Choose as Jobs Move," *New York Times,* April 11, 1991, p. B1.

12. Parents of the boomer generation find these trends equally frighten-

ing. The unpredictable swings in the local economy are all too reminiscent of earlier economic disasters they lived through as children in
the depression. As Simon Rittenberg sees it, things are just going
from bad to worse:

I think there are going to be a lot of psychological breakdowns
because of this economic uncertainty. I really do. I hope to hell it
doesn't happen and I don't think it will be as severe as what my parents went through [in the thirties], but I see it happening. You pick
up the *New York Times* this morning, Wang Corporation is laying off
two thousand people. Oh boy, that's a lot of people. Mobil Oil, Esso,
they're all laying off people. The economics of these takeovers that
are taking place and then selling these companies in parts only means
one thing: the people lose jobs, the companies do not exist after they
get through cutting them up.

13. After 1973 growth of real wages and thus growth of family income
    stagnated. As a result, individuals who came of age during this period
    face what Frank Levy calls an "inequality of prospects" relative to the
    generation that came before them. Levy, *Dollars and Dreams: The
    Changing American Income Distribution* (New York: W. W. Nor-
    ton, 1987); and Frank S. Levy and Richard C. Michel, *The Economic
    Future of American Families: Income and Wealth Trends* (Washing-
    ton, D.C.: Urban Institute, 1991).
14. See Kathryn Dudley, *End of the Line* (Chicago: University of Chicago
    Press, 1993). Dudley offers an interesting discussion of this Darwinist
    ideology in practice in Kenosha, Wisconsin, where autoworkers are
    being told they deserve to lose their jobs and standard of living to the
    white-collar elites since they had never really deserved these benefits
    in the first place.
15. In 1940 female participation in the labor force was 27.9 percent. By
    1944 it was up to 36.3 percent, dropping to 35.8 percent in 1945 and
    to 30.8 percent in 1946. *Historical Statistics of the United States:
    Colonial Times to 1970* (Washington, D.C.: U.S. Department of Com-
    merce, Bureau of the Census, 1975).
16. Arlie R. Hochschild, *The Second Shift: Working Parents and the Rev-
    olution at Home* (New York: Viking Press, 1989).
17. Marcia Millman, in her book *Warm Hearts and Cold Cash: How
    Families Handle Money and What This Reveals about Them* (New
    York: Free Press, 1991), suggests that parents often bestow money
    on their children or grandchildren. She is talking about people who
    have a net worth in excess of a half million dollars and income
    enough to support a lavish retirement. Most Pleasanton residents do
    not have resources like that. Indeed, most Americans do not have
    resources even close to that level.

18. To use William Julius Wilson's phrase. Wilson, *The Truly Disadvantaged: The Inner City, the Underclass, and Public Policy* (Chicago: University of Chicago Press, 1987).

19. Paul Kennedy, *The Rise and Fall of the Great Powers* (New York: Vintage Books, 1987).

2: Winners and Losers in the Eighties and Nineties

1. "Why Economists Fear the Deficit," *New York Times*, May 25, 1992, p. D1.

2. At the end of the 1980s, nearly 64 percent of the American population owned their own homes, down from a 1980 high of nearly 66 percent. U.S. Bureau of the Census, "Homeownership Trends in the 1980s," Series H-121, No. 2 (Washington D.C.: U.S. Government Printing Office, 1990). A 2 percent drop may not seem like much, but it takes a significant downturn to produce such a change in national averages. More important, however, is the direction of the trend.

3. By 1991 the national rate of homeownership had recovered to 64.1 percent. But this upturn masks the profound generation gap discussed in the next section.

4. Quoted in "Home Ownership: A Receding Dream," *New York Times*, October 20, 1991, sec. 10, pp. 1, 10.

5. Joint Center tabulations of the 1973, 1976, and 1980 American Housing Survey, and the 1983, 1987, and 1990 Current Population Survey, in "A Shift in Who Owns Homes," *San Francisco Chronicle*, November 29, 1991, pp. A1, A20.

6. See Leon F. Bouvier and Carol J. DeVita, "The Baby Boom: Entering Midlife," in *Population Bulletin* 46 (November 1991): 2-35.

7. The category includes single parents and unmarried individuals.

8. Denise Di Pasquale and William Apgar, "The State of the Nation's Housing, 1991" (Cambridge, Mass.: Joint Center for Housing Studies of Harvard University, 1991).

9. The 1990 median home value in the West was $126,200 and the ownership rate was 59 percent; in the Midwest, the median value was $62,000 and the ownership rate was 68.1 percent; the South had average values of $66,020 and an ownership rate of 66.2 percent; and the Northeast was in between with values of $124,000 and ownership rates of 61.3 percent. On a par with national averages, New Jersey shows an ownership rate of 64.9 percent.

10. White families headed by people under thirty-five lost ground by 12 percent during the same period.

11. U.S. Bureau of the Census, "Who Can Afford to Buy a House?" *Current Housing Report*, Series H121/91-1 (Washington, D.C.: U.S. Government Printing Office, 1991), p. 2, fig. 1.

12. Ibid., 5-6.
13. Prices increased from an average of $61,161 to $72,628, a major jump.
14. In constant 1989 dollars.
15. Median household incomes in the Northeast rose over this period by about $4,000; however, means sales prices of houses rose by more than $25,000. Hence the affordability gap increased even in the Northeast, where incomes improved.
16. "Don't Count on Baby Boomers to Hike Savings Rate," *Business Week,* November 21, 1988, p. 24.
17. Mary B. Schwartz, "First-Time Homebuyer Affordability: A Look Behind, A Look Ahead," *Research Paper for the National Association of Realtors, Forecasting and Policy Analysis Division* (February 1990): 17-22.
18. "Why Older People Are Richer than Other Americans," *New York Times,* November 3, 1991, sec. 4, p. 4.
19. "Age Old Questions on Wealth," *International Herald Tribune,* June 29-30, 1991, p. 14.
20. National Association of Realtors, Staff Study, "Demographics in the U.S.: The Segmenting of Housing Demand" (Washington, D.C.: National Association of Realtors, 1989), pp. 73-79.
21. To buy a median-priced starter home in the Northeast ($94,230), prospective owners must amass $20,452, the cost of a 20 percent down payment plus closing costs. This would require a minimum annual income of $33,260, a figure that exceeds by a considerable amount the average income of Northeastern renters according to the U.S. Bureau of the Census. Di Pasquale and Apgar, "The State of the Nation's Housing, 1991."
22. David Halle, *America's Working Man: Work, Home, and Politics among Blue-Collar Property Owners* (Chicago: University of Chicago Press, 1984), and Herbert Gans, *Middle American Individualism:*
    The Future of Liberal Democracy (New York: Free Press, 1988), make the point that the conservative politics of America's blue-collar and "middle-American" workers, particularly where housing integration is concerned, stems from the fact that home equity is their only mechanism for saving. Anything that threatens their property values, whether justified or not, strikes immediately at the heart of their long-term financial well-being.
23. This is especially true when we compare elderly Americans of the present period, those who were born in the twenties and before, with their own parents, born at the turn of the century. For the latter group, old age was nearly synonymous with poverty. Only in recent decades have we come to equate poverty with single parents or

inner-city minorities. Before the advent of social security, the elderly were by far the largest group of Americans living in poverty.

24. This point was reinforced by DiPasquale, a researcher at Harvard's Joint Center for Housing Studies, who noted that, "the increasing inability of younger renter households to cross the threshold of home ownership will affect not only their own lives, but the lives of their children." Quoted in "Homeownership: A Receding Dream."

25. As of 1990 the ratio of active workers contributing to the social security system to retirees drawing from it was five to one. By the year 2030, when the youngest baby boomers reach age sixty-five, 20 percent of all Americans will be over sixty-five and there will be only three active workers contributing to social security for every retired person drawing benefits. These ratios are frightening. It is not clear that the retirement system could survive this demographic profile without massive—politically untenable—increases in social security taxes.

26. "Buying a Home Is Still an American Goal," *New York Times,* June 30, 1991, pp. 1, 14.

27. The difficulties in accumulating a down payment for traditional single-family houses have pushed an increasing number of renters to invest in nontraditional housing. The California Association of Realtors found that condominiums had doubled from 14 percent of all homes in 1984 to 28 percent in 1990. Town houses with multiple master bedrooms are selling to single people who team up with friends to become joint owners. Mobile homes are growing in popularity as well: the total number of homes in the United States increased by 16 percent in the 1980s, but mobile homes grew by about 60 percent.

28. United States National Commission on Children, *Beyond Rhetoric: A New American Agenda for Children and Families: Final Report of the National Commission on Children* (Washington, D.C.: The Commission, 1991).

29. In a cruel twist of fate, declining prices has had a negative impact on postwar parents who have seen their equity plummet at a precipitous rate. They are depending upon that nest egg to fund their own retirement.

30. Bennett Harrison and Barry Bluestone, *The Great U-Turn: Corporate Restructuring and the Polarizing of America* (New York: Basic Books, 1988).

31. "The 1980s: A Very Good Time for the Very Rich," *New York Times,* p. 1.

32. Household wealth is defined as the total of what it owns (stocks and bonds, housing and other real estate, checking and savings accounts, and so forth) minus what it owes in debts (mortgage loans, credit card balances, and business loans).

33. "Fed Gives New Evidence of 80's Gains by Richest," *New York Times,* April 19, 1992, p. 1.

34. For more on this thesis, see Kevin Phillips, *The Politics of Rich and Poor* (New York: HarperCollins, 1990).

35. The average pay of CEOs of large companies more than doubled in real terms in the 1980s. Peter Passell, "Those Big Executive Salaries May Mask a Bigger Problem," *New York Times,* April 20, 1992, p. A1. See also Louis Uchitelle, "No Reason for Executive Pay," *New York Times* March 18, 1991, p. D1; and Monci Jo Williams, "Why Chief Executives' Pay Keeps Rising," *Fortune,* April 1, 1985, pp. 66–68.

36. Quoted in "Fed Gives New Evidence of 80's Gains by Richest."

37. Data cited from "Trapped in the Impoverished Middle Class," *New York Times,* November 17, 1991, sec. 3, pp. 1, 10.

38. Levy and Michel, *The Economic Future of American Families: Income and Wealth Trends* (Washington, D.C.: Urban Institute, 1991), p. 7. For further information on trends in income and wealth accumulation, see Levy, *Dollars and Dreams: The Changing American Income Distribution* (New York: W. W. Norton, 1987). He analyzes the same issue for the 1980 census.

39. Levy and Michel, *The Economic Future of American Families,* make this point as well.

40. Levy and Michel, *The Economic Future of American Families,* p. 10. Emphasis mine.

41. "Getting Whittled in the Middle," *Washington Post National Weekly Edition,* November 18–24 , 1991, p. 37.

42. In 1987 dollars adjusted for inflation.

43. This study identified three basic trends. (1) Between 1967 and 1980, 35.5 percent of the poor moved into the middle-income group. But during the 1980s, this slowed to 30.4 percent. (2) During the thirteen-year period ending in 1980, 6.2 percent of the middle-income individuals fell into the lower class. After 1980 this trend accelerated: middle-income Americans descended into the lower class at the rate of 8.5 percent. (3) Before 1980, 6.3 percent of the middle class became wealthy. During the 1980s, 7.5 percent made this fortunate transition. The combination of the these three trends was a sizable increase in income inequality in the United States. See Greg J. Duncan, Timothy Smeeding, and Roger Willard, "The Incredible Shrinking Middle Class," *American Demographics* 14 (May 1992): 34–38.

44. Ibid. Smeeding, Duncan, and Willard, analysts of the Panel Study of Income Dynamics, attribute these income shifts to technological changes in the workplace that have led to the stagnation of real earnings among the young and less educated and a growth in earnings among the better educated and more experienced workers.

45. For a more detailed discussion of this point, see William B. Johnson and Arnold E. Parker, *Workforce 2000: Work and Workers for the 21st Century* (Indianapolis, Ind.: Hudson Institute, 1987).

46. Harrison and Bluestone, *The Great U-Turn,* p. 113.

47. Johnson and Parker, *Workforce 2000,* p. 31, writing for the Hudson Institute, dispute this picture in its entirety. They argue that while income inequality is greater within the service sector, it is not the major cause of wage stagnation. The demographic argument holds that the flattening of the wage curve is a response to the flood of women and young people into the labor market, a move that has depressed average wages but will slowly dissipate as these newcomers move up the ladder. Harrison and Bluestone (*The Great U-Turn*) dismiss this argument: "After accounting for the business cycle, for productivity and for the shrinkage of manufacturing jobs, the growing proportion of baby boomers in the total workforce contributes nothing to an explanation of low wages. Older workers have experienced a U-turn in their fortunes as well, so that age itself provides no clear explanation of the changing wage pattern" (p. 125).

48. Harrison and Bluestone, *The Great U-Turn,* p. 127.

49. Ibid., p. 128.

50. The term was coined by Bluestone and Harrison to describe the wave of plant shutdowns in the Midwestern and Eastern industrial states, a trend made possible by government tax write-offs and the lure of nonunionized labor in other parts of the country (and offshore). Bluestone and Harrison argue, in *The Deindustrialization of America: Plant Closings, Community Abandonment, and the Dismantling of Basic Industry* (New York: Basic Books, 1982), that this was a secular trend that resulted in a basic disinvestment in American industry and the wholesale elimination of millions of good jobs.

51. Moreover, there are productivity problems in the service sector as well. Growth in productivity was only .7 percent per year in the service industries, compared to 2.7 percent annual increases in manufacturing productivity throughout the 1980s. "Executives Expect Many '91 Layoffs to Be Permanent," *New York Times,* December 16, 1991, pp. A1, D9.

52. See Newman, *Falling from Grace: The Experience of Downward Mobility in the American Middle Class* (New York: Free Press, 1988), for more on the subjective impact of managerial unemployment.

53. "This Time, the Downturn Is Dressed in Pinstripes," *Business Week,* October 1, 1990, pp. 130–31.

54. Ibid., p. 131.

55. Andrew Sum, director of the Center for Labor Market Studies at

Northeastern University, quoted in "Laid-Off Bosses Scramble in a Changing World," *New York Times*, July 12, 1992, p. E6.

56. See Katherine S. Newman, "Uncertain Seas: Cultural Turmoil and the Domestic Economy," in *America at Century's End,* ed. Alan Wolfe, (Berkeley: University of California Press, 1991), pp. 112–30.

57. More than 100,000 people lost their jobs in New York City between 1988 and 1991. "All Walks of Life Now Converge in New York City's Jobless Lines, " *New York Times*, April 20, 1991, p. A1. New York City lost 8.7 percent of its jobs between 1989 and 1991. "New York Logs 500,000 Jobs Lost since 1989, a Record high," *New York Times*, April 16, 1991, p. B1.

58. Peter Passell, "The Age Gap: Sins of Omission," *New York Times*, May 27, 1992, p. D2.

59. See Levy and Michel, *The Economic Future of American Families*, p. 109. For more on the problems of the poorly educated American worker, see McKinley Blackburn, David Bloom, and Richard Freeman, "The Declining Economic Position of Less Skilled American Men," in *A Future of Lousy Jobs? The Changing Structure of U.S. Wages*, ed. Gerald Burtless (Washington, D.C.: Brookings Institution, 1990).

60. This figure compares to the one in ten college graduates who were overqualified for their jobs in the late 1960s. Labor Department economists predict that college enrollments will outpace the growth of professional and managerial jobs for many years to come, so that by the year 2005 nearly 30 percent of the nation's college graduates will be working as file clerks, assembly-line workers, or some other occupation that does not require higher education. "More College Graduates Taking Low-Wage Jobs," *New York Times*, August 7, 1991, p. C5.

61. "U.S. Birth Rate Nears 4 Million Mark," *New York Times*, October 31, 1989, p. A18.

62. Arlene Skolnick, *Embattled Paradise: The American Family in an Age of Uncertainty* (New York: Basic Books, 1991).

63. "Rate of Marriage Continues Decline," *New York Times*, July 17, 1992, p. A19.

64. These staggering increases have begun to level off as the biological clocks of millions of boomer women have started ticking louder.

65. Cited in "The Work Week Grows: Tales from the Digital Treadmill," *New York Times*, June 3, 1990, sec. 4, pp. 1, 4. Juliet Shor's recent book, *The Overworked American* (New York: Basic Books, 1992), notes that despite our reputation as a society of increasing leisure time, the majority of American households are working 140 hours more on the job in a year than twenty years ago. We cannot afford to take time off because we need our jobs more than ever before and cannot forgo wages for leisure or illness.

66. Married couples with or without children make up just 55 percent of the nation's 91.9 million households, down from 60 percent in the past decade. "Percentage of Marrieds Is Smallest in 200 Years," *USA Today,* June 11, 1991. Indeed, according to the Census Bureau, one in four Americans age eighteen and older has never married, up from 1970 when only one in six was "never married. " See "Rate of Marriage Continues Decline." This shift has left nearly 23 million people living alone, an unprecedented number. In 1980, "nonfamily" households made up 27 percent of the nation's households; that figure rose to 30 percent by 1990, most of whom (85 percent) were single people.

67. A pattern due in part to the financial difficulty of floating a middle-class living on a single income.

68. American Demographics study cited in "Parenthood II: The Nest Won't Stay Empty," *New York Times,* March 12, 1989, p. A30.

69. "More Young Men Hang on to Apron Strings," *New York Times,* June 16, 1991, pp. A1, A18.

70. Women marry at younger ages than men do, and it is likely that some of the difference noted here is attributable to the relative ease with which women can marry out of their natal households.

71. Levy and Michel put the matter this way: "The net wealth of those families headed by a young person with at least some college education was 66% higher than that of families headed by a young person with a high school education or less." *The Economic Future of American Families,* p. 65.

3: The Making of the Boomers

1. See Herbert Gans, *The Levittowners: Ways of Life and Politics in a New Suburban Community* (New York: Vintage Books, 1967), for a good review of contrasting perspectives on the suburbs in the 1950s and 1960s. The first series of sociological reports on suburbia was written by William H. Whyte, Jr., and later published as part of his book *The Organization Man* (Garden City, N.Y.: Doubleday Anchor Books, 1957). Later writings, including novels, criticized the suburbs and suburbanites as alienated, atomized, and depersonalized. Literary and social critics created an image of suburban culture as oppressively conformist, intellectually debilitating, and politically dangerous. In *Working Class Suburb* (Berkeley: University of California Press, 1960), Bennett Berger dubbed this image the "myth of suburbia."

2. In *The Urban Villagers* (New York: Free Press, 1962), Herbert Gans shows that among the urban Italian Americans he studied, social connections were built around sibling ties and the peer group.

3. Suburbia has attracted relatively little attention from the social science community. Urban areas have long been the focus of sociological and anthropological attention, from Robert E. Park, *The City* (Chicago: Chicago University Press, 1925) and the classics of the Yankee City series, for example, W. Lloyd Warner and Paul S. Lunt, *The Status System of a Modern Community* (1942; Westport, Conn.: Greenwood Press, 1973), to later studies like William Whyte, *Streetcorner Society* (Chicago: University of Chicago Press, 1955); Gans, *Urban Villagers;* and Elliot Liebow, *Tally's Corner* (Boston: Little, Brown, 1967). Suburbia enjoyed a brief flurry of interest with the publication of Berger's *Working Class Suburb and* Gans's *The Levittowners,* but there have been few serious investigations of suburban life since then. Mark Baldassare, *Trouble in Paradise: The Suburban Transformation in America* (New York: Columbia University Press, 1986); and M. P. Baumgartner, *The Moral Order of a Suburb* (New York: Oxford University Press, 1988), stand out as recent exceptions, but the latter is focused specifically on problems of dispute settlement.

4. Even the classic studies of the past (for example, Gans, Berger) focused more on social organization (civic groups, social clubs, coffee klatches, local government, and so forth) than on culture, understood as the values, expectations, and socially constructed meaning of suburban aspirations. Gans's *Middle American Individualism: The Future of Liberal Democracy* (New York: Free Press, 1988) deals with some of these cultural issues for suburban dwellers who are not comfortable enough to be middle class, but it this book is primarily devoted to diagnosing political conservatism.

5. See Glen H. Elder, Jr., *Children of the Great Depression: Social Change in Life Experience* (Chicago: University of Chicago Press, 1974).

6. For more on the social impact of the Great Depression on families, see Mirra Komarovsky, *The Unemployed Man and His Family* (1940; New York: Octagon Books, 1971); or Paul F. Lazarsfeld, *Marienthal: The Sociography of an Unemployed Community* (Chicago: Aldine, 1971).

7. See Elder, *Children of the Great Depression,* for a masterful study of the social and psychological effects of growing up during the depression.

8. To use Glen Elder's phrase.

9. Some boomers define themselves as risk averse as compared with their parents, whereas they want security before they launch themselves into family lives, their parents simply plunged ahead.

10. Pooling resources among extended families is common even today among the nation's pool. See Carol Stack, *All Our Kin* (New York:

Harper and Row, 1974). But it is precisely the linkage of "sharing" and poverty that made this structural adaptation so hard to manage among the stable, employed, white working class during the depression, for those people were working toward an "American-style" nuclear household that achieved independence from extended kin of the immigrant generation.

11. Federal work relief programs such as the Civilian Conservation Corps and the Works Progress Administration were begun almost immediately after FDR's inauguration in 1933, along with grants-in-aid to states to be used for emergency unemployment relief. The Social Security Act was signed in August 1935. These measures were critical in enabling families to survive the depression, but they were enacted four to six years after the onset of serious hard times. See Walter I. Trattner, *From Poor Law to Welfare State: A History of Social Welfare in America* (1974; New York: Free Press, 1984), pp. 257–84.

12. See chapter 2 for more on this. The same point applies with even greater force to the postboomer generation now in its early twenties.

13. This is not to suggest that the war was a picnic on the home front, for it brought hardships of its own. Housing was in short supply, and millions of families "doubled up," taking in their grown daughters and grandchildren for the duration. Ordinary goods of all kinds were unavailable. Men who stayed behind to go to college or to work were subject to ridicule. Nevertheless, those whose experience of World War II was confined to domestic shores, were spared the bloodshed and devastation faced by Europeans.

14. Though as Kenneth Jackson notes, the postwar builders deliberately segregated blacks from whites and were supported in their efforts by mortgage lenders whose policy of grading neighborhoods was based in large part on racial composition. See Jackson, *Crabgrass Frontier: The Suburbanization of America* (New York: Oxford University Press, 1985), pp. 207–9.

15. This is interesting in view of the interest shown by many of Pleasanton's 1970 graduates in issues of race relations, the career of Martin Luther King, Jr., and so forth.

16. I speak here mainly of Pleasanton parents who were raised in working-class homes by manual laborers and who became skilled blue-collar labor or up-from-the-shop-floor factory management in their own adult lives.

17. Popular songs such as "Down in the Boondocks" and "Leader of the Pack" drew attention to the theme of class division by presenting stories of lovers kept apart by their parents or communities as a result of their different backgrounds.

18. The popular 1980s film *Dirty Dancing* plays with the same themes: working-class boy meets middle-class girl, with the class gulf adding spice to an otherwise ordinary love story.

19. Barbara Ehrenreich has written about how the discovery of the working class catalyzed a "fear of falling." She argues that the cloistered middle class woke up one day to find that there was something other than the middle class in the United States and that this very discovery reinforced the problematic nature of social mobility in the United States. Ehrenreich suggests that parents suddenly realized that it was up to them to provide the drive and ambition that would push their kids over the hump. Ehrenreich, *Fear of Falling: The Inner Life of the Middle Class* (New York: Pantheon Books, 1989). There is much truth to her analysis; the cultural problems attending the credential-laden process of joining the middle class are legion, precisely because membership has become ever more a matter of laying claim to M.D.'s, Ph.D.'s, and M.B.A.'s. Gone (largely) are the days when a prosperous businessman just passed the family firm on to the next generation and every son just had to wait for it. Now more than ever before, parents find themselves responsible for creating the right kind of personality in their children, the kind that wants to strive in all the necessary institutional domains. As we have seen in chapter 2, even this is no longer enough, and the "fear of falling" is hardly an abstract concern; falling is exactly what many members of the baby-boom generation are doing.

20. I borrow a phrase here from Sylvia Hewlett's *A Lesser Life: The Myth of Women's Liberation in America* (New York: William Morrow, 1986). Readers interested in a more thorough treatment of domestic life in the 1950s are referred to her chapter on the subject, also entitled "The Cult of Domesticity."

21. Child rearing has always straddled the fine line between art and science. In the twentieth century, science has had the upper hand in the sense that experts on raising children emerged as specialists with a mass market for their advice. The inexact nature of our understanding of human development is apparent from the fact that the content of these admonitions has fluctuated from an emphasis on strict discipline, an aversion to cuddling, and scheduled feedings in the 1920s and 1930s to the approach inspired by Benjamin Spock, of loving support, understanding, tolerance, and demand feeding. As far back as Ruth Benedict's classic *Patterns of Culture* (Boston: Houghton Mifflin, 1934), anthropologists have told us that child-rearing practices are central to the way a society works on individuals, making them part and parcel of the cultures they will later participate in as adults.

22. Simone de Beauvoir, *The Second Sex* (1952; New York: Vintage Books, 1974); Betty Friedan, *The Feminine Mystique* (New York: W. W. Norton, 1963).

23. In *The Unexpected Community: Portrait of an Old Age Subculture* (Berkeley: University of California Press, 1978), Arlie Hochschild argues that the elderly engage in a similar kind of "altruistic surrender," in that they too tend to live through their children and derive a sense of identity and satisfaction from the achievements of others. In a curious sense, the mothers of Pleasanton were in a similar cultural position. They lived through their kids because they could not participate directly in the adult (male) work world.

24. Barbara Ehrenreich discusses the breadwinner role and its effects on men in *The Hearts of Men: American Dreams and the Flight From Commitment* (New York: Anchor Books, 1983).

25. The great developers of the era—Levitt, Eichler, and a host of others—had the solution: tract houses that could be produced relatively cheaply and quickly, the perfect item for a young couple looking to start out with something modest and move up as finances permitted. See Jackson, *Crabgrass Frontier*, for more on planned suburbs.

26. Composed and performed by the great Berkeley radical singer Malvina Reynolds.

27. See Jackson, *Crabgrass Frontier*, for a more thorough discussion of the relationship between transportation and suburban development.

28. See Kathryn Dudley, *The End of the Line*, for a more thorough discussion of this point. Newman, in *Falling from Grace*, explores the issue with respect to intragenerational downward mobility.

29. Indeed, Glen Elder, Jr., argues that deprivation itself, living through hard times, produced more self-sufficient people in the long run. The longitudinal studies of depression survivors show that those who really suffered in their youth emerged in adulthood as more resilient and well-adapted individuals. See Elder, *Children of the Great Depression*.

4: The Problem of the Moral Mother

1. One might argue, however, that the controversy that has surrounded Hillary Clinton throughout the 1992 campaign is a very public indication of the continued division in American culture over the role of women in private and public life. See "The Hillary Factor," *Newsweek*, July 20, 1992, pp. 38–39.

2. Indeed, it might be argued that the whole industry of scientific mothering came about because of the possibilities for a new, expanded technocratic middle class in the postwar era. The model of the "good

mother" as a woman devoted solely to the nurturing of children was almost exclusively a middle-class phenomenon, one that came increasingly to depend on a woman's willingness to accept personal responsibility for the psychological development of her child. As Christopher Lasch argues in *The Culture of Narcissism: American Life in an Age of Diminishing Expectations* (New York: W. W. Norton, 1979), pp. 278–89, Dr. Spock (author of the best-selling *Baby and Child Care,* first published in 1946) is wrongly blamed for the excesses of child-centered permissiveness. In fact, Spock and other child-rearing experts of the 1940s and 1950s focused their attention primarily on the parent, not the child. Parents (assumed to be the mother, of course) were instructed to "trust themselves" and respond spontaneously to their child's needs, advice that hardened into what Lasch calls a "cult of authenticity." Raising a happy, well-adjusted child came to depend on being a happy, well-adjusted adult—a state of being that, ironically, women could only achieve by anxiously consulting the growing legions of child care experts.

3. Arlie Hochschild, *The Unexpected Community: Portrait of an Old Age Subculture* (Berkeley: University of California Press, 1978).

4. Working-class women have always been on the job. However, as Louise Lamphere points out in her study *From Working Daughters to Working Mothers: Immigrant Women in a New England Industrial Community* (Ithaca, N.Y.: Cornell University Press, 1987), women working in New England textile mills during the late eighteenth century were primarily young and single.

5. Betty Friedan, one of the founding mothers of the feminist movement, ultimately concluded that this one-sided message was a mistake. She argued that the movement had alienated mothers by ignoring "family" concerns. Friedan, *The Second Stage* (New York: Summit Books, 1981).

6. In *Abortion and the Politics of Motherhood* (Berkeley: University of California Press, 1984), Kristin Luker attributes the conflict on abortion to a cultural division between uneducated, working-class women and professional, middle-class women. Here the clash has less to do with class. Both of these women are of working-class origin and both are teachers. But it does have to do with an ideological rift that has superseded what might have been class origins to take on a life of its own.

7. This is in contrast to Kathleen Gerson's argument in *Hard Choices: How Women Decide about Work, Career, and Motherhood* (Berkeley: University of California Press, 1985). Gerson looks at a group of women who began adulthood with high career aspirations but veered toward motherhood and domesticity when they encountered

poorly rewarded jobs and structural barriers to occupational mobility.

8. A point made in somewhat different terms by Micaela di Leonardo, who notes that women are responsible for kinship work among Italian Americans. See di Leonardo, *The Varieties of Ethnic Experience: Kinship, Class, and Gender among California Italian-Americans* (Ithaca, N.Y.: Cornell University Press, 1984).

9. Subjective interpretations of life events depend on the symbolic frameworks through which individuals conceptualize the meaning of those events. Historical experience and life-cycle differences can shape interpretive frameworks in distinctive ways. See Katherine S. Newman, "Symbolic Dialects and Generations of Women: Variation in the Meaning of Post-Divorce Downward Mobility," *American Ethnologist* 13 (May 1986): 230–52.

10. While Phyllis Schlafley comes to mind here, I do not mean to imply that her right-wing sentiments in any way capture the views of these women. Their politics vary across the spectrum, and few would embrace the extreme tendencies of Schlafley's movement. Where they do intersect, however, is in their shared grievance against the women's movement, not for the ways it promoted women's rights, but for the ways that it appeared to denigrate domestic life.

11. In her essay on the aberrant 1950s, Sylvia Hewlett challenges this idea by showing that before and after the 1950s women worked. It was only during this hyperdomestic era, says Hewlett, that the ideal of the cloistered mother took hold as a reality. See Hewlett, *A Lesser Life: The Myth of Women's Liberation in America* (New York: William Morrow, 1986).

12. This way of calculating a woman's social value is a common refrain in working class culture, particularly among women who are strongly opposed to abortion. See Luker, *Abortion and the Politics of Motherhood.*

13. Ibid. Luker argues that for the former, reproductive rights present a challenge to the "market value" of the virgin bride and therefore a threat to the economic security of traditional women who need a powerful device for binding men to them. The latter are less dependent on traditional male-female relations because they are capable of making a living on their own and can therefore afford their independence. Indeed, they insist upon it through the vehicle of the pro-choice movement.

14. Interestingly enough, it was the stay-at-home mothers of the 1950s that produced the rebellious generation of the 1960s, the generation that still excites more comment on the subject of moral decadence than any other. Nonetheless, because a mother's morality is typically

connected to the fate of her children, the war over proper motherhood is waged in terms of the moral bearings of children and the
imagined injuries to same.

15. See Richard Easterlin, *Birth and Fortune* (New York: Basic Books,
1980).

16. While the participation of women in the labor force has risen sharply
over the past three decades, over the past two years the percentage
of women entering the labor market has leveled off. Economic stagnation, rising college enrollment, and the sudden increase in the
birth rate have all contributed to this plateau. Louis Uchitelle,
"Women's Push into the Work Force Seems to Have Peaked for
Now," *New York Times,* November 24, 1990, p. 1.

17. Newman, *Falling from Grace: The Experience of Downward Mobility in the American Middle Class* (New York: Free Press, 1988).

18. On the growing wage disparities between educated and noneducated
men, see McKinley 1. Blackburn, David E. Bloom, and Richard B.
Freeman, "The Declining Position of Less-Skilled American Males,"
Working Paper no. 3186 (Cambridge, Mass.: National Bureau of Economic Research, 1989).

19. This is not to say that cultural conceptions of motherhood and
fatherhood have not changed; it is to say that the changes have
been slow and incremental, not revolutionary. Despite recent portraits of recombinant families such as that drawn by Judith Stacey,
*Brave New Families: Stories of Domestic Upheaval in Late Twen-
tieth Century America* (New York: Basic Books, 1990), we have
not entered a postmodern heaven where it is perfectly acceptable
to organize family life around single parenthood, dual careerism,
divorce and remarriage, gay couples, or any other form of non-
orthodoxy. That these configurations exist, and exist in large numbers, is not the point. They have not replaced the dominant
imagery of the Ozzie-and-Harriet family no matter how prevalent
they have become, and no matter how much agony this hegemony
of traditionalism poses for those who live differently. Alternative
family structures remain the "marked category," examples of difference that merely reconfirm the norm, the centrality of the nuclear
family, where Mother is the moral center of the universe and Dad
is the arbiter of external links between the family and the workplace.

20. This is especially true in high-cost areas of the Northeast, but it is a
problem in so many parts of the United States today that it has
become a major generational burden.

21. This is, of course, a simplistic rendering of the past. Birth rates plummeted during the Great Depression for many of the same reasons that

younger boomers have put off having children today: financial constraints.

5: The Spoiled Generation

1. In 1950, the unemployment rate was 5.2 percent; it rose to only 5.4 percent in 1960. Bureau of the Census, *Statistical Abstracts of the United States* (Washington, D.C.: U.S. Department of Commerce, 1991).
2. In a sense this congruity should not be surprising. Middle-class postwar parents in Pleasanton were often of working-class origins themselves. Today's middle-class boomers, who are themselves of blue-collar (Pleasanton) origins, are structurally equivalent to them.
3. See Todd Gitlin, *The Sixties: Years of Hope, Days of Rage* (New York: Bantam Books, 1987); Abbie Hoffman, *The Best of Abbie Hoffman* (New York: Four Walls Eight Windows, 1989); Peter Collier, *Destructive Generation: Second Thoughts about the Sixties* (New York: Summit Books, 1989); Lauren Kessler, *After All These Years: Sixties Ideals in a Different World* (New York: Thunder's Mouth Press, 1990); and Gregory N. Calvert, *Democracy from the Heart: Spiritual Values, Decentralism, and Democratic Idealism in the Movement of the 1960s* (Eugene, Oreg.: Communitas Press, 1991).
4. See Newman, "Symbolic Dialects and Generations of Women: Variation in the Meaning of Post-Divorce Mobility," *American Ethnologist* 13 (May 1986): 230–52.

6: Illegitimate Elites and the Parasitic Underclass

1. Jonathan Rieder shows how this belief shapes the way ethnic whites think about their own social standing relative to African Americans in his book *Canarsie: The Jews and Italians of Brooklyn against Liberalism* (Cambridge, Mass.: Harvard University Press, 1985). On the same point, see Alan Wolfe, *Whose Keeper?* (Berkeley: University of California Press, 1990).
2. See David Matza, "The Disreputable Poor," in *Class, Status and Power: Social Structures in Comparative Perspective,* ed. Richard Bendix and Seymour Martin Lipset (New York: Free Press, 1966), pp. 289–302.
3. In this retrospective tale, the contributions made by the federal government in the form of low-interest mortgages, the GI Bill, and the like are rarely cited, a point discussed at length in chapter 3.
4. This is a variant of a theme that appears in David Halle, *America's Working Man: Work, Home, and Politics among Blue-Collar Prop-*

erty Owners (Chicago: University of Chicago Press, 1984). Halle talks about blue-collar suspicion of the wealthy; here we see an ethnic twist on the same idea.

5. These sentiments might surprise Andrew Hacker, author of *Two Nations: Black and White, Separate, Hostile, Unequal* (New York: Scribner's, 1992), who writes: "As Asians find places in the economy, they are allowed to move upward on social and occupational ladders. Middle-class whites do not object if Asian children attend their local schools or populate their neighborhoods" (p. 10).

6. For a far more complete discussion of anti-Asian legislation and public opinion, see Ellis Cose, *A Nation of Strangers* (New York: William Morrow, 1992).

7. I say new form of nativism only because it is normally found among lower class populations locked in direct economic competition in the labor market. Competition for resources is clearly central to the nativist response of Pleasanton residents to their Asian neighbors, but it is less the result of labor-market conflict and more a matter of intergenerational mobility and international economic decline.

8. In their classic work *The American Occupational Structure* (New York: Free Press, 1977), Peter M. Blau and Otis Dudley Duncan stress that an individual's occupational position is the single best indicator of class.

9. Because this research was based upon the composition of Pleasanton in 1970 and 1980, very few Asian families fell into the interview sample. In those years, there were few nonwhite families in Pleasanton. Were this study to be replicated today, the composition of the sample would be very different.

10. Robert N. Bellah et al., *Habits of the Heart: Individualism and Commitment in American Life* (New York: Harper and Row, 1985).

11. "The Tonight Show," NBC television, December 3, 1990.

12. Ralph's point is amplified in more scholarly studies of tax burdens, some of which show that increasingly taxes are being paid (1) by individuals and less by corporations, particularly those that can take advantage of generous write-off provisions and (2) more by middle- and low-income workers and less by the wealthiest individuals. See Donald Barlett and James Steele, *America: What Went Wrong?* (Kansas City: Andrews and McMeel, 1992), pp. 47–48.

13. While suburbs began as bedroom communities, newer suburbs have become the locus of manufacturing industries and other economic activities. Suburbs like these, with good commercial sales and high property values, suffer less fiscal strain. Mark Baldassare, *Trouble in Paradise: The Suburban Transformation in America* (New York: Columbia University Press, 1986).

14. For a discussion of these policy initiatives, see Lawrence M. Mead and Laurence E. Lynn, "Should Workfare Be Mandatory? What Research Says," *Journal of Policy Analysis and Management* 9 (Summer 1990): 400–404.

15. Aid to Families with Dependent Children accounted for 0.9 percent of the federal budget in 1991, while food stamps cost the federal purse another 1.5 percent. The states spent 2.2 percent of the revenues on AFDC in the same year. Center on Budget and Policy Priorities quoted in "Politics of Welfare: Focusing on the Problems," *New York Times,* July 5, 1992, pp. 1, 13.

16. See John Kenneth Galbraith, *The Culture of Contentment* (Boston: Houghton Mifflin, 1992); and William Julius Wilson, *The Truly Disadvantaged: The Inner City, the Underclass, and Public Policy* (Chicago: University of Chicago Press, 1987).

17. On this last point, see Jonathan Kozol's indictment of school spending patterns, *Savage Inequalities: Children in America's Schools* (New York: Crown Publishers, 1991).

18. This is essentially the point made by conservatives like Charles Murray, *Losing Ground: American Social Policy, 1950–1980* (New York: Basic Books, 1984); and Laurence Mead, *The New Politics of Poverty: The Nonworking Poor in America* (New York: Basic Books, 1992).

19. Studs Terkel, the well-known oral historian of American culture, provides a longer and more detailed look at the racial divide that separates blacks and whites in the United States in his recent book *Race: How Blacks and Whites Think and Feel about the American Obsession* (New York: New Press, 1992).

20. George would probably react favorably to the kinds of proposals to end welfare issued by authors like Mickey Kaus, even though they involve increasing public sector employment. See Kaus, *The End of Equality* (New York: Basic Books, 1992).

21. In his book on welfare policy, conservative analyst Lawrence Mead argues that America's underclass is growing, not because there are too few jobs to go around, but because the poor are simply unwilling to work in jobs like those described in this quote. Mead gives academic voice to the sentiments of many in the affluent suburbs who are suspicious of the nonworking poor. See Lawrence Mead, *The New Politics of Poverty.*

22. Jonathan Rieder made a similar point in his book *Canarsie: Jews and Italians against Liberalism.* Rieder is speaking of white urban dwellers who moved out of the Lower East Side of New York for less dense communities in Brooklyn, only to discover that minorities were interested in the same area. He explains the resistance of whites

to desegregation by saying that they could not flee any farther and were worried that the social problems they left behind in the city would follow them to the community in which they had invested their life savings. The people in Pleasanton are not as lacking in options as Rieder's Canarsians may be. But they share with the working class of Canarsie a sense of being stuck in the political arena with no one to represent their views.

23. Claude Lévi-Strauss, *Structural Anthropology* (1958; New York: Basic Books, 1963). As Lévi-Strauss has shown, however, there are other ways to reduce the dissonance of contradiction. He has raised the examination of oppositional ideas to a high art in his work on mythology.

7: The Fractured Generation

1. The latest of which is menopause. See Gail Sheehy, *The Silent Passage* (New York: Random House, 1992).

2. In recent years there has been a resurgence of interest in the relevance of historical scholarship among anthropologists dissatisfied with the atemporal quality of much ethnography. Eric Wolf (*Europe and the People without History* [Berkeley: University of California Press, 1982]), among others, has pointed out the impossibility of understanding the "ethnographic present" without a full appreciation of the historical past. Marshall Sahlins (*Islands of History* [Chicago: University of Chicago Press, 1985]) exemplifies a related theoretical thrust in showing how events in Hawaiian history were made meaningful only by reference to a prior mythological/historical structure into which such moments as the arrival of Captain Cook were interpolated. However, most of what this historical movement has produced in anthropology involves a reconstruction of the conditions under which the ethnographic present was produced. In this chapter I argue for another form of rapprochement between anthropology and history, one that asks how a set of historical events created a "cultural dialect" that then followed a generation throughout its history. On this model, generations—particularly those that are forged in cataclysmic conditions—carry with them aspects of culture that other generations do not share as immediate experience. These orienting themes structure the moral experience of generations throughout their lifetimes. In this sense, historical experience moves with a generation rather than remaining merely a backdrop to later events. I take inspiration for this perspective from the long-standing literature in sociology on the "life course." See, for example, Glen Elder, Jr., *Children of the Great Depression: Social Change in Life Experience*

(Chicago: University of Chicago Press, 1974), which focuses on the intersection of cohort and time but generally fails to draw out the long-term cultural implications of the life-course model.

3. See Barbara Ehrenreich, *Fear of Falling: The Inner Life of the Middle Class* (New York: Pantheon Books, 1989); and Todd Gittlin, *The Sixties: Years of Hope, Days of Rage* (New York: Bantam Books, 1987).

4. After 1970 almost half of those assigned lottery numbers could feel safe. Twenty-one percent of high school graduates served in Vietnam, while only 12 percent of college graduates saw service. Gitlin, *The Sixties,* p. 412.

5. It would be a rank exaggeration to suggest that *all* of Pleasanton's progeny embraced this oppositional stance. On the whole, the hotbed of resistance to adult authority—symbolized in actions and in unconventional dress—was occupied by the middle class. Working-class kids in the community did not take too kindly to the long-haired countercultural types. More than a few amateur hippies were harassed or beaten up at the hands of blue-collar boys in Pleasanton High School.

What was at stake between these antagonistic camps was more than style, even if style was the most visible catalyst of the tension. Middle-class kids in Pleasanton were busily expressing rejection and disdain for the very elements of the good life that blue-collar families were working double overtime to afford. For although Pleasanton was a heterogeneous town, with a healthy mix of the well-to-do and the struggling, it was clearly easier for some to afford than others. And for the others, whose families had barely arrived in the lower middle class, the spectacle of "rich" kids shrugging their shoulders with contempt at the advantages of privilege was more than the working-class boys, who had no such silver spoon, could take.

At the time the language of class division was submerged in a far more immediate dispute. The "jock" set was antagonized by the "long-haired" clique's contempt for patriotism, as it was expressed in the heat of the antiwar movement. For whatever doubts they had about Vietnam as a cause, they were quite certain that the United States remained "the best country on earth." As Kyle Gordon, a blue-collar son of Pleasanton put the matter:

I went down to the draft board when I was eighteen and got my draft card. I was able to pick a college deferment and didn't. I maintained a 1A military status the whole time Vietnam was going on. I told my mother, don't worry, I'm not going to enlist, but if they call me I'm going. Those were my feelings. I have always loved this country. I don't think there's a better one on earth. We're not as good as we think we are, either militarily or economically, but we're still the land of the free and we have a lot to be thankful for. I would have been willing to go to Nam. Didn't want to and to this day I tell people, 'There but for the grace of God go I.' I wasn't a war hawk, but I wasn't a dove either.

Yet as Barbara Ehrenreich, Robert Bellah, and a host of other "diagnostic" writers have pointed out, the middle class has long dominated the center stage of our culture. Hence, while recognizing the conflict that infused the sixties generation over the legitimacy of the Vietnam War, the middle-class rebel remains the standard-bearer for the sixties generation.

6. Made all the more tranquil by the chilling effect of McCarthyism on college campuses. See Ellen Schrecker, *No Ivory Tower: McCarthyism and the Universities* (New York: Oxford University Press, 1986).

7. From a feminist perspective, this revolt should not be minimized. Girls began to reject the way society expected them to look, insisting upon their own independence. As Frances Anderson, another 1970 graduate of Pleasanton High, put it:

There had always been a dress code at school. Girls couldn't wear pants. I remember one day forty girls, myself included, walked into school wearing pants. It was hard to throw forty girls out. The dress code was dropped.

8. Todd Gitlin's account of the 1960s points out that the antecedents of these anti-establishment attitudes were to be found in the 1950s. For an account of these themes in scholarship and popular culture, see Gitlin, *The Sixties,* chap. 1.

9. Robert Bellah and his coauthors discuss the importance of institutions and the ways ordinary people operate through them. They argue that institutions, not individuals, are the locus of engagement in social policy in the United States. Here I try to show that even in a period that many count as the most anti-institutional of recent decades, most young people were committed to exactly this model of social responsibility. Robert Bellah et al., *The Good Society* (New York: Knopf, 1991).

10. This divide remains unresolved thirty years later and indeed threatens to grow wider, as racial conflict in places like the Crown Heights section of Brooklyn seem to demonstrate. To find out what happened in Crown Heights, see Scott Minerbrook and Miriam Horn, "Side by Side, Apart," *U.S. News and World Report,* November 4, 1991, pp. 44–46; and Sam Allis, "An Eye for an Eye," *Time,* September 9, 1991, p. 20.

11. Tradition, particularly as it applied to mothering, did come back to haunt the sixties generation. See chapter 4 for more on this.

12. McCarthyism is probably more responsible for this unfortunate truth than anything else. All it took in some circles during the early 1950s was a mild embrace of innocuous liberal ideas to ruin someone's career in academia, the arts, politics, and even science. We like to think these days are over, but one glance at the career problems of academic Marxists tells us otherwise. See Paul A. Attewell, *Radical Political Economy since the Sixties: A Sociology of Knowledge Analysis* (New Brunswick, N.J.: Rutgers University Press, 1984). In the 1990s many liberals concerned with maintaining a civilized tone on campus have found themselves clobbered with the label, "politically correct" by conservatives worried about the diminution of the traditional emphasis on Western culture and preferential admissions policies. This kind of mudslinging makes it hard to remember what kinds of principles and ideals underlie social change, for the labeling (and its career consequences) inevitably get in the way.

13. Robert Bellah et al., *Habits of the Heart: Individualism and Commitment in American Life* (New York: Harper and Row, 1985).

14. See Newman, *Falling from Grace: The Experience of Downward Mobility in the American Class* (New York: Free Press, 1988).

15. See chapter 2 for more on the boomerang phenomenon.

16. See Newman, *Falling from Grace.*

17. Herbert J. Gans, *Middle American Individualism: The Future of Liberal Democracy* (New York: Free Press, 1988).

18. Richard Sennett and Jonathan Cobb, *The Hidden Injuries of Class* (New York: Vintage Books, 1972).

19. For a discussion of how the current generation of young people seems to be "delaying" adulthood, see Susan Littwin, *The Postponed Generation: Why American Youth Are Growing Up Later* (New York: William Morrow, 1986).

8: The Politics of Generational Division

1. "It's No Wonder Clinton Rejects the Boomer Tag," *Los Angeles Times,* July 16, 1992, p. E4.

2. Older boomers, who grew up in a time of political activism, tend to vote in greater numbers than those who entered adulthood a decade later, during a period of government retrenchment. In 1972, 50 percent of all those aged eighteen to twenty-four voted, while in 1980 only 40 percent of this group went to the polls. Felicity Barringer, "Younger Boomers Are Found Less Well Off," *New York Times,* January 4, 1992, p. 26.

3. "A Baby Boomer Elite Yearns to Take Part in a Clinton Presidency," *Wall Street Journal,* July 16, 1992, p. 1

4. During the 1980s, some anthropologists began to focus on age as an important social variable, building upon long-standing ethnographic interests in societies organized by "age sets." Most of the newer research focuses on age as an aspect of the life course (see especially Jennifer Keith and David Ketzer, *Age and Anthropological Theory* [Ithaca, N.Y.: Cornell University Press, 1984]). But some anthropologists have also begun to look at the cultural significance of cohorts. For an excellent example of the latter view, see Elizabeth Colson, "The Reordering of Experience: Anthropological Involvement with Time," *Journal of Anthropological Research* 40 (no. 1; 1984): 1-13.

5. There are good reasons for this allergy: how do we set the boundaries of generations, how do we sort out the relative importance or power of characteristics that crosscut generations (like race) when compared to generation, and so on? The fact that individuals are present during the course of earthshaking events does not, in and of itself, guarantee that they will understand their existence to have been shaped forever after by that experience. Glen Elder's landmark study of the impact of the Great Depression shows that major differences developed in the lives of young people who lived through the 1930s, depending upon exactly how old they were or what kind of life transitions they were poised to embark upon when the economy crashed. See Elder, *Children of the Great Depression: Social Change in Life Experience* (Chicago: University of Chicago Press, 1974). Elder notes that those most devastated by the depression were young people set to enter the labor market when all their prospects disappeared. For the rest of their lives, this single fact marked their experience, leaving them shaken, and not a few of them embittered. They were never able to lay claim to the careers they wanted, the standard of living they had hoped for, the marriages they had wanted, all because the depression hit them at a particularly vulnerable moment. Children who were five years younger, who were sheltered at home during the depression joined the armed forces and then moved into a booming labor market after World War II. Which of these two groups should we denote as the "depression generation"?

The question of boundaries—of who belongs most squarely inside a generation, is best understood not by rigid demarcations of birth dates but by looser bounds of experience and memory. We would probably remain truest to the layman's understanding of generation by suggesting conceiving of generations as "fuzzy sets" (to use the language of mathematicians), with degrees of membership that are not equally strong. Imagine a core at the middle of people who are unambiguously identified with a particular generational experience, and then wrap concentric circle around the core that express a less tightly integrated identification with, for example, the depression generation. The farther one moves out from the core, the "fuzzier" the sense of identification becomes. See David Ketzer's excellent review article on the concept of generations, "Generation as a Sociological Problem," *Annual Reviews of Sociology* 9 (1983): 125–90.

6. Robert Wohl's lyrical study of the generation that fought World War I captures this sentiment of separation vividly in his effort to pin down the essential meaning of generational identity:

A historical generation is not defined by its chronological limits or its borders. It is not a zone of dates; nor is it an army of contemporaries making its way across a territory of time. It is more like a magnetic field at the center of which lies an experience. . . . What is essential to the formation of a generational consciousness is some common frame of reference that provides a sense of rupture with the past and that will later distinguish the members of the generation from those who follow them in time.

See Wohl, *The Generation of 1914* (Cambridge, Mass.: Harvard University Press, 1979), p. 210.

Hence, cataclysmic events that have the power to create strong generational identities often cleave nations. The insiders who stand at the magnetic center Wohl describes feel bound to others similarly situated with an intensity matched in strength only by the distance they feel from those on the outside. Bystanders to the earthshaking movements of the past and present sense the energy and intensity of these commitments but cannot partake of them. Indeed, among those who sit on the outskirts of a great generation, there is often a feeling of envy, lack of defined identity, and an inchoate sense that they do not count in the same way as their more sharply defined cousins. See also Maurice Halbwachs, *The Collective Memory* (New York: Harper Colophon, 1980).

7. E. J. Dionne, Jr., *Why Americans Hate Politics* (New York: Simon and Schuster, 1992).

8. One could argue that plans for the first-time home buyer and watered-down day-care bills do represent a response to boomer demands. There is some truth to this, but they are weak, not central, to the political mission of the major parties, and interestingly enough, they are never articulated in terms of the politics of age.

9. "Angry Taxpayers Reject 44% of New Jersey School Budgets," *New York Times,* May 2, 1992, p. B1.

10. See Jean Scandlyn, "When the Social Contract Fails: Inter-Generational and Inter-Ethnic Conflict in an American Suburb," (Ph.D. thesis, Columbia University, 1992).

11. One thing that is "in it for them" is the preservation of the value of

their own real estate. The quality of the local public school is essential to property values. On this count, retirees should be concerned to keep quality high. Unfortunately, this interest conflicts with the desire to hold down tax rates, a losing battle in the 1980s.

12. "Educators Complain Business Tax Breaks Are Costing Schools," *New York Times,* May 22, 1991, pp. A1, A23.

13. A college degree is an important hedge against wage losses. The wages of college graduates relative to high school graduates were higher in 1987 than at any other time since 1963. But as Lawrence Mishel and David M. Frankel observe, the average college graduate was still earning less in 1987 than in 1971. The increased wage gap between college and high school graduates reflects "a modest increase in the demand for college-educated workers, not an across-the-board, economy-wide trend toward higher skilled and higher wage jobs." See Mishel and Frankel, *The State of Working America, 1990–91* (Armonk, N.Y.: Economic Policy Institute, M. E. Sharpe, 1991).

14. At the University of California, Berkeley, this was particularly sensitive where the admission of students of Asian origin were concerned. Grade-point averages and test scores would have placed Asian students at the top of the admissions list to such a degree at Berkeley that virtually no room would be left for other ethnic groups, including whites. Responding to this, university officials proposed to rely in part on extracurricular activities, admissions essays, and other unquantifiable characteristics for admissions. Ethnic and racial groups on all sides of this dispute were at each other's throats because access to Berkeley, as well as the rest of the University of California system, is becoming increasingly restricted. See Daniel Seligman, "College in California: The Numbers Game," *Fortune,* February 11, 1991, p. 146; and James S. Gibney, "The Berkeley Squeeze," *New Republic,* April 11, 1988, pp. 15–17.

15. For a look at the favored treatment of the postwar generation by the feds and the comparatively unfavorable plight of the boomers, see Laurence J. Kotlikoff, *Generational Accounting: Knowing Who Pays—and When—for What We Spend* (New York: Free Press, 1992).

16. Richard Lamm, "Again, Age Beats Youth," *New York Times,* Op-Ed, December 2, 1990, p. A32.

17. Lamm is quick to note that Medicare policies were hardly designed for millionaires and that they have been responsible for pulling poverty-stricken seniors out of harm's way far more often than they have been used to coddle the very wealthy. His point, also echoed by H. Ross Perot, is both that a far larger share of our resources go to the elderly than to any other demographic group and that we do not

means test the benefits we provide.

18. Perhaps the baby-boom generation should be satisfied with the prospect that they too will one day be the beneficiaries of policies that enhance the lives of the elderly. As we saw in chapter 2, there is reason to question whether the nation will be able to afford such largesse when this colossal generation is ready for retirement. Yet so little attention has been paid to the problems we are likely to see in the social security system (when a small number of workers—today's children—are paying into a system that will have to care for the enormous boomer generation) that the conflicts that will undoubtedly emerge over unbearable tax burdens have barely registered in the public mind. See Kotlikoff, *Generational Accounting.*

19. Mark Featherman, "The 80's Party Is Over, . . . " *New York Times,* Op-Ed, September 24, 1990.

20. This particular complaint may have unpleasant racial dimensions as well. The increasing fertility rates of minorities, particularly Hispanics, in the United States may well mean that whites in the boomer generation will be more dependent on racial minorities to pay for their retirement needs than has ever been the case in the past. This is but one more reason for the country to attend to the racial tension growing in the cities and suburbs. For the social security system to work as it was designed, a degree of intergenerational and cross-racial commitment will be needed.

21. Bill Clinton is the only national politician who articulated a program akin to those of the postwar era. He has argued that a national "education bank" should be created that would allow young people to borrow money for college, to be repaid through public service jobs that would rebuild the nation's infrastructure.

Index